Hub-and-Spoke Cartels

Hub-and-Spoke Cartels

Why They Form, How They Operate, and How to Prosecute Them

Luke Garrod, Joseph E. Harrington, Jr., and Matthew Olczak

The MIT Press
Cambridge, Massachusetts
London, England

The MIT Press would like to thank the anonymous peer reviewers who provided comments on drafts of this book. The generous work of academic experts is essential for establishing the authority and quality of our publications. We acknowledge with gratitude the contributions of these otherwise uncredited readers.

This book was set in ITC Stone Serif by Westchester Publishing Services. Printed and bound in the United States of America.

Library of Congress Cataloging-in-Publication Data

Names: Garrod, Luke, author. | Harrington, Joseph Emmett, 1957– author. | Olczak, Matthew, author.
Title: Hub-and-spoke cartels : why they form, how they operate, and how to prosecute them / Luke Garrod, Joseph E. Harrington Jr., and Matthew Olczak.
Description: Cambridge, Massachusetts : The MIT Press, [2021] | Includes bibliographical references and index.
Identifiers: LCCN 2021003131 | ISBN 9780262046206 (hardcover)
Subjects: LCSH: Cartels.
Classification: LCC K3854 .G37 2021 | DDC 343.07/2—dc23
LC record available at https://lccn.loc.gov/2021003131

10 9 8 7 6 5 4 3 2 1

Contents

5   Collusion to Exclude Rival Firms   159

6   General Assessment of Hub-and-Spoke Cartels   213

7   Competition Law and Hub-and-Spoke Collusion   223

Preface

When competitors are concerned with the intensity of competition, they may choose to form a cartel whereby they replace their independent conduct with coordination intended to limit how aggressively they compete. Most cartels are composed exclusively of those firms that ought to be competing. However, there is a particular brand of cartel that, in addition to those firms, includes a firm that resides either upstream or downstream from them. Referred to as a hub-and-spoke cartel, they have been observed on both sides of the Atlantic in a wide variety of markets, including consumer products, such as automobiles and toys; industrial products, such as insulation and paints; and services, such as insurance and movie theaters.

As we hope to convince the reader, the inclusion of an upstream seller or a downstream buyer in a cartel substantively affects how the cartel operates and how it should be prosecuted. It is also essential for understanding why a cartel forms. For all these reasons, we believe this book's investigation of hub-and-spoke cartels is warranted.

Collusion is a subject for which economics and the law are intrinsically intertwined. The conduct of cartel members is influenced by the need to achieve a stable and profitable outcome, which depends on economic forces related to incentives and the design of strategies but is also constrained by the legal environment, which manifests itself in practices for avoiding detection. However, most analyses of collusion fail to bring together the economic and legal strands of the story. Economics journals publish mathematical or econometric studies of collusion that are impenetrable to anyone lacking formal mathematical and statistical training. Law or policy journals publish studies by legal scholars that, while offering a rich description of collusive practices and properly relating the cases to jurisprudence, do not adequately deal with incentives and, more broadly, the economics of collusion. Our approach is to blend economic and legal analyses in order to provide a more comprehensive picture of hub-and-spoke cartels.

While this book is relevant to anyone with an interest in collusion, it is intended for scholars and practitioners, whether trained in economics or the law. With the exception of some technical appendices, the presentation is nonmathematical and presumes only that the reader is comfortable with economic reasoning at the level at which an antitrust or competition lawyer converses.

For economic scholars, the book offers a collection of facts that could be useful for theoretical and empirical modeling of cartel formation and collusive practices.[1] Given that the book is the only comprehensive and systematic study of hub-and-spoke cartels, it should be useful to practitioners engaged in litigation involving suspected hub-and-spoke collusion. Our analysis of many past cases would assist in constructing a theory of harm and establishing that a set of vertical relationships forms a horizontal agreement. Finally, a consumer who is upset for having paid too much for a toy, an e-book, or a pound of cheese may like to learn how the cartel responsible for the harm inflicted on them operated.

We very much appreciate the comments and suggestions of Bill Page and three anonymous reviewers and, on an earlier version of this book, those of Steve Davies, Morten Hviid, Nic de Roos, Juan-Pablo Montero, Barack Orbach, Peter Ormosi, Tom Ross, Pierluigi Sabbatini, and Alexis Walckiers. We also benefited from discussing our preliminary thoughts with participants at the 2018 International Symposium on Imperfect Forms of Collusion hosted by Stellenbosch University. The diligent research assistance of Hsiang-Yen (Sam) Huang, Asad Hussain, Sin Chit (Martin) Lai, and Richard Pletan is gratefully acknowledged. We recognize with gratitude the financial support of the Carol and Lawrence Zicklin Center for Business Ethics Research at the Wharton School of the University of Pennsylvania.

1 Introduction

1.1 What Is a Hub-and-Spoke Cartel?

A cartel is a collection of firms that supply a market and agree to coordinate their behavior for the purpose of restraining competition. Their resulting conduct is referred to as collusion. Most commonly, collusion takes the form of firms coordinating on a common price above the competitive level, which raises their profits and harms buyers. Alternatively (or along with agreeing on prices), a cartel may limit competition by coordinating complementary services, product traits, advertising, manufacturing capacity, or other variables. Indeed, any way in which firms compete could be the basis for forming a cartel for the purpose of limiting that mode of competition. Rather than directly constraining competition for customers, collusion may instead involve a subset of firms acting collectively to harm other firms that are not part of the cartel. They may engage in coordinated exclusionary actions—such as predatory pricing—to either drive those firms out of the market or make it more difficult for them to compete. Again, consumers are harmed, because they lose those excluded firms as effective suppliers.

The subject of this book is cartels that include an upstream supplier to or downstream buyer from the firms that are constraining competition. Such a cartel is referred to as a hub-and-spoke cartel, where the *spokes* are the colluding firms in a market and the *hub* is the firm that resides either upstream or downstream from those firms. Competition between spokes is being restrained by collusion, and the hub is facilitating that collusion. The horizontal agreement present among the spokes is referred to as the *rim*, for it connects the conduct of the spokes. In the canonical hub-and-spoke cartel, that agreement to restrain competition arises not from direct communications between the spokes but rather from bilateral communications between the hub and each spoke. In some hub-and-spoke cartels, the spokes may communicate directly, but the central communication protocol involves a spoke communicating with the hub.

To make this description more concrete, let us consider two hub-and-spoke cartels that arose in the market for children's toys. In the late 1990s in the UK, toy retailers Argos and Littlewoods coordinated to charge supracompetitive prices for certain toys they both sold. Collusion was initiated and orchestrated by the manufacturer of those toys, Hasbro. Argos and Littlewoods reached this illegal agreement without ever having communicated directly; all their communications were through Hasbro. As depicted in figure 1.1, the upstream manufacturer was the hub and the two downstream retailers were the spokes.

This arrangement was flipped around with a hub-and-spoke cartel in the US toy market in the early 1990s. Toy manufacturer Hasbro was not the hub but rather a spoke. Along with several other toy manufacturers, it was approached by retailer Toys "R" Us to form a cartel to exclude discount competitors to Toys "R" Us. More specifically, the agreement was for Hasbro, Mattel, Fisher-Price, and other toy manufacturers not to supply discount retailers with any of the toys they supplied to Toys "R" Us. The structure of this hub-and-spoke cartel is depicted in figure 1.2.[1]

A hub-and-spoke cartel differs from the typical cartel in that it encompasses a firm that operates in a part of the supply chain that is distinct from where competition is being restrained. It is also distinguished from cartels encompassing a third party that, while assisting in the restraint of

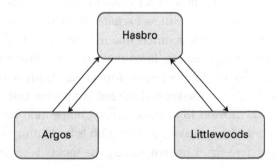

Figure 1.1
Information flows in toys (UK).

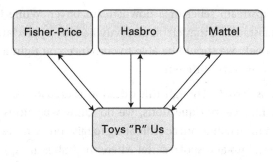

Figure 1.2
Information flows in toys (US).

competition, neither supplies nor buys from the cartel's members. Examples of such third parties include the consulting company AC Treuhand in the organic peroxides cartel,[2] a Swiss accounting firm in the lysine cartel,[3] and a taxi driver in a bidding ring of stamp dealers (Asker 2010). With a hub-and-spoke cartel, that third party has a vertical relationship with the firms that are limiting competition.

1.2 Why Study Hub-and-Spoke Cartels?

The objective of this book is to investigate hub-and-spoke cartels to understand them and develop legal strategies for prosecuting them.[4] Before we go any further, you may be asking why a separate study of this particular brand of cartel is warranted. To address that question, let us begin by posing the four questions central to the study of cartels and collusion. First, why do cartels form? What conditions are conducive to cartel formation, and which firms choose to participate? Second, how do cartels operate? Over what variables do firms coordinate? How is the collusive outcome monitored for compliance, and what is the punishment when there is evidence of noncompliance? What is done to avoid detection? Third, how effective is collusion? How long do cartels last, and how significant is their impact on conduct, outcomes, and welfare? Fourth, how does one detect and prosecute cartels? What distinguishes collusion from competition, and what evidence is necessary and sufficient to establish that there is an illegal agreement? The reason for a separate study of hub-and-spoke cartels is that the answers to most of those questions are different when the cartel includes an upstream seller or a downstream buyer. While the evidence we offer to substantiate that claim can only be fully appreciated after having read the book, we should be able to convince you right away that the answers are likely to be different.

Why do cartels form? Though this question is arguably the least understood of the four central questions, we do know why firms in a market would benefit from collusion: coordinating to raise prices raises their profits. Now consider a hub-and-spoke cartel where the hub is an upstream manufacturer or distributor and the spokes are downstream retailers. Just as with a regular cartel, downstream retailers would find it attractive to jointly charge higher prices. But what about the upstream supplier? What is its incentive to aid the spokes in that enterprise? Given that collusion will mean lower sales by the downstream retailers, it implies lower demand for the upstream supplier, which would appear to harm it. Thus, it is not immediately clear why an upstream supplier would participate. To make it yet more puzzling, some of the cartels we'll be studying were initiated by an upstream firm. For example, the hub-and-spoke cartel in the UK toy market was the brainchild of upstream manufacturer Hasbro. Analogously, consider a cartel with a downstream retailer acting as the hub to coordinate upstream supplier-spokes to exclude a rival to the retailer-hub, as exemplified by the cartel in the US toy market. It is clear why the downstream retailer would participate, but what about the upstream suppliers? Exclusion means they lose a source of demand, which certainly does not sound appealing. For these reasons, the decision to form and participate in a hub-and-spoke cartel is likely to be based on incentives that are distinct from those of a cartel that does not comprise an upstream seller or downstream buyer.

How do cartels operate? A critical part of a cartel's modus operandi is communication. Firms communicate to coordinate on a particular collusive outcome and to share information relevant to monitoring cartel members for their compliance with that outcome. With a standard cartel, all members typically communicate with each other. In contrast, communications occur in a less direct manner with a hub-and-spoke cartel. Primarily—and often exclusively—the firms that are restraining their competition do not communicate directly. Rather, each firm (spoke) communicates with a particular upstream supplier or downstream buyer (hub), which then shares information with other firms (spokes). Thus, the hub is the nexus in this communication network and plays a role that is generally absent in standard cartels. The hub is also special when it comes to monitoring and enforcing the collusive agreement. Because it is an upstream seller or downstream buyer, the hub has access to information that other firms may lack and has the power to deny supply or refuse to buy, which can be a formidable punishment to induce compliance with the agreement. For all these reasons, the hub is a singular player in the cartel, which means hub-and-spoke cartels are expected to operate differently from standard cartels.

How effective is collusion? Because hub-and-spoke cartels form for different reasons and operate in different ways, we expect them to be differentially effective. As an upstream supplier generally prefers that downstream retailers price lower and sell more, the inclusion of that supplier as the hub could constrain the extent of the rise in retail prices. If upstream manufacturers are forced to participate in a cartel to exclude a rival to the downstream hub and find their participation unprofitable, that could make collusion less stable and thereby shorten its duration. It could also be the case that coordination is more difficult because spokes do not communicate directly and instead go through the hub. On the other hand, the additional information and instruments possessed by the hub for monitoring and enforcing an agreement may make collusion more effective. Thus, there is reason to believe that the success of a hub-and-spoke cartel may differ from that experienced by standard cartels.

How are cartels detected and prosecuted? All the hub-and-spoke cartels we will be studying were prosecuted for unlawful collusion.[5] Thus, concerns about detection and prosecution can be as relevant for hub-and-spoke cartels as they are for regular cartels. In practice, cartels are detected in all sorts of ways, and one of them is when communications surrounding an unlawful agreement are discovered. Such a discovery may be less likely with a hub-and-spoke cartel because direct communications are between an upstream supplier and a downstream buyer, which is to be expected under competition. Furthermore, evidence of some overt act of communication between firms in a market that allows them to coordinate their behavior is necessary to obtain a conviction. However, in most hub-and-spoke cartels, rival firms never communicate directly. Thus, the "smoking gun" evidence of communication between competitors is absent. Convicting a hub-and-spoke cartel requires establishing that a series of vertical relationships—between the suspected hub and each suspected spoke—constitute a horizontal agreement among the suspected spokes. It follows that the enforcement of competition law is a bit different when the cartel is a hub-and-spoke cartel.

In sum, whether the objective is to understand or prosecute collusion, the associated analysis is likely to be different when that collusion emanates from a hub-and-spoke cartel. Therein lies the rationale for a study of hub-and-spoke collusion.

An important issue that this book will not address is the welfare effects of hub-and-spoke cartels. Generally, cartels are thought to harm consumers and reduce social welfare. If the only effect of collusion is to raise prices, then that is indeed true and is the end of the story. However, even if firms coordinate only on prices, there can be an impact on firms' other choices, for firms compete not just on prices but also, for example, on service, product quality, and advertising. By coordinating on higher prices, nonprice competition can be expected to intensify for two reasons. First, each cartel member still desires to sell more, so if price competition is neutralized, then firms will use nonprice instruments, such as more advertising, to attract more demand. Second, higher collusive prices make each additional sale more profitable, which increases the return to these nonprice instruments and thus promotes nonprice competition. Thus, if firms are colluding on prices, we expect consumers to be harmed by the higher prices but to benefit from more service or some other nonprice choice. It is even theoretically possible for nonprice competition to intensify to such a degree that consumers are made better off from price collusion.[6] However, the available evidence is that it is very likely that consumer and social welfare will decrease when firms coordinate so competition is reduced, which is why cartels are per se illegal and unlawful by object.[7]

Although the welfare effects of hub-and-spoke collusion and of the particular cartels examined are a worthy topic of study, our book does not investigate them. With regard to the latter, we lack the evidence to be able to make such an assessment. Furthermore, a welfare analysis is not relevant to the central questions our investigation is designed to address, as we now explain.

In exploring why cartels form and how they operate, it is possible that taking account of the implications of price collusion for nonprice variables could be relevant to understanding cartel formation. However, we found no evidence of this. All the cartels we examined were formed to raise prices or exclude rivals. There was no evidence to suggest the cartel was formed to increase service or some other nonprice dimension, or that the implications of price collusion on these other variables were part of the calculus in forming a cartel and designing the collusive arrangement.[8]

In exploring the prosecution of cartels, welfare effects are not relevant to their illegality, because hub-and-spoke cartels are per se illegal, as we explain in chapter 7. Assessing the welfare effects of a hub-and-spoke cartel could be relevant for deciding whether a cartel is prosecuted. A competition authority may choose to focus resources on the most welfare-reducing anticompetitive activities, while plaintiffs may only litigate when harm is large and thus so are the possible damages to be collected. A welfare analysis is also necessary for determining whether hub-and-spoke cartels should be per se illegal or instead subject to a rule of reason that balances benefits and costs. All these questions deserve examination, but we choose not to address them here.

1.3 Approach and Overview

The approach of this book is to construct the most comprehensive collection of case studies on hub-and-spoke cartels and analyze them through the lens of economic reasoning. We have identified three classes of hub-and-spoke cartels, each analyzed in three parts. The first part of the analysis offers an economic framework applicable to that class. It provides insight into why those cartels form and how they operate. The second part is a description of the hub-and-spoke cartels in that class. To the extent that such information is available, each case study addresses:

- *Formation* Who initiated collusion, and what was their objective?
- *Coordination* How did the hub and spokes coordinate? How did they communicate, and what was the role of the hub?
- *Enforcement* How did the hub and spokes monitor conduct for compliance? How did the hub and spokes punish when there was evidence of noncompliance?
- *Efficacy* How effective was collusion, and did it benefit all cartel members?
- *Prosecution* What was the disposition of the legal case?

The third part draws general lessons from those case studies. In particular, it distills elements common to these cartels and identifies how they differed.

In creating a collection of hub-and-spoke cartels, our goal was to be as comprehensive as possible, subject to three criteria. The first was whether there is compelling evidence of collusion. While a conviction was sufficient to meet that criterion, it was not necessary, for many cases settle without a judicial decision. Though innocent firms may settle for financial reasons, the cases included here contained enough evidence that we were convinced that collusion was present. The second criterion was whether there is adequate documentation for identifying some critical features of the collusive scheme.[9] The third criterion was whether communication between competitors was primarily through an upstream supplier or downstream customer, which we take as the defining trait of a hub-and-spoke cartel. For most cases, communication between competitors was totally absent (at least according to the documented record). In a few cases, there was some direct communication between spokes, which supplemented the bilateral communication between the hub and a spoke.[10]

After an exhaustive search, 16 cases were found that satisfied these criteria. They are listed in table 1.1.

Table 1.1 demonstrates that while prosecuted hub-and-spoke cartels go back to the mid-1930s, the vast majority of cases date from the 1980s onward. This is in line with the general increase in cartel prosecution around this time. It is worth noting that the earliest documented case of a hub-and-spoke cartel occurred in the Canadian sugar market in 1887. This case (summarized in section 3.4) is not included in our main sample, since it occurred prior to the introduction of Canada's competition law in 1889 so communications between the hub and spokes were unconstrained.[11]

In spite of a limited number of cases in our sample and the usual sample selection bias associated with cartel studies,[12] we believe the study delivers on its goal of substantively improving our understanding of hub-and-spoke collusion.

This book developed out of previously unpublished work by the authors: a working paper by Joseph Harrington (2018) and uncirculated research by Luke Garrod and Matthew Olczak (2018). The aim of the latter work was to use four UK hub-and-spoke cartels to shed light on the economic incentives of the cartel members, as well as their roles in helping to coordinate, monitor, and enforce the agreement. A limitation of that study is that the sample comprises only one of the three classes of hub-and-spoke cartels identified here. Harrington (2018) analyzes a larger—but still restricted—sample that

Table 1.1

List of hub-and-spoke cartels

Market	Country	Years of operation[a]
Automobile retailing	US	1979–1980
Bread	Canada	2001–2017
Chicken	Chile	2008–2011
Commercial insurance	US	1998–2004
Dairy products	UK	2002–2003
Desiccant	UK	2000–2003
Drugstore, perfumery, and hygiene products	Belgium	2002–2007
e-books[b]	US	2009–2013
Fiberglass insulation	US	1999–2003
Movie exhibition	US	1934–1935
Paints and varnishes	Poland	2003–2006
Pharmaceutical products	US	1956
Replica football kits	UK	2000–2001
Specialty pipe	US	1981–1984
Toys	UK	1999–2001
Toys	US	1989–1997

[a] The first year of operation was the first year in which there was evidence of communication relevant to collusion. The last year of operation was either when there was evidence that the firms were no longer coordinating or, when that evidence was absent, the year of the first judicial decision ruling against the cartel.

[b] There was also a similar case brought in this market by the European Commission. However, while recognizing the communication through a downstream supplier, the infringement was based on direct communication between suppliers (OECD 2019). Thus, we focus on the US case, where the hub-and-spoke agreement was integral to the case.

spans two of the three classes of hub-and-spoke cartels investigated here and primarily focuses on the coordinating practices of those cartels. Thus, this book is more comprehensive in terms of the cases covered and the features of the cartels described. This allows us to develop a deeper understanding of why hub-and-spoke cartels form, how they operate, how effective they are, and how best to prosecute them.

Hub-and-spoke cartels have long been recognized as a phenomenon in economic and legal circles, so there is an existing body of research work, though it is slim. Odudu (2011), Sahuguet and Walckiers (2013, 2014), Zampa and Buccirossi (2013), Van Cayseele (2014), and Orbach (2016) raise some of the economic and legal issues regarding hub-and-spoke collusion but do not provide a comparative analysis of hub-and-spoke cartels to address the questions of this book.[13] There is also a small body of theoretical work on hub-and-spoke collusion, which includes Van Cayseele and Miegelsen (2013), Sahuguet and Walckiers (2017), and Shamir (2017), as well as some papers motivated by the e-books case (which are referenced in chapter 5). What is missing from the literature is a comprehensive and systematic study of hub-and-spoke collusion. This book fills that gap.

The book is organized as follows. Effective collusion requires that firms decide to participate in a cartel, coordinate in some collusive arrangement, and act to maintain that arrangement. Chapter 2 examines when we can expect those three conditions to be satisfied for a hub-and-spoke cartel. It sheds light on collusion in the absence of direct communication between competitors and when a third party participates that has a vertical relationship with the firms that are restraining competition. Chapters 3–5 are the core of the book, with one chapter on each of the three classes of hub-and-spoke cartels we have identified. Chapter 3 covers cartels for which the hub is an upstream manufacturer or wholesaler and the spokes are downstream retailers or distributors, where the cartel's objective is to raise downstream prices. Chapter 4 turns to cartels for which spokes are upstream suppliers and the hub is a downstream intermediary. The goal of these cartels is to raise the prices of upstream suppliers that are charged to buyers who use the downstream intermediary. The cartels in chapter 5 have a downstream distributor or customer as the hub and upstream suppliers as the spokes, with the objective of excluding a rival to the downstream firm. Where needed, a mathematical economic analysis is provided to substantiate our claims. This can be found in the technical appendices to chapters 3 and 5 (sections 3.5 and 5.5, respectively). Chapter 6 draws some general lessons from chapters 3–5. The analysis in chapters 2–6 focuses on economic factors and is relevant regardless of how a jurisdiction's competition law treats hub-and-spoke cartels. For those jurisdictions that find such cartels unlawful, chapter 7 examines some of the issues and challenges in prosecuting hub-and-spoke collusion. The primary challenge is to determine when a series of vertical agreements form a horizontal agreement. We also offer a new legal approach with specific strategies for proving that there is a horizontal agreement in spite of the lack of direct communication between competitors.

2 General Analysis of Hub-and-Spoke Collusion

Collusion is a particular mode of conduct designed to constrain competition in order to yield a supracompetitive (or collusive) outcome that delivers higher profits for firms. Typically, a supracompetitive outcome takes the form of prices above competitive levels, though it could also involve limiting supplies, restricting manufacturing capacity, prohibiting advertising, or constraining other variables by which firms compete. A supracompetitive outcome is sustained by firms adopting *collusive* strategies. A collusive strategy is composed of three crucial components. First, it describes the collusive outcome, such as high prices or a market allocation scheme (e.g., allocating customers or territories across cartel members). Second, it describes how firms will be monitored for compliance with that collusive outcome. For example, monitoring prices when they are publicly available (such as with a cartel of retailers) or monitoring sales as part of a market allocation scheme (which is common with intermediate goods cartels). Third, a collusive strategy provides the punishment to be imposed should there be evidence of noncompliance. Intended to provide incentives to comply, that punishment could be reversion to competition or some other conduct that would harm the noncompliant firm (e.g., aggressively competing for its customers). Collusion is the adoption of collusive strategies, and the collusive or supracompetitive outcome observed in the market is the manifestation of using those collusive strategies.

2.1 Collusion Requires Participation, Stability, and Coordination

Having stated what collusion is, what is required for it to occur? For a group of competing firms to shift from competition to collusion, three conditions must be satisfied, which we refer to as participation, stability, and coordination.[1] Participation refers to the discrete event whereby firms engage in forming a cartel. Participation may start with just one firm adopting the objective of constraining competition and then acting as an entrepreneur to attract other firms to this nefarious enterprise. The decision to pursue collusion is presumably motivated by the prospect of higher profits, so the participation condition is more likely to be satisfied when the incremental profits from collusion are higher. There could be a triggering event—such as a sharp decline in profits—that leads firms to adopt the view that competition ought to be replaced with collusion. Some cartels—such as in the markets for citric acid (Connor 2008) and graphite electrodes (Levenstein and Suslow 2004)—formed after experiencing a significant decline in price-cost margins that was apparently caused by more aggressive competition.

Just because collusion is profitable, it does not follow that the participation condition will be satisfied. One reason is that the prospect of detection and penalties may discourage firms from pursuing cartel formation. Even if the expected incremental profit exceeds the expected penalties, managers may be disinclined to collude because of a reticence to engage in unlawful behavior or uncertainty as to whether other firms would participate (given that attempting to collude can be unlawful as well). Though it is not well understood what sparks cartel formation, it is important to remember that the pursuit of collusion is a conscious, well-defined decision by firms and is a necessary first step for collusion to occur.

Let us suppose the participation condition is satisfied so (at least some) firms want to collude. However, as elsewhere in life, wanting something does not mean having something. For collusion to occur, it must also be feasible to collude. That is, a collusive arrangement (i.e., collusive strategies) must exist that, if adopted by firms, would result in a collusive outcome and firms would find it in their best interest to go along with it if other firms are expected to do so. When such a stable collusive arrangement exists, we say that the stability condition is satisfied.

The challenge for meeting the stability condition is that the adoption of a collusive outcome creates an incentive for firms to deviate from it. Given that a collusive outcome involves departing from the competitive outcome (e.g., pricing above the competitive level or choosing not to compete for some customers), a firm could increase its current profit by deviating from the collusive outcome (e.g., by lowering its price or selling to those customers). It is that short-run temptation to deviate that poses a challenge for the stability of any collusive outcome. For all firms to behave as prescribed by the collusive outcome, each firm must believe that a departure from it is sufficiently likely to be detected and punished. A firm must view the short-run gain in profit from cheating as being exceeded by the expected future loss associated with detection of their deviation and its subsequent punishment (such as a temporary price war or the indefinite breakdown of collusion). Hence, a supracompetitive outcome will arise and persist only if there exists a self-enforcing collusive arrangement where *self-enforcing* means that each firm prefers to abide by it rather than act differently.

Thus far, we have described the internal stability condition, which ensures that all cartel members find it best to implement the collusive outcome. There is also the external stability condition, which ensures that the collusive outcome is not upset by the actions of noncartel firms (when the cartel is not all-inclusive) or by the entry of new firms into the market. Entry barriers are critical to preventing a collusive arrangement from collapsing because of these external actors. In sum, the stability condition is satisfied when there exists a stable collusive arrangement, which means it is resistant to internal and external forces that might upset it.[2]

Even if firms *want* to collude (so the participation condition is satisfied) and firms *can* collude (so the stability condition is satisfied), it does not immediately follow that firms *will* collude. This brings us to the coordination condition. Making a move from competition to collusion is not always straightforward or assured of success. Firms must communicate if they are to achieve a state of mutual understanding that competition is to be replaced with collusion. This state of mind is what competition law refers to as an *agreement*, which, according to the US Supreme Court, is when firms have a "unity of purpose or a common design and understanding, or a meeting of minds"[3] and "a conscious commitment to a common scheme designed to achieve an unlawful objective."[4] This perspective is echoed by the EU General Court, which refers to it as firms having "joint intention"[5] and a "concurrence of wills."[6] All these terms focus on the same mental state: mutual understanding among firms that they will restrict competition in some manner. Achieving that common state of mind is what the coordination condition is all about.

When firms engage in express communication (e.g., unfettered natural language that is not lawyered up), coordination can fail because the veracity of their communications is questioned. A firm may not believe another firm when it says it will raise its price or stay away from rival firms' customers. To make achieving mutual understanding even more challenging, firms may not speak so expressly in order to avoid engaging in a per se (or by object) violation of competition law. Instead, they may deploy nonexpress means of communication that, while less incriminating, are also less effective in achieving a mutual understanding not to compete. Even when firms' messages are understood, coordination can fail because of disagreement. For example, there are many instances in which collusion is not realized because of a bargaining breakdown over how to allocate market demand.[7] Getting past the challenges of communication and bargaining, the coordination condition is satisfied when firms are able to achieve mutual understanding that firms are colluding as well as how they are colluding (i.e., the collusive arrangement).

Summing up, collusion occurs when firms intend to replace competition with collusion (participation condition), there exists a stable collusive arrangement (stability condition), and firms are able to orchestrate a coordinated shift from competition to collusion (coordination condition).

2.2   Participation, Stability, and Coordination Conditions for a Hub-and-Spoke Cartel

Given this general understanding of what must transpire for collusion to emerge in a market, let us discuss when these three conditions are satisfied for a hub-and-spoke cartel. The canonical cartel comprises firms that are alternative suppliers in a market and but for collusion would be competitors for some common set of customers. A *hub-and-spoke cartel* augments that collection of firms with a firm that resides either upstream or downstream. The *spokes* of a hub-and-spoke cartel are the suppliers in a market (which are the sole members of the canonical cartel), and the *hub* is the upstream supplier or downstream customer that facilitates collusion by the spokes. The mutual understanding of a collusive arrangement among the spokes is referred to as the *rim*, for it connects the spokes. It is the rim that transforms a series of vertical relationships into a horizontal agreement.

There are two general ways in which the hub plays a substantive role in collusion. First, the hub is the nexus in a communication network. Generally, the spokes do not communicate directly and instead engage in bilateral communications with the upstream or downstream hub. Through these bilateral communications, the hub seeks to achieve mutual understanding of a collusive arrangement among the spokes and thereby satisfy the coordination condition. Second, the hub has a transactional role with each spoke because it is a buyer or seller, which has implications for satisfying the participation and stability conditions. Let us explore how the hub affects collusion by buying from or selling to the spokes and as the conduit for communications between the spokes.

2.2.1 Participation

As already noted, a reduction in prices may induce firms to form a cartel. Such a source for satisfying the participation condition also occurs with hub-and-spoke cartels. As we will document, some hub-and-spoke cartels formed in response to complaints by downstream retailers to an upstream supplier that retail profit margins were too low or that a particular downstream retailer was competing too aggressively. Thus, a common motivation for standard cartels also pertains to hub-and-spoke cartels.

There are, however, sources of cartel formation unique to hub-and-spoke cartels. For example, an upstream supplier may be interested in raising wholesale prices but believe that downstream buyers would resist the increase unless they could be assured of higher retail prices to preserve their margins. Or consider a downstream retailer that is faced with tough competition from a class of competitors. A strategic response to that downstream retailer is to form a hub-and-spoke cartel that coordinates upstream suppliers to exclude those competitors by denying them supply. In both these instances, the impetus for the cartel is coming not from the firms that will ultimately coordinate their conduct but rather from the firm that has a vertical relationship with them. Here, the participation condition is satisfied for a hub-and-spoke cartel but would not have been satisfied for a standard cartel.

2.2.2 Coordination

Turning to the coordination condition, collusion requires that competitors achieve some level of mutual understanding that they are constraining competition and how they plan to do so (i.e., the collusive scheme). In a hub-and-spoke cartel, this mutual understanding is largely (if not exclusively) achieved by firms communicating indirectly through an upstream supplier or downstream customer. Compared to when competitors communicate directly, indirect communication may be less effective for two reasons. First, messages between spokes may lose information in the process of going through the hub. Collusion requires that each firm achieve some level of trust with the other cartel members so that it is confident that they will abide by the collusive outcome. With face-to-face direct communication, it is not just words that create that trust; it may be how words are expressed (emphasis, inflection, hesitation), facial expressions, eye contact, and body language. Experimental research has shown that this extraneous information from direct interaction provides useful cues for cooperation.[8] However, when firms communicate through a third party, all but the words get stripped away. In addition to the loss of those other facets of communication, errors may be introduced as the hub forgets to convey something said by a spoke or mistakenly inserts something that a spoke did not say. Messages communicated through a hub are then apt to be less rich, less accurate, and less precise than when conveyed directly, and that could make it more difficult for firms to achieve mutual understanding of a collusive arrangement.

Second, the hub may intentionally distort messages or otherwise control the conversation between spokes because it is not a neutral third party.[9] Common sense suggests that messages between two parties are more likely to be informative if the preferences and interests of the two parties are more closely aligned. If two people have a mutual interest in meeting up, then individual A has every incentive to accurately convey where she will be at a particular time to individual B. In contrast, if A does not want to meet with B, then A will have an incentive not to reveal where she will be and, consequently, B would be naive to believe what A has told him. More generally, the following property has been established in a simple game-theoretic model (Crawford and Sobel 1982) for which individual A has some private information, A sends a message about that private information to individual B, B draws an inference from that message about A's private information, and B takes an action that affects both A and B.[10] If the interests of A and B are fully aligned, then messages are shown to be fully informative, and if the interests of A and B are diametrically opposed, then messages are fully uninformative. If the interests of A and B are partially aligned, then messages are partially informative and increasing the alignment of interests results in more informative messages. Thus, when it comes to considering the effectiveness of communication between cartel members for achieving mutual understanding, a key driver is how aligned their interests are with regard to the collusive outcome.

The relevance of that theory to hub-and-spoke cartels is that messages conveyed by the hub to a spoke may only be partially informative because their interests, while not entirely in conflict, are not fully coincident either. Collusion will impact competitors in a market differently from an upstream supplier or a downstream customer. For example, downstream retailers can benefit from a rise in retail prices, while an upstream supplier will be harmed by the lower demand for its product (because of lower downstream demand). However, higher retail prices could allow the upstream firm to raise its wholesale price, which would benefit it. Or higher retail prices could induce retailers to provide more service, and that will benefit the upstream supplier by generating more demand. Hence, collusion can benefit both the hub and spokes but in different ways. This means that all parties could agree that collusion is desirable but have different ideas as to the most desirable collusive outcome. Given that there is some misalignment of interests, there is scope for deception by the hub, which would make communication less effective and make it more difficult to satisfy the coordination condition.

To exemplify how different interests can lead to message distortion, consider a hub-and-spoke cartel in which a manufacturer is the hub (e.g., Hasbro), retailers are the spokes (e.g., Argos and Littlewoods), and the collusive outcome has retailers raise their prices, which will then support a rise in the wholesale price. A retailer will be concerned with avoiding a situation in which it raises its price only to find that other retailers did not raise their prices, for such an outcome would cause the retailer to suffer a decline in demand and profit. Thus, a compliant retailer incurs a cost for participating in failed collusion and, critical for the current discussion, this cost is likely to be more severe for a retailer than for the upstream manufacturer. With the manufacturer undervaluing the risk that the retailers face, it may then try to mislead them in order to enhance the chances of collusion. For example, the manufacturer might tell each retailer that the other retailers have agreed to raise their prices when they have said no such thing. The manufacturer benefits if this tactic succeeds in inducing all retailers to raise their prices, and it is only modestly harmed (relative to any complying retailers) if it fails. Such an incentive to mislead could make communication problematic. If the spokes believe the hub is always inclined to say that all other spokes have agreed to collude (whether or not it is true), then the hub's announcements would be uninformative to the spokes. In such a situation, the hub would be unlikely to succeed in establishing mutual understanding among the spokes. In sum, mutual understanding among firms may be more problematic when they communicate indirectly, because each firm is not sure what other firms are saying and hearing and the upstream or downstream firm that is intermediating may have an incentive to engage in acts of omission or deception.

Thus far, our discussion has focused on how communication between competitors is less effective when it is conducted through an upstream or downstream hub. However, there are ways in which the presence of a hub can make communication more effective. First, the credibility of a hub's messages may be enhanced because of its relations with a spoke, which go beyond participating in a collusive arrangement, and that could act as a countervailing force to the sources of incredulity just described. From its previous business dealings with a spoke, a hub may have established a reputation it can draw on. With regard to future business dealings with a spoke, a hub will want to maintain a reputation for providing accurate information and following through on its promises, and that will make its messages more credible. In contrast, direct communication between rival firms in a market is not common in a competitive environment. This means that the members of a standard cartel cannot draw on an existing reputation for veracity (and incentives for maintaining such a reputation) when they communicate with each other, while an upstream supplier or downstream customer can do so in the context of a hub-and-spoke cartel.

A second advantage may come from more frequent communications in the case of a hub-and-spoke cartel. Direct communication between competitors is inherently suspicious from a legal perspective, and that could cause the members of a standard cartel to limit the frequency of communication in order to reduce the chances of detection and lessen the amount of incriminating evidence. In contrast, communication between an upstream seller and a downstream buyer is to be expected under competition. While the content of that communication is problematic when it involves collusion, that the parties are communicating is not. The routine nature of communication within the vertical chain is a factor that makes it easier for a hub-and-spoke cartel to satisfy the coordination condition.

In discussing the efficacy of communication in a hub-and-spoke cartel, we should remember that direct communications between firms in a standard cartel are also imperfect. Cartel members' interests are not fully aligned, which leaves scope for deception when communicating. While a higher common price is likely to benefit all cartel members, so their interests are probably well aligned in that dimension,[11] their preferences among different market allocations are in pure conflict because market allocation is a zero-sum game: when one firm is given a higher market share, some other firm must receive a lower market share. Thus, two cartel members' interests are opposed when it comes to market allocation, though they may largely coincide concerning price. Not surprisingly, some communication in standard cartels is duplicitous and uninformative.[12] In comparison, an upstream supplier might care little about the market allocation scheme (i.e., how its supply is divvied up among the downstream firms) but have preferences different from those of spokes regarding price (for a rise in downstream prices can lower the upstream firm's profits and raise the downstream firms' profits). The point is that the degree of alignment of interests between colluding firms is different from the degree of alignment between an upstream hub and downstream spokes or a downstream hub and upstream spokes in a hub-and-spoke cartel, and that has implications for the effectiveness of communication.

Finally, let us note that when a spoke conveys a message to the hub with the intent that the message be shared with another spoke, any incentive for it to mislead another cartel member that would have existed with direct communication is likely to remain when the communication is indirect through the hub. Furthermore, theoretical research has shown that the presence of an intermediary between communicating parties can only reduce the informativeness of those parties' messages.[13] This suggests that replacing direct communications between spokes with indirect communications through a hub will tend to make communication less effective.

2.2.3 Stability

Turning to the stability condition, the presence of an upstream or downstream firm in the collusive arrangement has implications for the collusive outcome, monitoring, and punishments.[14] The first key point is that the hub will participate only if it finds it profitable to do so; that is, if its profits are higher under collusion. This simple observation has several implications. As already mentioned in the context of the participation condition, the collusive outcome can have a different character depending on whether the cartel is formed at the instigation of an upstream firm or a downstream firm. For example, the collusive outcome might be the coordinated exclusion of competitors to the hub, which would only come about when the hub initiated cartel formation. If the purpose of the cartel is to raise the upstream hub's wholesale price, then downstream retail prices may be raised to the minimum level necessary for the downstream spokes to accept that wholesale price increase. However, if the downstream retailers are the ones to initiate collusion, they are likely to strive for higher retail prices though they will be constrained in that prices cannot rise so high that the upstream firm's demand declines to a point where its profits are lower. In contrast, if the downstream firms sought to collude without a hub, retail prices would not be so restricted and thus could be even higher. Or consider an upstream manufacturer that is concerned that raising retail prices on its products may cause consumers to switch over to other manufacturers' products carried by those same retailers. In at least one case, the upstream hub requested that the retailers raise the prices of those other products. While that will enhance the hub's profits (as it would limit the extent of switchers), it will also raise the profits of the spoke, which will have an incentive to unilaterally increase the prices of rival brands anyway. In various ways, the inclusion of a firm upstream or downstream in the cartel can alter the form and profitability of the collusive outcome.

When the initial impetus for collusion comes from the spokes, the collusive outcome must increase the profits of the spokes and the hub. Of course, the spokes could instead pursue a standard cartel, in which case it is not constrained to ensure that the hub benefits from it. That they do not do so suggests there are some advantages to involving a firm with which they have a vertical relationship. However, if it is the hub that initiates collusion—for example, in order to engage in exclusion against some of its rivals—then it is actually not necessary that the spokes earn higher profits from collusion compared to competition. It is enough that each spoke finds it in its best interest to collude *given that all other spokes are expected to collude*; that is, it is an equilibrium for spokes to participate in the collusive scheme. Collectively, spokes could be worse off from collusion, but, individually, each spoke goes along because it is better than the punishment that would be inflicted on it for not complying. As we will see, this possibility is relevant for understanding some hub-and-spoke cartels designed to exclude rival firms.

Irrespective of whether the instigation for collusion came from the hub or spokes, that the hub controls information flows could allow it to influence the collusive outcome. For example, suppose a retailer communicated to the manufacturer that it would like all retailers to raise prices by 15% but the manufacturer prefers a 10% increase. Given that the manufacturer is the information gatekeeper, it could convey to the other retailers that this retailer's pricing intention is to raise its price by 10%. More generally, given its strategic position in the communication network, the hub may choose to distort communications between the spokes in order to push the collusive outcome in a direction that it favors.

With regard to monitoring compliance with the collusive outcome, it could be more effective with a hub-and-spoke cartel because the hub is in a better position to monitor. As part of normal business practices, the hub is regularly communicating with the spokes, whether it is to take orders (in the case of an upstream supplier) or place them (in the case of a downstream customer). Those interactions provide opportunities to collect information useful for monitoring. For example, when visiting stores, it would be easy for an upstream supplier to observe the prices that a retailer is charging and thus whether it is setting collusive prices. In addition, if the spokes are engaging in their own monitoring, the hub can collect that information when interacting with the spokes. If a downstream buyer acquires evidence from several upstream suppliers that a particular upstream supplier is not in compliance, that provides a compelling basis for implementing a punishment against that upstream supplier. Given the hub's vertical relationships with the spokes, it is well situated to collect and disseminate information relevant to monitoring, and with more effective monitoring comes more effective collusion.

The hub may possess instruments to induce spokes to comply with the collusive outcome, and that richer set of punishments would expand the set of stable collusive outcomes. One instrument is the refusal to sell to or buy from a spoke. If the hub is an upstream supplier, it could threaten to limit, delay, or deny supply to a downstream retailer that is undercutting the collusive price. Such a threat would help stabilize collusion in two ways. First, the prospect of foregone profit resulting from not having the supply to sell would induce retailers to comply. Second, in response to a retailer undercutting the collusive price, compliant firms are inclined to lower their prices to stave off the loss of demand. However, if the deviating retailer does not have the supply to fully meet the additional demand, then the demand loss to compliant firms is lessened, which could make them inclined to continue to charge the collusive price. Analogously, if the hub is a dominant downstream retailer, then it could threaten to refuse to purchase from noncompliant upstream suppliers.[15] A second instrument is the use of side payments to stabilize collusion. The hub could offer monetary transfers to those firms that comply—for example, in the form of rebates—which would provide additional incentives for the spokes to abide by the collusive arrangement. While monetary transfers could occur between firms in a standard cartel, they are more likely to create suspicion than if they were from a supplier or customer.[16]

2.3 Summary and Final Remarks

Summing up, collusion occurs when firms decide to replace competition with collusion (participation), when firms communicate to achieve mutual understanding of a collusive arrangement (coordination), and when that collusive arrangement is self-enforcing in that all firms find it in their best interest to implement the supracompetitive outcome, given how it is to be monitored and enforced (stability). The presence of an upstream or downstream firm in a cartel can affect whether there is a stable collusive arrangement, whether firms are able to coordinate on it, and whether firms participate by seeking to form a cartel. A cartel may form only because of the initiative and entrepreneurship of the hub. Compared to when firms communicate directly, coordination may be more or less difficult in a hub-and-spoke cartel. Indirect communication through a firm that may have incentives to filter or distort messages could make communication less effective. On the other hand, an upstream supplier or downstream customer might communicate more frequently and have more credibility because it has legitimate reasons to communicate with these firms. Lastly, the presence of a hub can affect the set of stable collusive arrangements because the collusive outcome is constrained by the need to enhance the profits of the hub as well as those of the spokes (though the latter may not always be required), but, at the same time, monitoring and punishments are likely to be more effective because the hub has information (as a buyer or seller) and instruments (e.g., denying purchases or sales) at its disposal that are not available to the spokes. There are then a rich set of differences between how a hub-and-spoke cartel operates and how standard cartels operate.

Finally, there are likely to be differences regarding the detection and prosecution of collusion when the cartel is of the hub-and-spoke variety. As opposed to direct communications between competitors, indirect communications through a hub leave less of an evidentiary trail. In practice, prosecuting those cases is more challenging because plaintiffs must argue that these vertical relationships embody a horizontal agreement.[17] Firms may then be more inclined to collude through a hub-and-spoke cartel because plaintiffs find it more difficult to prove that firms have colluded. In addition, bilateral communications between a seller and a buyer would not create suspicion, which means that detection is less likely. However, whether the firms involved in a hub-and-spoke cartel appreciate the illegality of their actions is unclear. If they communicate somewhat openly about cartel activities under the false assumption that their actions are lawful, the actual probability of being found to have participated in an illegal cartel may exceed what is perceived by the firms. Also enhancing the probability of detection is that a hub-and-spoke cartel may require the involvement of a large number of employees, who range from senior staff tasked with organizing the arrangement to lesser staff members who operationalize it by passing messages between the hub and spokes. This could mean that there are more people who could "blow the whistle" or accidentally "let the cat out of the bag." In contrast, standard cartels can often be restricted to the senior staff members who determine the prices.[18] It is unclear, however, whether the involvement of more employees is because hub-and-spoke cartels inherently require more people to operate or reflects the beliefs of the parties that their actions are not illegal.

In order to flesh out this general theoretical discussion, chapters 3–5 examine a diverse array of hub-and-spoke cartels across each of the three classes we have identified. For each class, the economic framework considers the three crucial components of a collusive strategy we identified earlier: the collusive outcome, monitoring, and punishment. That analysis provides insight into why the specific class of cartels forms and how it operates. Each cartel is then examined with the goal of addressing the following questions: How was collusion initiated? How did firms coordinate? What was the collusive outcome, and how was it monitored and enforced? Did collusion benefit all firms? What was the role of the hub? What was the effect of collusion on prices and other market variables?

3 Collusion to Raise Downstream Prices: Upstream Supplier as Hub

In this chapter, we discuss the economics of hub-and-spoke cartels when the hub is located upstream. In section 3.1, we explore how vertical relationships operate under competition, and we consider the implications for hub-and-spoke cartels. Section 3.2 examines 10 hub-and-spoke cartels, and section 3.3 distills some general lessons from these cases. Section 3.4 is an appendix that covers the historically interesting case of a Canadian sugar cartel. Section 3.5 is a technical appendix that includes some of the underlying economic theory.

3.1 Economic Framework

A vertical supply chain is a sequence of firms in which one firm supplies an input to another firm in the production chain and at the end of this sequence is a firm that supplies a final good or service. Given this interdependence, the decision of a firm at one stage of the supply chain will affect the choices and profits of firms at other stages of the supply chain. Because the incentives of these firms may not be aligned, what one firm chooses to do could have adverse effects on firms at other points in the vertical chain, and this could prove to be detrimental to the chain's total profits. Consequently, these firms may engage in vertical agreements to influence or restrict the decisions of other firms, with the aim of better aligning their incentives. This can, in principle, benefit all firms when it raises the total profits of the vertical chain.

A hub-and-spoke cartel can be viewed as a special type of vertical agreement. In this chapter, it involves a horizontal agreement among downstream competitors that is facilitated by an upstream firm. Before we start examining such cartels, it will be useful to first review competitive conduct and performance within vertical chains. In forming a hub-and-spoke cartel, firms will be seeking to improve on their results under competition, so we will need to understand how competition leaves room for both upstream and downstream firms to earn higher profits. While our discussion pertains to many different types of vertical chains, it is most relevant when the upstream firm is a manufacturer and the downstream firm is a retailer. Thus, we will often use these terms.

3.1.1 Competitive Benchmark

We begin by assessing how a firm's pricing decisions affect the profits of firms operating at a different stage of the supply chain. A manufacturer's wholesale price will affect the profits of the manufacturer and the retailers, though in opposite directions. If we hold constant the quantity sold to final consumers (which is appropriate if downstream prices are held fixed), a manufacturer's profit will be increased by a higher wholesale price for its product, but this will decrease the profits of the retailers, as they now face a higher cost.

Turning to the price that a retailer charges to final consumers, its effect on profits is more complex. If the wholesale price is held constant, an upstream manufacturer will prefer lower retail prices for its brand because this will induce final consumers to buy more from retailers, who in turn will buy more from the manufacturer. Consequently, at a given wholesale price, the manufacturer's profit will be higher when retail prices are lower. In contrast, a retailer trades off the higher demand from a lower retail price against the lower profit earned per unit. Because a retailer will choose a price that maximizes its profit and is not concerned with the impact on the manufacturer's profit, it will typically price too high from the perspective of the manufacturer. Though competition between retailers will limit the magnitude of this effect as it forces retail prices down, it will not entirely eliminate it as long as retailers have some market power to price above cost.[1] Thus, at the competitive prices charged by retailers, the manufacturer would benefit from retail prices being reduced (and remember we are holding the wholesale price fixed). The retailer's price imposes a negative externality on the manufacturer in that a higher price reduces the manufacturer's profit and that effect is not taken account of (or internalized) by the retailer.

This misalignment of pricing incentives between upstream and down-stream firms can lead to outcomes that are inefficient for the vertical chain in the sense that there are alternative feasible choices that could raise the total profits of the vertical chain and possibly make all firms better off. Of particular importance is the inefficiency referred to as "double marginaliza-tion" (Spengler 1980). To explain this inefficiency, consider a monopoly supplier that sells its product to a monopoly retailer at a fixed wholesale price per unit.[2] Suppose the manufacturer has all the bargaining power, so it can dictate the level of the wholesale price to the retailer. In order to maximize its profit, the manufacturer will choose the wholesale price as a monopoly markup over its marginal cost, and the retailer will then add a monopoly markup of its own. The problem of double marginaliza-tion arises because when the manufacturer and retailer independently set their markups, neither considers that a higher markup lowers the profits of the other. If they accounted for their markup's effect on the other firm in the vertical chain, they would ensure that there is only one monopoly markup imposed on the product. In other words, they would internalize the externalities they impose on each other by acting as a vertically inte-grated monopolist that would set the price that maximizes total profits. If they did not do so, two monopoly markups would be imposed and the profits of the chain would not be maximized, because the resultant retail price would be too high.

Another important decision for the vertical chain is a retailer's choice about how much to invest in raising demand through instruments other than price. Such activities include advertising the product, employing highly motivated sales representatives to assist potential customers, and offering aftersale services. These activities will benefit both retailers and the manu-facturer through increased sales. However, in deciding how much to spend on nonprice demand-enhancing activities, a retailer will not take into account the effect of these activities on the manufacturer's profits. As a result, given that such activities are costly to the retailers, they will invest less than the manufacturer desires.

We have consequently identified a second inefficiency, which is under-investment in retail service provision. The root of this inefficiency is that the retailer incurs all the cost but does not reap all the benefit, because the manufacturer claims some of the higher profit. Because of this external-ity, there will be underprovision of these services from the perspective of maximizing the total profits of the vertical chain. Furthermore, this inefficiency is exacerbated when retailer competition is more intense. Given that more intense competition lowers retail prices, the smaller retail profit margin means a smaller return from raising demand. Hence, a retailer may invest little even though more investment would yield higher profits for the vertical chain; the problem is that those profits are largely going to the manufacturer because of low retail margins. Even when retail margins are not low, underinvestment occurs when the increased demand is not fully appropriated by the retailer making the investment and is partly received by competing retailers (Telser 1960). This occurs when investments are nonexcludable (i.e., a retailer cannot prevent another retailer from benefiting from the investment). For example, a consumer can access the high-quality services provided by a retailer (e.g., an offline retailer with an attractive showroom and helpful sales personnel) but then purchase the product from a rival retailer that provides little or no service and is able to sell at a lower price because it does not incur the costs related to service (e.g., an online retailer). Consequently, retailers have an incentive to free ride on the service provision of their rivals, and retailers will underinvest in anticipation of such free riding. In light of this inefficiency, the total profits of the vertical chain could be increased if all retailers were to invest more.

As the preceding analysis has shown, competition leaves room for the vertical chain to do better because retailers price too high (because of double marginalization) and invest too little in demand-enhancing activities (because the manufacturer and other retailers free ride on a retailer's investment). Vertical agreements offer solutions to correct these inefficiencies. For example, the provision of exclusive territories can solve free riding by other retailers. If a retailer is the only one who sells in a geographic area and consumers in that area are constrained to buy from that retailer (e.g., they cannot buy online), then any increase in demand resulting from that retailer's investment will be claimed by that retailer. While the manufacturer still appropriates part of the additional profits—in which case some inefficiency remains—a vertical agreement giving a retailer exclusivity to an area can partially alleviate it. An agreement that will help correct the remaining inefficiency would be for the manufacturer to subsidize the retailer's investment, which is feasible when that investment is observable, such as in the case of advertising.[3]

Our focus will be on correcting the inefficiency of double marginalization, which is most directly relevant to our analysis of hub-and-spoke collusion.

One solution to the double-marginalization problem is for the supplier to fix the retail price at the level that maximizes the profits of the vertical structure, which means lowering the retail price by removing the second markup that would otherwise be imposed by the retailer. Such an agreement could take the form of a manufacturer setting a maximum price that retailers are allowed to charge (also known as maximum resale price maintenance). In some jurisdictions, such vertical agreements are unlawful, which prevents their use.[4]

A second solution to double marginalization lies in the type of contract that determines the terms of trade between the manufacturer and retailers. Rather than have the retailer pay a constant wholesale price for each unit it buys from the manufacturer, suppose the pricing arrangement is a two-part tariff consisting of a constant wholesale price per unit and a fixed fee (which essentially is a payment made to have the right to buy the good). Consider the case of weak intrabrand competition so retailers offering the same brand are nearly local monopolies. The upstream supplier could avoid double marginalization by setting its unit wholesale price equal to its marginal cost so it does not impose a margin on the product. With the wholesale price equal to the manufacturer's cost, the retailer will be acting like a vertically integrated monopolist when it sets its retail price. As a result, the retailer earns monopoly profits, which the manufacturer can then extract by setting the fixed fee equal to those profits. Furthermore, when there is more intense intrabrand competition between the retailers so each retailer imposes a smaller than monopoly markup, the supplier is able to set its wholesale price above its marginal cost to ensure that the retailers remain incentivized to set the retail price of an integrated monopolist. Then, similar to before, the manufacturer can set the fixed fee equal to the retailer's profit in order to extract the remaining rents from the retailers that are not captured by the wholesale price markup.

3.1.2 Collusive Outcome

With that background on the operation of a vertical chain under competition, let us now consider the incentives to form a hub-and-spoke cartel. The first observation is that it is not clear why an upstream supplier would facilitate collusion among downstream retailers, which serves to raise downstream prices. Suppose the upstream firm charged a two-part tariff to solve the double-marginalization problem. A two-part tariff extracts all possible profits from the retailers, so there is nothing to be gained (and in fact something to be lost) by facilitating retailers' coordination to raise prices. However, in spite of their theoretical appeal in correcting inefficiencies, two-part tariffs (and other nonlinear pricing schemes) are not as common in practice as theory would suggest. That is a puzzle that goes beyond the current study. It is sufficient for our purposes that charging a fixed wholesale price per unit (and no fixed fee) is quite common in the markets we'll be examining, which means that total profits for the vertical chain are not maximized and therefore there is the possibility that the upstream and downstream firms could jointly be better off through some form of collusion.

However, there is a bigger challenge that double marginalization poses for explaining the presence of hub-and-spoke cartels. Let us return to the setting where there is a monopoly supplier, but now suppose there are several retailers so the market structure is more closely related to the hub-and-spoke cartels in our sample. As before, suppose the manufacturer charges a fixed wholesale price per unit and has all the bargaining power. Hence, it will choose the wholesale price as a monopoly markup over its marginal cost, and retailers add a positive retail price-cost margin on top of that markup. Given that retail prices are already too high from the perspective of the manufacturer, it would only harm itself by acting as a hub to coordinate retailers to raise their prices even higher. Thus, the presence of double marginalization would seem to undermine the basis for forming a hub-and-spoke cartel.

For the reader who is versed in (and perhaps trained by) Robert Bork's *The Antitrust Paradox* (1993), the rationale for a hub-and-spoke cartel would seem as problematic as for many other vertical restraints. Applying the logic to the current setting, the "single monopoly profit" theory espoused by Bork states that an upstream monopolist has the ability to extract all possible profits without the need for hub-and-spoke collusion. Indeed, this is what we explained earlier when the upstream monopolist uses a two-part tariff in selling its good to downstream firms. Given that there is no more profit to be had, an upstream firm would not participate in a cartel with downstream firms. Should the upstream firm be constrained by only being able to charge a wholesale price (and no fixed fee), full monopoly profit is not obtained because of double marginalization, but then collusion that raised downstream prices would only exacerbate that inefficiency and lower the upstream monopolist's profit. Again, the upstream firm would not choose to be part of such a hub-and-spoke cartel. By this Borkian logic, it makes no sense for a hub-and-spoke cartel to be created for the purpose of raising wholesale and retail prices. Thus, if there is collusion, then it must instead be for some efficiency-enhancing goal that, if anything, benefits consumers. The following view continues to be held: "One type of alleged hub-and-spoke conspiracy involves a manufacturer acting as a hub that facilitates a conspiracy among its retailer spokes through a vertical contract that restricts the ability of retailers to compete in the sale of the manufacturer's products. Unless there are efficiencies associated with such purely intrabrand contracts, it does not make sense for the manufacturer to voluntarily restrict retailer competition in this way" (Klein 2020, 131–132).

This economic theory is part of the Chicago school of antitrust and, like much theory of the Chicago school, it is correct *but only under certain restrictive assumptions*. The particular restrictive assumption in this case is that the upstream firm has all the bargaining power when negotiating with the downstream firms. When one departs from that extreme assumption, it can be mutually profitable to the upstream manufacturer and downstream retailers to raise downstream prices. Contrary to the Chicago school, there is a rationale for hub-and-spoke collusion and, under that rationale, consumers are harmed, as we will now explain.

Thus far, our analysis has assumed that the manufacturer has all the bargaining power, so it is able to dictate the type of contract or terms of trade. In contrast, when it does not dominate bargaining, it is possible that the manufacturer will have an incentive to facilitate collusion between the retailers in order to raise retail prices along with the wholesale price. To understand how this can happen, consider the other extreme, where retailers have all the bargaining power so they are dictating the terms of trade to the manufacturer. Each retailer will force the upstream supplier to set its wholesale price equal to its marginal cost (along with refusing to pay a fixed fee, in the case of a two-part tariff); hence, the manufacturer's profits will be zero. Suppose further that intrabrand competition is very intense, so retail prices are close to cost. In that case, total profits in the vertical chain are basically nothing because the wholesale price is close to the manufacturer's cost and retail prices are close to retailers' costs. With that as the competitive scenario, a hub-and-spoke cartel that coordinated a price rise among retailers would raise retailers' profits, and the manufacturer could benefit as well if the wholesale price was raised (by an amount less than the rise in retail prices). This would allow upstream and downstream firms to earn profits when previously they were earning none.

Hub-and-spoke collusion can benefit both upstream and downstream firms not just under the extreme assumptions that the downstream firms have all the bargaining power and downstream competition is intense. To explore the matter more generally, we develop a formal theoretical analysis in section 3.5 but summarize the main insight here.

Assume there is a monopoly supplier that sells its product to final consumers through two retailers. The products sold by the retailers are imperfect substitutes, and each retailer negotiates a (constant) wholesale price with the supplier. A model of bargaining is assumed that parameterizes how bargaining power is distributed. It encompasses the entire span of possibilities: where the upstream firm has all the power, the downstream firms have all the power, they have equal bargaining power, and so on. The outcome of bargaining is determined according to the parties' relative bargaining strengths (as captured by the bargaining power parameter) along with properties that describe the bargaining environment faced by the firms. One of those properties is the trade-off between a retailer's profit and the manufacturer's profit from different outcomes;[5] for example, in response to an increase in the wholesale price, how much the manufacturer's profit rises (because of a higher markup) and how much a retailer's profit falls (because of a lower markup). When a rise in the wholesale price lowers retailers' profits a little while increasing the manufacturer's profits a lot, bargaining will tend to lead to a higher wholesale price (and retailers will pass on a proportion of those costs to final consumers through higher retail prices). A second crucial property of the bargaining environment is the situation faced by a firm when it fails to come to an agreement (in bargaining theory, this is known as the disagreement or threat point). If the manufacturer and a retailer fail to come to an agreement, the former can fall back on selling more to the other retailer, while the latter is left without any inputs to buy. In that situation, the cost of bargaining breakdown is more severe for a retailer than for the manufacturer, so the retailer will be more willing to accept a higher wholesale price in order to reach an agreement.

When retailers have sufficiently strong bargaining power compared to the manufacturer, there will be a collective incentive to coordinate on raising retail prices because it will increase the total profits for the vertical chain. This is because, absent collusion, a retailer will be able to negotiate a low wholesale price when its bargaining position is strong, and this in turn will result in a low retail price. Consequently, when enough of the bargaining power lies downstream, retail prices will be below the vertically integrated monopoly price. Hence, forming a hub-and-spoke cartel to raise retail prices toward this level will raise the profits of the vertical chain. In contrast, when enough bargaining power lies upstream, retail prices will exceed the vertically integrated monopoly price. In that situation, a hub-and-spoke cartel would not form, because higher retail prices would lower total profits for the vertical chain, in which case it is not possible for both the upstream and downstream firms to benefit. While a rise in retail prices might raise retailers' profits, the rise in the wholesale price required to make the manufacturer better off would reduce retail margins to the point where retailers end up worse off in spite of the higher retail prices. In sum, the formation of a hub-and-spoke cartel designed to raise downstream prices can occur when downstream firms have sufficient bargaining power.

A second important driver of hub-and-spoke collusion is product substitutability, which, in our setting, is the propensity with which consumers are willing to switch from one retailer to another. A greater degree of product substitutability will lower retail prices, which then provides greater scope to profitably raise retail prices toward the vertically integrated monopoly level and thereby raise total profits for the vertical chain. This result occurs for two reasons. First, as is standard in models of competition, greater substitutability intensifies intrabrand competition between retailers, which lowers retail prices and margins. The lower retail margins are, the more likely that increasing retail prices will raise total profits for the vertical chain. Second, greater product substitutability affects bargaining in such a way that the negotiated wholesale price is lower, and this lowers retail prices, which again provides room to jointly raise wholesale and retail prices and make both upstream and downstream firms better off.[6]

Having identified two factors instrumental for a rise in retail prices to increase total profits for the vertical chain, the theory in section 3.5 goes on to demonstrate how retailers can share the collusive rents with the upstream supplier. The challenge lies in that higher retail prices reduce retail demand, which then lowers the manufacturer's demand, implying that, if the wholesale price is unchanged, the manufacturer's profit must fall. Under certain market conditions, it has been shown to be possible to raise the wholesale price (along with retail prices) so collusion benefits the manufacturer while still benefiting the retailers. Nevertheless, there is a limit on how high the wholesale price can rise, because it does lower retailers' profits and thereby risks having collusion harm retailers, in which case they would not participate. However, as long as retailers have enough bargaining power and products are sufficiently substitutable, there will be a range of wholesale prices for which both the manufacturer's and retailers' profits are higher because of the higher retail prices generated by hub-and-spoke collusion.

There are some other relevant factors not covered by the theory in section 3.5 (for reasons of mathematical tractability), which we will address with an informal analysis here. Generally, a cartel can raise total upstream and downstream profits from a coordinated increase in retail prices whenever the sum of the upstream and downstream markups is less than the markup of a vertically integrated monopolist. Cartel formation is not profitable when the markups of the manufacturer or retailers are already large so that condition is not satisfied. Hence, any factor that limits the markup of the manufacturer or retailers could facilitate hub-and-spoke collusion. Interbrand competition— so the upstream manufacturer faces competition for its brand from a rival manufacturer—is one such factor. It has the potential to constrain a manufacturer's ability to charge a high wholesale price because retailers can turn to selling more of the rival manufacturer's brand, and it may also increase competition at the retail level. Both effects imply that it is less likely that prices will be too high because of double marginalization, and thus there is more room for upstream and downstream firms to benefit. However, while interbrand competition may increase their willingness to form a hub-and-spoke cartel in order to raise retail prices, it will also constrain the cartel's ability to profitably implement those increases, because of the presence of a rival brand to which consumers can switch. Indeed, in the extreme case where the rival brand is a perfect substitute, a higher retail price for the hub's brand will cause it to have no demand. Consequently, strong interbrand competition may prevent the emergence of a hub-and-spoke cartel. When it is not strong enough to deter cartel formation, it will still constrain the magnitude of the rise in retail and wholesale prices.

There are at least three ways in which hub-and-spoke cartels could mitigate the effects of interbrand competition. First, the hub could encourage the spokes to supply the hub's brand exclusively or to promote the hub's brand over its rivals' by, for example, allocating it more shelf space. This is likely to be a more successful strategy when the cartel encompasses all retailers because it may be able to exclude the other brands from the market, thereby completely eliminating interbrand competition. Second, in addition to raising the price of the hub's brand, the spokes could raise the price of rival brands as well. It may be possible for the spokes to do so unilaterally. That is because if the price of one brand has increased, the retail demand for the other brands will rise, which gives a retailer a unilateral incentive to raise the prices of rival brands. Third, the downstream cartel members may encourage a rival manufacturer to participate in the hub-and-spoke cartel or form a separate hub-and-spoke cartel. This may enable the retailers to increase the rival brand's price by more than they could achieve unilaterally, and this dampening of interbrand competition may benefit both manufacturers.

As already emphasized, a coordinated increase in retail prices that raises total vertical chain profits is not enough to induce formation of a hub-and-spoke cartel, because, while retailers benefit from it, it is also essential that the upstream hub does as well or it would not participate. Thus far, the focus of our discussion has been on using a higher wholesale price to ensure that the upstream hub's profits are higher. As we'll see in the cases, there are other methods that can make the upstream firm better off. Rather than pay a higher wholesale price, retailers could provide monetary payments, thereby directly transferring some of their gains in order to ensure the upstream hub's willingness to go along. Alternatively, retailers could engage in demand-enhancing activities that increase the manufacturer's profits by raising its demand (rather than raising the price it is paid). Retailers may naturally be willing to invest more in such activities because of the higher margin on units sold. A fixed retail price also eliminates the free-rider problem, by removing the ability of rival retailers to undercut the price of a retailer that makes these investments, but retailers may invest even more in order to ensure that the manufacturer benefits from collusion. Other examples will arise in the cases.[7]

The preceding analysis showed that it is possible for both the upstream firm and downstream firms to earn higher profits by coordinating on an increase in the wholesale price and a common increase in retail prices. Hence, it can be in their collective interest to form a hub-and-spoke cartel. Suitable market conditions include sufficient retailer bargaining power and retailers that are sufficiently substitutable from the perspective of consumers.

A presumption in that analysis is that retailers are sufficiently alike so that if one retailer benefited from a common hike in retail prices, then that would be true for all retailers. That condition need not always hold. What is particularly problematic is when one or a few retailers are focused on increasing market share. Such a corporate goal manifests itself with prices below those of rival retailers in order to attract more customers.[8] This poses an obstacle for collusion in that a retailer driven by market share may prefer the competitive outcome, with low margins but growing market share, to the collusive outcome, with high margins and stable market share. Bringing such a retailer into the collusive fold may then be challenging. However, as we discuss at the end of this section, the upstream supplier can be instrumental in solving that problem, with the implication that a hub-and-spoke cartel can succeed where a cartel comprising only retailers would fail.[9]

Though all the upstream and downstream firms may find collusion attractive, there is still the matter of who takes the initiative to make it happen. In some cases, that initiative arises with one or more of the downstream retailers expressing their dissatisfaction with the low level of retail margins to the upstream supplier. To agree to assist them in the raising of retail prices, the upstream supplier will require compensation, which, as already discussed, can be achieved with a higher wholesale price. That begs the question of why retailers would choose to bring in the upstream supplier when doing so would require transferring some of their collusive rents to it. In chapter 2, we discussed how inclusion of an upstream hub can make collusion more effective, and more insight into that matter is provided here. In other cartel cases, it is the upstream supplier that initially expresses a desire to cartelize. Its objective is to raise wholesale prices— perhaps because of a rise in its own costs—and, in order to get retailers to go along with a rise in their input prices, it orchestrates a rise in retail prices to ensure that retail margins remain constant or rise.

Having developed some understanding of why upstream and downstream firms would want to collude, the next step is to understand how it is done. How do hub-and-spoke cartels operate to implement higher prices and earn higher profits? Having agreed on a higher wholesale price and higher retail prices, implementation of that collusive outcome requires *monitoring* to determine whether firms are complying and then *punishing* when there is evidence of noncompliance. We consider each of these in turn.

3.1.3   Monitoring

We begin by outlining how firms might want to cheat on the collusive outcome and then consider how compliance can be monitored. Let us start with
the upstream supplier, which, as part of the collusive arrangement, is to
raise its wholesale price to a particular level. If retailers set their prices at the
agreed collusive level, the upstream supplier has no incentive to lower its
wholesale price, because it would be reducing its profit margin without experiencing a change in sales (given that those sales are determined by retailers'
prices). It may possibly have an incentive to deviate to a higher wholesale
price to extract a higher profit, but there would be no gain from such an act.
Given that retailers would learn of this deviation from the agreed collusive
wholesale price prior to choosing their demand from the upstream supplier and prior to setting retail prices, any such departure by the upstream
supplier would cause collusion to unravel before it gets started. Thus, there
would be nothing gained from raising the wholesale price above what was
agreed.

The more relevant temptation for the upstream supplier resides in coordinating with one of the retailers to cheat. What it could do is offer a secret
discount to a retailer with the understanding that the retailer would cut
its price. To see how such a move could raise the upstream supplier's current profit, note that, holding wholesale prices fixed, the upstream supplier earns higher current profit if a retailer sets a lower price; the upstream
firm's profit per unit is the same (because it is charging the same wholesale
price) and now it is selling more to retailers because retailers are selling
more (because of the deviating retailer's lower price). This profit gain to the
upstream supplier will still be present if its wholesale price is slightly lower,
as long as the reduction in its profit margin is exceeded by the rise in the
number of units sold. Next, note that a downstream retailer will be more
inclined to undercut the collusive price when the wholesale price it pays is
lower, because it is then earning a higher profit for each additional unit it is
now selling at that lower retail price. Putting these two points together, the
upstream supplier may be tempted to offer a secret discount to one retailer
if doing so induced that retailer to undercut the collusive price. Deterring
such a deviation will require monitoring and being able to threaten the
upstream and downstream firms with a sufficiently severe punishment.

While the aforementioned coordinated deviation between the upstream
hub and a downstream spoke is a possibility, it is one that, to our knowledge,

has not been a concern of actual hub-and-spoke cartels and thus may not be a practical concern for the stability of hub-and-spoke collusion. The deviation of greater relevance is that a downstream retailer undercuts the collusive retail price on its own in order to increase profits by raising its sales. As will be revealed in our study of cartel cases, retailers commonly expressed such a concern about their rivals and there are documented episodes of such a deviation having occurred.

What can a hub-and-spoke cartel do to monitor downstream firms' retail prices in order to assess their compliance with the collusive arrangement? Even in the absence of collusion, monitoring of retailers' prices occurs because it is natural for a retailer to observe what its competitors are doing, not just in terms of prices but also marketing, product variety, and other variables by which they compete. This information is collected by reading advertisements, conducting store visits where shelves are checked for products and prices, and the like. This observational practice would most likely continue even when the firms are colluding on price because retailers are likely to continue to compete on nonprice dimensions. Thus, simply continuing what was done before will result in some level of price monitoring. Furthermore, for the upstream manufacturer or wholesaler, monitoring is often a by-product of supplying retailers when it means showing up at stores (though in some instances they may only be appearing at distribution centers). As part of hub-and-spoke collusion, that practice can be modified to ensure that the manufacturer records the retailer's prices when supply is delivered.

Though there is already a natural level of monitoring, it is not clear that its frequency and precision are sufficient to neutralize incentives to undercut the collusive price. Of course, the firms can engage in additional monitoring by showing up at rivals' stores on a more frequent basis to check on prices. However, monitoring is costly and, as a public good, is likely to be underprovided. It is a public good because when a firm monitors another firm for compliance, it is benefiting all members of the hub-and-spoke cartel by making the cartel more stable. Because all firms benefit but only the firm that does the monitoring incurs the cost, the monitoring firm will not monitor as much as it should from the collective perspective of the cartel. In addition, a cartel member may be inclined to free ride on the monitoring of others, letting them incur the expense. In sum, retailers' prices are public information and thus, in principle, detections can be observed.[10]

Furthermore, there will naturally be some level of monitoring, but whether it proves to be sufficient for cartel stability is unclear.[11]

If a retailer or the manufacturer has information that a retailer has been pricing too low, it is crucial that the information be shared, but there may be reasons not to do so. Suppose the anticipated punishment in response to an episode of cheating is that firms stop colluding for some time and return to competitive pricing. If retailer A learns that retailer B has been undercutting on price, does it want to inform the upstream hub, which might then inform the other retailers and possibly bring forth competitive prices? Or suppose it is the upstream supplier that has detected the undercutting? It is actually experiencing higher sales and earning higher profits because a retailer lowered its price. Reporting this episode to other retailers may lead to the collapse of collusion with not just lower retail prices but also a lower wholesale price. Thus, there may be incentives not to share knowledge of price deviations. On the other side of the ledger, failure to share information may lead to more frequent episodes of deviation, which could cause the permanent shutdown of the cartel. That risk would incentivize full reporting.

3.1.4 Punishment

When there is evidence of noncompliance, one form of punishment is for retailers to lower their prices, along with the upstream supplier lowering its wholesale price. This could involve a temporary or permanent return to competitive prices or a temporary shift to prices below competitive levels, perhaps even below cost. Such a punishment is common for regular cartels and, in particular, would be available to a cartel comprising only retailers. One appeal of a hub-and-spoke cartel is that the inclusion of the upstream supplier expands the set of punishments. In response to a retailer undercutting the collusive price, the upstream supplier could raise the wholesale price to the noncompliant cartel member. Another punishment, which is the one that will be the focus of our attention, has the upstream firm constraining how much is supplied to the price-cutting retailer. This could mean limiting supply, delaying supply, or denying supply outright for some length of time.[12]

There are several unique features of a punishment that restricts supply to a noncompliant retailer. First, it can be more detrimental than a punishment based on competitive pricing. Suppose both punishments were to be imposed for the same length of time. Competitive pricing will generally allow the retailer to still earn a profit, while a complete denial of supply would result in no profit.[13] Furthermore, firms are typically concerned about how they perform relative to competitors (which may be because managerial compensation is based on measures of relative performance). A firm with limited supply from the manufacturer (or that faces a higher wholesale price than its rivals) will underperform other firms in the market, which will intensify the punishment.

Second, limiting supply to the retailer that deviated actually benefits the other retailers, for they now have more sales because of the constrained supply of the noncompliant retailer. Returning to our discussion of the incentives to monitor and share information, retailers would be more inclined to detect and report price cutting, because now the punishment would raise its sales and profits because of the reduction in the deviating firm's supply.

Third, while limiting supply to a noncompliant retailer may be a more potent punishment, we need to be concerned with the incentives of the upstream supplier to implement it. If retailers are perfectly substitutable, then the lost sales from the retailer that is denied supply will be entirely made up by increased sales from the other retailers, as customers switch over to them. In that situation, the upstream supplier's sales and profits are unaffected; it is earning the same profit from denying supply as it earned prior to the deviation. However, if retailers are not perfectly substitutable, then the upstream supplier's sales and profits will be lower from having limited or denied supply to one of the retailers; some of its customers will not move their demand to other retailers. With lower total demand at the retail level, the upstream firm will face lower demand.

However, what is crucial for providing the upstream supplier with the incentive to go through with a punishment that limits how much it supplies to one of the retailers is that the profit it would earn from doing so be higher than the profit it would earn from not doing so. Suppose that failure to follow through on the agreed punishment would result in the collapse of collusion. In that case, the upstream supplier will be inclined to deny supply as long as the profits it earns from the collusive outcome associated with supplying the remaining retailers exceeds the profits it would earn under competition. That condition is more likely to hold when the retailer supplies a smaller proportion of the cartel's total quantity and when the retailers' products are more substitutable. Under such conditions, denying supply is likely to have only a small negative effect on the manufacturer's profits. However, if it means punishing a retailer with many stores, then the upstream firm might not be inclined to deny supply to such a chain. In that situation, threatening a large chain with not supplying it if it undercuts the collusive price would not be credible, because the upstream supplier would not find it in its best interest to go through with the threat. In such a situation, one alternative is to limit, but not fully deny, supply and do so for only a limited length of time. The punishment is then not as costly for the upstream supplier, which might therefore find it optimal to implement it. Of course, the punishment is also less severe, so it will be less of a deterrent to a large chain undercutting the collusive price.

There is, however, a challenge to enforcing a punishment of denying supply when multiple retailers deviate over time. Assume there was a deviation and the upstream supplier denied supply to that retailer. With the lost demand from one retailer, would it be credible to deny supply to a second retailer that also deviated? Even if it was credible, how about denying supply to a third retailer that deviated? At some point, the lost demand from not supplying so many retailers would make such a punishment untenable. However, there is a fix to this problem. Suppose when a second retailer deviates, the upstream supplier denies supply to it but then renews supplying the first retailer that deviated. If collusion is stable so the anticipation is that deviation is rare, a retailer that considers deviating cannot count on a later deviation to get it off the hook. In that situation, it is credible to deny supply to a deviating retailer, because the upstream supplier anticipates losing only one retailer's sales, regardless of how many retailers actually end up deviating. Anticipating that credible and severe punishment, retailers will be inclined to abide by the collusive arrangement and charge high retail prices.

To conclude, let us return to the challenge associated with aggressive retailers who are willing to accept low profit margins in order to grow their market shares. Because they may prefer competition (because it provides an opportunity to raise its market share) to collusion (where its market share will be kept around its current level), their participation in the cartel is problematic. However, if the punishment is denial of supply, then noncompliance means a *reduction* in market share. In that case, this retailer is faced with two alternatives: charge collusive retail prices and maintain its market share or undercut collusive retail prices and lose market share because supply is restricted or fully denied. The inclusion of the upstream supplier in the cartel is then able to make collusion succeed even with such aggressive retailers, and it does so by drawing on a richer set of punishments.

3.1.5   Resale Price Maintenance as an Alternative to Hub-and-Spoke Collusion

For a manufacturer desiring its retailers to sell its products at higher prices, an alternative to a hub-and-spoke cartel may be (minimum) resale price maintenance (RPM). With RPM, the manufacturer specifies a price level and requires retailers (typically, authorized dealers) to either price at that level or price at least as high as that level.[14] Thus, a manufacturer who finds price competition excessive (for whatever reason) can force retail prices higher by imposing RPM and setting a minimum price above the prices that were occurring under competition. It may also be the case that it is the retailers who request that the manufacturer adopt RPM in order to suppress price competition.

The practical appeal of RPM over hub-and-spoke collusion is that a manufacturer can impose it on each retailer rather than having to coordinate with all retailers to adopt some common collusive price, which, as we have documented, can be a protracted and challenging exercise. This is especially true when some retailers have been pricing aggressively in order to raise their market shares, for then coordinating on a common collusive price gets in the way of that objective. Under RPM, those retailers would be forced to toe the line by raising their prices.

The problem with RPM is that it is not always an option for firms, because it is unlawful in many jurisdictions. In the EU, RPM is a hardcore restriction[15] that falls under Article 101(1) of the Treaty of the Functioning of the European Union, which prohibits those agreements that appreciably restrict or distort competition (para. 5). While it is possible for a firm to plead an efficiency defense under Article 101(3) (para. 60), such defenses are not typically accepted. Competition law in the UK is similar.[16] With RPM off the table, hub-and-spoke collusion becomes the next best alternative for raising retail prices.

Until 2007, RPM was not an option in the US either. RPM was per se illegal, which meant that firms could not use an efficiency defense to justify the use of this vertical restraint. However, with the US Supreme Court's decision in *Leegin* (2007),[17] RPM is now judged by the rule of reason. That means a firm using RPM is only in violation of the law if the harm to consumers from higher prices is shown to exceed any consumer benefits generated by RPM. As the court noted, "The economics literature is replete with procompetitive justifications for a manufacturer's use of resale price maintenance . . . [and] although the empirical evidence on the topic is limited, it does not suggest that efficient uses of the agreement are infrequent or hypothetical."[18]

The primary benefit from higher retail prices is that retailers are induced to engage in more nonprice competition, which would benefit consumers through the provision of more service.[19] One factor that the court found would heighten concerns about anticompetitive effects from RPM is when retailers, rather than the manufacturer, propose it, for then it may be driven more by retailers' desire for higher prices and less by the manufacturer's desire for more demand-enhancing service.

In any case, such issues appear moot. While, in principle, RPM can be found illegal in the US under the rule of reason, that is unlikely to occur because, in practice, cases are rarely brought. It is not far off the mark to say that effectively RPM is now per se legal in the US. In such an environment, there is little need to pursue hub-and-spoke collusion when the objective is to reduce intrabrand competition and raise retailers' prices. Of course, there is still a role for hub-and-spoke cartels in the US when the goal is to constrain interbrand competition, as exemplified by the cases in chapter 4, and exclude rivals, as with the cases in chapter 5.

The US aside, RPM is not a viable option in many jurisdictions, because of its illegality and local enforcement practice, in which case a manufacturer and retailers will find a hub-and-spoke cartel a relevant strategy for raising prices.

3.2 Cases

Here we offer 10 cases in which an upstream firm assisted downstream firms to coordinate raising downstream prices.

3.2.1 Toys (UK)
The setting is the UK market for toys and games.[20] At the time of this case, Hasbro was the leading toy manufacturer in the UK, producing household brands such as the action figure Action Man and the board game Monopoly.

At the retail level, toys and games were sold through a variety of outlets, including specialist toy stores, such as Toys "R" Us, mixed retailers that sold more than just toys, such as Woolworth's, and catalog retailers, such as Argos and Littlewoods. Large toy retailers were supplied directly by Hasbro, but smaller ones tended to be supplied indirectly through Hasbro's network of independent distributors.

Argos and Littlewoods differed from other High Street stores, because their offerings were presented in a catalog and purchased over the counter in a warehouse rather than displayed in a store. Argos and Littlewoods published two catalogs per year: one for the spring/summer (S/S) season and the other for the autumn/winter (A/W) season. The latter is considered more important because of the high demand for toys and other products leading up to Christmas.

In this case, the hub was Hasbro and the spokes were Argos and Littlewoods (the latter is also often referred to by its catalog's name, Index). The cartel was active for the A/W catalogs of 1999 and both the S/S and A/W catalogs of 2000 and 2001. Initially, the cartel was limited to Hasbro's Action Man collection and its core games (including Monopoly). These were high-volume, well-advertised products for which pricing had been particularly aggressive. However, starting with the S/S 2000 catalog, the scope of the cartel was expanded to include other popular Hasbro products. Hasbro's objective was to coordinate toy retailers to charge recommended retail prices (RRPs) rather than price below them.

Having learned that retailers were "unhappy with the margins they were receiving on Hasbro's branded products,"[21] in October 1998 Hasbro organized a meeting among its key employees to develop initiatives to raise retail margins. As noted by Hasbro sales director David Bottomley, "The listing and pricing initiatives came about as a result of low margins that were [a] concern across the entire industry and shared by Argos and Littlewoods."[22]

The "pricing initiative" was for retailers to charge the RRP. The "listing initiative" was for Hasbro to offer rebates to retailers to induce them to continue stocking certain Hasbro products that were in jeopardy of being removed from a toy retailer's offerings. These initiatives were developed by Hasbro employees Ian Thomson (business account manager for Littlewoods) and Neil Wilson (business account manager for Argos) and were supported at a senior level by Mike McCulloch, the head of marketing and sales, and sales directors David Bottomley and Mike Brighty.

Bottomley of Hasbro felt that "Argos and Littlewoods were key to the success of the pricing initiative since they were the market leaders—if they could be persuaded to maintain prices at RRP then other retailers would follow suit."[23] Consequently, Hasbro entered into a dialogue with the two retailers to encourage them to support the pricing initiative. While at the outset Hasbro also discussed its pricing initiative with other retailers, further communication was considered unnecessary. As explained by Mike McCulloch, "Initiative was discussed with other retailers. Other retailers were always going to follow prices of Argos and [Littlewoods] Index. So other retailer[s] felt whatever Argos and Index did was crucial to strategy. . . . As far as other retailers [are] concerned, [there was] no need to communicate; they had bought into [the] initiative, and were happy to follow Argos['s] price lead."[24]

In contrast, getting Argos and Littlewoods to charge RRPs in the first place required that each be assured by Hasbro that the other would do so:

> Argos is generally accepted as the price setter and leader in the market. However, Hasbro considered that Argos would have been very unlikely to make a commitment to follow Hasbro's RRPs unless it was reassured that doing so would not result in its catalogue prices being undercut by those in the Index catalogue [of Littlewoods]. Littlewoods is the main catalogue competitor to Argos. . . . Argos and Littlewoods monitor, in particular, each other's prices very closely and produce regular analyses showing how often each undercuts and is undercut by the other. Since both companies offer a price-match guarantee, neither can afford to have prices that are seriously out of step with the other. It was therefore necessary to reassure Argos that Littlewoods would also be committed to RRPs. For its part Littlewoods required the same assurance of commitment by Argos.[25]

This concern of mutual compliance was especially acute with their catalog prices. As catalogs were issued only twice a year, a retailer could find itself at a price disadvantage for six months if it complied with the RRPs and the other retailer did not:

> Both Argos and Littlewoods were concerned about undercutting by any retailer, but each had a special concern about undercutting by the other. This was because they were the largest catalogue retailers, directly competing with each other, and because their retailing formats meant that they both had to commit themselves to a price for a forthcoming season without knowledge of the other's intention except for the previous catalogue which was, by definition, out of date. Further, unlike with ordinary retailers where an agreement to price at X could be given public effect on the next day or within a very short space of time, any "agreement" or "understanding" that the other catalogue retailer would price at an

agreed price (say RRP) would not be seen to be implemented until much later when it would be too late to change one's own catalogue.[26]

Starting in late 1998, members of Hasbro's sales team were speaking with Argos's buyers about having retailers charge the RRPs. The initial reaction of the retailers was not encouraging:

> Littlewoods was concerned about the feasibility of Hasbro's pricing initiative and in particular expressed doubts about Hasbro's ability to prevent undercutting by Argos. Ian Thomson states in his witness statement: "It was at this point that Mike McCulloch intimated . . . that he had been having discussions with the major opposition (Argos) and they were of the same opinion, i.e. that they could not agree to the new pricing structure for fear of being undercut. It did need the agreement of both parties in order for the plan to work, but that if Index would agree to go along with it then Mike McCulloch, using this knowledge, was confident that he could persuade them to do the same. John McMahon [of Littlewoods] said that he would play ball and go along with the plan but if they (Argos) reneged on the deal and did not stick to the retail prices in their 1999 Autumn Winter Catalogue and he (Index) did, he would be seriously disadvantaged. If this happened as a result he would do some serious price cutting in the next Index catalogue launch."[27]

Intent on surmounting such skepticism, Hasbro engaged in extensive bilateral communications with Argos and Littlewoods. The goal was for Argos and Littlewoods to commonly believe they would charge the RRPs. These communications also involved finding levels for the RRPs that would be acceptable to both retailers:

> Hasbro set the RRPs after separate discussions with Argos, Littlewoods, and other retailers. . . . Argos and Littlewoods then selected, independently from each other, the Hasbro products they would include in their catalogues. Neil Wilson, Hasbro's account manager for Argos, describes how the pricing initiative then worked in practice: "When I was given the products selected for the catalogue, I established which were the common products carried by the majority of retailers (not specifically Index) and asked Argos what its price intentions were in relation to each of these products. I did not do this for products that were not common. I informed Argos what the Hasbro RRPs for the common products were and asked them whether any of our RRPs were a problem for them to match. . . . Having determined Argos' pricing intentions and passed these on to the other account managers within Hasbro, I received information from those account managers regarding the intentions of other retailers to go with RRPs. I then reverted to Argos and said, without being specific, that it was my belief that the future retail price of a product would or would not be at the RRP. I told Argos which products this related to. I never mentioned the name of the retailer who was involved or

quantified exactly the price that retailer would go out at. I simply said to Argos that it was my belief from what retailers told us that this or that product would or would not be at the RRP."[28]

Neil Wilson of Hasbro was communicating with Argos, and Ian Thomson of Hasbro was communicating with Littlewoods. The two of them shared information with the common objective of having each retailer become confident that the other retailer would charge the RPPs on the Hasbro products that they commonly carried:

> [David Bottomley states:] "It is incorrect to suggest that Neil and Ian were acting unilaterally in putting together this proposal: it was based on detailed discussions and conversations that they had with Argos and Littlewoods about pricing at RRPs. Each was aware that similar discussions were taking place with the other and that a big effort was being made to get all retailers to price at RRP." Neil Wilson states: "Argos were fully aware that the pricing initiative involved Hasbro talking to other retailers." . . . Ian Thomson states: "There was no doubt that Alan Burgess [Littlewoods's buyer of boys' toys] knew that I was passing on to the Argos account handler (Neil Wilson) the contents of our discussion and that I would confirm the Argos intentions back to him after Neil had concluded his discussions with Argos."[29]

The Office of Fair Trading (OFT) found "no evidence that Argos and Littlewoods spoke directly" and that "confidential information was exchanged between them with Hasbro acting as the fixer or middleman."[30] In spite of the initial concerns of Argos and Littlewoods that the other would undercut the RRPs and the lack of direct communication between them, Hasbro felt that they achieved the exchange of assurances required for the pricing initiative to work:

> [David Bottomley, Neil Wilson, and Ian Thomson made] it clear that there was an informal agreement, understanding or tacit arrangement whereby Argos and Littlewoods co-operated with Hasbro by indicating that they would or might price the particular products in question at or near RRP on the understanding that the other retailer would also do so, at the same time making it clear again and again that if the other reneged, the former would immediately respond.[31] Bottomley . . . states that "what existed between Hasbro and Argos and Hasbro and Littlewoods was an understanding that, because of the obvious benefit to everyone in the industry, prices would be at or near RRP."[32]

While the pricing initiative started on a restricted set of products, it was soon extended to other categories because, as conveyed in a meeting at Hasbro, "It was crucial that we maintained retail price stability as far as possible across our key brands so that the initiatives could succeed."[33] Given the initial success of the pricing initiative, there was cautious optimism: "Littlewoods' reaction to Hasbro's proposal was similar to Argo[s]'s reaction: it was positive, but also concerned about undercutting."[34] Argos's senior buyer Sue Porritt "felt it was great that Hasbro could help maintain retail price stability but said that Argos would react if it was undercut in order to remain competitive."[35]

Obtaining a state of common understanding among retailers to implement the proposed collusive strategy was just the starting point for effective collusion. Argos and Littlewoods continued to be concerned that its rival would undercut the RRPs, in spite of its announced intention to abide by them (as conveyed by Hasbro). The resulting consequences if Littlewoods was undercut were hinted at by Alan Cowley, a Littlewoods buyer of toys, in an email to Ian Thomson of Hasbro on December 28, 2000:

> Reference our conversation pre Christmas regarding Hasbro's late decision to reduce the price of the Tweenies soft toys featured in the Index SS01 catalogue. Fortunately for both of us we were in fact able to amend the selling prices at the last minute due to an unexpected delay in catalogue production. This however literally meant "holding up the presses", entailing an additional cost of £4000 which will be debited to your account shortly. I will not elaborate on the consequences if we had been unable to do so, resulting in our being undercut by Argos and other High St outlets, especially when you had earlier been so insistent that we all went out at the same price![36]

To limit the incidences of undercutting, "Argos and Littlewoods would . . . often inform Hasbro if they intended to reduce the price of a Hasbro product during a catalogue season,"[37] and presumably Hasbro would pass on this information to other retailers. Furthermore, Hasbro would also pass on information regarding rivals' prices when they became aware that either Argos or Littlewoods had decided not to price at the RRP. One such episode occurred on May 25, 2000, when Neil Wilson emailed Ian Thomson and Mike Brighty to inform them that "Argos have confirmed that Interactive Pikachu will be at 23.75 not 23.99 for A/W. Please advise [Littlewoods] Index accordingly."[38] In his witness statement, Wilson stated that he expected Thomson "to contact Index to inform them that the prevailing market price for this product was likely to be below the Hasbro RRP, without mentioning Argos specifically."[39] Following this, "Ian Thomson 'phoned Alan Burgess [Littlewoods's buyer of toys] to make him aware of the issue and that he could change his pricing if he wanted to. He [Burgess] thanked me [Thomson] for passing on the information but did not commit on how he was going to act; he was going to think about it.' The Interactive Pikachu toy was priced at £23.75 in the A/W 2000 catalogues of both Argos and Littlewoods."[40]

The importance of monitoring was very much recognized by Hasbro. However, given the transparency of Argos's and Littlewoods's prices, their focus was on other retailers who were not considered part of the cartel. Ian Thomson of Hasbro noted, "The emphasis on price monitoring now was to ensure that our other customers would fall in line so that Argos and Index would be confident that our plan was working throughout the U.K. This would reduce the risk of them going back to price cutting in the following catalogues."[41]

Given their concerns about having higher prices than their rivals, Argos and Littlewoods were also incentivized to monitor. However, rather than contacting the deviator directly, they would inform Hasbro. For example, Neil Wilson of Hasbro stated:

> If [Argos] found out that a retailer was not at the Hasbro RRP, they contacted me to find out why there was a difference. When Argos called me about the apparently lower price of another retailer, they contacted me to see if Hasbro could do something about it, i.e. get the other retailer to go back to RRP. The understanding was that if Hasbro could give Argos an assurance that the other retailer would put the price back up to the RRP, Argos would also remain at the RRP. If not, Argos would have to make a decision about how it would price the product—usually by matching the competitor's price.[42]

He also described how the process operated within Hasbro:

> Once I had spoken to Argos, I contacted the account manager in Hasbro who dealt with the retailer in question. He or she in turn called the buyer of the retailer who had the lower price. The account manager sought to find out why the price was lower and to persuade the retailer to go back to the RRP. Often the lower price turned out to be a temporary promotion, for instance to clear out stock, or a simple mistake, as most retailers were eager to charge RRPs. I then informed Argos whether we were able to do anything and either provided the reassurance they sought or said that we could do nothing. Argos knew that this was the process that was going on.[43]

In the OFT's decision, there is documented evidence that this approach was successful. For example, according to Ian Thomson of Hasbro,

> During the Autumn Winter sales period of 2000 Woolworth's had decided to price Standard Tweenies at £12.99 (?). (This may not have been the price but it was around £2.00 less than everyone else and did happen.) I was asked to go back

to Index (this was either by David Bottomley or Mike Brighty [Hasbro sales direc-
tors]) and warn them that this was either happening or had happened and that
we would be talking to Woolworth's in order to get them to put the price back up.
I phoned Alan Cowley [a Littlewoods toy buyer] and passed on the news that it
was only a temporary problem and that someone was talking to Woolworth's and
I was sure that the retail price would go back up. Woolworth's did put the price
back up very soon after.[44]

That the cartel was successful at coordinating the prices of Argos and
Littlewoods is also evident in figure 3.1, which shows the percentage of
products in common between Argos and Littlewoods that had the same
price in their respective A/W and S/S catalogs. Recall that the cartel covered
the A/W catalogs of 1999 and both the A/W and S/S catalogs of 2000 and
2001. The pricing initiative was initially limited to Hasbro's core games
and its Action Man collection, until the A/W 2000 catalog, where it was
extended to include other key Hasbro brands. Figure 3.1 shows that virtually all common products had the same price in the final catalog before the
cartel was detected, almost all of which were at Hasbro's RRPs. In contrast,
almost no common products had the same price three years earlier.

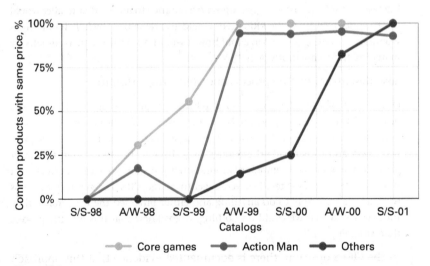

Figure 3.1
Percentage of products in common between Argos and Littlewoods that had the
same price in their respective A/W and S/S catalogs. *Source*: Data from CA/98/8/2003
Agreements between Hasbro UK Ltd, Argos Ltd & Littlewoods Ltd fixing the price of
Hasbro toys and games, [2004] 4 UKCLR 717 at 56.

Although there is no data in the decision related to the effects of the cartel on other retailers' prices, the head of marketing and sales at Hasbro, Mike McCulloch, did report to the OFT that "the impact of the new Hasbro 1999 Terms by Argos and Index was felt throughout the trade and nearly all of our customers stuck to the price points because Argos and Index, who were the price leaders, had demonstrated that the new strategy was working."[45] Furthermore, it was noted by the OFT that "in practice RRPs were generally adhered to and that the more this was observed to happen the more smoothly Hasbro's initiative worked, with less need for Hasbro's active involvement in facilitating the arrangements."[46]

These statements suggest that the cartel was successful in achieving its aim of limiting intrabrand competition beyond Argos and Littlewoods and that this became easier over time. Likewise, the OFT also stated that there was likely to be an effect on interbrand competition:

> Given the strong market position of Hasbro in some of the branded toys specified in the agreement, for example boys' toys and games and puzzles, it is difficult to believe that an agreement that fixed these prices at a level that was higher than they would otherwise have been would not have had a similar effect on the competing products of other manufacturers within that market. It is reasonable to assume that if the prices of Hasbro's products were higher than they would otherwise be, then prices of competing brands could be maintained at prices that were higher than those that would have prevailed had there been no agreement.[47]

Any such increase in the retail prices of rival brands would benefit Hasbro by reducing the number of consumers that switch away from Hasbro products.

The pricing initiative was designed to benefit retailers by increasing retail margins because "margins in toys tend to be relatively low . . . [and] margins are even more limited in the case of highly promoted branded toys such as those produced by Hasbro."[48] As the OFT noted, the intense intrabrand competition meant that Hasbro could not raise retail margins by simply lowering wholesale prices: "This was an industry that had been fiercely competitive with retailers eager not to be beaten on price, particularly on key lines, such as these. There was clearly a risk for Hasbro that any attempts to increase retailer margins by reducing list [wholesale] prices would simply result in all the benefit being passed on to the consumer with no change in the overall margins for retailers. But the [pricing initiative] 'arrangements' were deliberately designed to have the effect that retailers did not need to discount and [they] knew this."[49]

Consequently, the main benefit of the pricing initiative for Hasbro was to raise retail profit margins, which would reduce its concern that its products would be delisted by some toy retailers in favor of more profitable toys. To the contrary, Hasbro claimed that "there was no gain to Hasbro from the 'arrangements' as list prices (i.e. wholesale prices) also fell over the period that the 'arrangements' were in place."[50] However, the OFT argued that Hasbro may have still benefited because its wholesale prices could have fallen further absent the cartel. Furthermore, contemporaneous with the pricing initiative, Hasbro was trying to reduce the complexity of its rebate scheme, such that Hasbro "may well have reduced the overall level of rebates at the same time as the list [wholesale] prices fell."[51] To support the latter, the OFT stated that Hasbro's profit margins on its core games did not seem to fall as much as their average wholesale price.

In describing the resolution of the legal case, let us begin by referencing an email sent by Ian Thomson and Neil Wilson that informed some of their superiors of their pricing initiative: "Neil and I have spoken to our respective contacts at Argos and Index and put together a proposal regarding the maintenance of certain retails within our portfolio. This is a step in the right direction and it is fair to say that both Accounts are keen to improve margins but at the same time are taking a cautious approach in case either party reneges on a price agreement."[52]

In response, they received an effusive email from Hasbro sales director Mike Brighty: "Ian . . . This is a great initiative that you and Neil have instigated!!!!!!!!! However, a word to the wise, never ever put anything in writing, its highly illegal and it could bite you right in the arse!!!! suggest you phone Lesley and tell her to trash? Talk to Dave. Mike"[53]

The OFT did "bite them in the arse," as they found that all three firms had infringed the Competition Act of 1998. Penalties of £17.28 million and £5.37 million were levied on Argos and Littlewoods, respectively. The penalty for Hasbro was calculated to be £15.59 million, which it avoided by receiving amnesty for cooperating with the OFT. Hasbro's leniency application was triggered by a separate OFT investigation that looked into whether Hasbro had imposed resale price maintenance on a number of the independent distributors that Hasbro used to supply small toy retailers.[54]

Argos and Littlewoods appealed the OFT's decision to the Competition Appeal Tribunal (CAT), which then dismissed the appeal. However, in a separate judgment, the CAT reduced the penalties that the OFT had imposed on

Argos and Littlewoods to £15.0 million and £4.5 million, respectively. The CAT's judgment was taken to the Court of Appeal by Argos and Littlewoods on the grounds that there were no communications between the two retailers and such communications were necessary to conclude that there was an agreement or concerted practice. The Court of Appeal sided with the CAT, saying that "Argos must have known or could have reasonably foreseen that its discussion with Hasbro reflected Hasbro's discussions with other retailers. In our view such conduct was a 'form of practical coordination' which knowingly substituted practical cooperation for the risks of competition. In particular, those reciprocal contacts reduced uncertainty on Argos' part as to what other retailers' pricing intentions were, and reduced uncertainty on Hasbro's part on what Argos' prices would be. That, in turn, facilitated Hasbro's conversations with other retailers, especially Littlewoods, with a view to ensuring that they too priced at RRPs."[55] In other words, downstream firms can have an exchange of assurances by communicating through an upstream firm.

3.2.2 Desiccant (UK)

Desiccant is an absorbent that keeps the space dry between the two panes of glass in an insulated glass window unit.[56] At the time of the case, there were approximately 4,000 producers of insulated glass units in the UK, and desiccant manufacturers typically supplied them through distributors. UOP was one of the two main manufacturers of desiccant in the UK, and it used four distributors: UKae, Thermoseal Supplies, Double Glazing Supplies Group (DGS), and Double Quick Supplyline (DQS). These firms were found by the UK Office of Fair Trading (OFT) to have operated an unlawful collusive agreement, which the firms referred to as "the Policy," under which the distributors sought to dampen price competition.

Although the OFT's focus was on the period beginning March 1, 2000 (when the UK's Competition Act came into force), the Policy had been in place for some time, possibly since 1989, when UOP entered the desiccant market. Initially, the Policy appears to have been an agreement to allocate customers across distributors. It later developed into a pricing agreement, and UOP assisted in implementing coordinated price increases for distributors in 2001 and 2002. The agreement continued until the cartel was detected in 2003.

The hub in this case is the manufacturer (UOP), and the spokes are four distributors (UKae, Thermoseal Supplies, DGS, and DQS). As we will describe, there were many bilateral communications between UOP and a distributor. These communications served to coordinate on price increases and disseminate reports relevant to monitoring compliance. In contrast to many hub-and-spoke cartels, there were also some occasional meetings attended by UOP and multiple distributors, and some direct communications between the distributors. However, most of the communications occurred bilaterally between the hub and a spoke.

Let us begin by examining the means by which the distributors coordinated on a price increase in 2001 and then turn to the 2002 price increase. During 2000, UOP regularly received complaints from its distributors that their prices were being undercut by their rivals. In response, UOP invited its four distributors to a meeting to be held on November 3, 2000. The meeting was attended by UOP's sales manager and the managing directors of UKae, Thermoseal, and DQS. DGS declined to attend because of its poor relationship with Thermoseal.

Tony Scullion, sales manager at UOP, prepared notes for this meeting that outlined the distributors' concerns of an "increasing number of 'tit for tats' with the overall outcome being a downward spiraling of prices."[57] Although Scullion denied circulating these notes among the distributors, at least one of the distributors received a copy of them, and it is clear that one purpose of the meeting was to prevent future retail price undercutting by the distributors. Also discussed at this meeting was UOP's intention to impose a 4% wholesale price increase on its distributors. The distributors resisted this proposal and demanded higher margins and instead a wholesale price reduction. Scullion stated, "Because of the strongly adverse reaction to my proposal it was eventually agreed that UOP would not implement a price increase to the distributors—instead the distributors would increase their list price of UOP desiccant by 4 per cent, thereby allowing them to increase their margin. The distributors also asked me to provide them with a letter which they could present to their customers as justification for their price increase."[58]

According to Garry Ealing, managing director at UKae, it was also agreed at the meeting that the retail price increase would be coordinated among the distributors: "As the 4 per cent increase was to be explained as an increase in price from the manufacturer, it was in both the UOP distributors' and UOP's interests to ensure that the price increase was implemented into the market place at the same time by all the UOP distributors. This would reinforce the fact to customers that this price increase was due to a price increase imposed on them by UOP, the manufacturer."[59] While some cartels stagger price increases in order to avoid giving the appearance of coordinated conduct, the distributors here desired simultaneous price increases in order to (misleadingly) signal to customers that the increase resulted from a common rise in the wholesale price, as opposed to firms independently seeking to raise their markups.

Given DGS's absence from the meeting with the other distributors, Scullion had a separate meeting with DGS on November 15, 2000, which involved its managing director, Derek Aucott. A couple of days later, Scullion made the other distributors aware that this meeting had taken place and then sought to coordinate on the exact implementation date of the agreed price increase, saying, "I have now met with Derek and can confirm that he was in agreement with the majority of the issues that we discussed at Callow Hall. I can therefore minute the following actions: 5. Pricing: It has been unanimously agreed that there would be a 4 per cent price increase for UOP products in the UK market, to be implemented on 22nd January 2001. Please prepare your sales team for this."[60]

However, disagreement ensued regarding the implementation date. On January 3, 2001, Scullion sent a fax to the four distributors, suggesting other possible dates and providing them with the letter to use to falsely justify the retail price increase to their customers:

> As discussed in November last year please find attached a fax giving advice of a 4 per cent price increase for UOP desiccant. This is to allow [distributor] to implement a price increase in the market and does not represent a price increase from UOP to [distributor]. The intention is to allow [distributor] to increase margins on UOP products, and hopefully gain an added incentive to sell more product as a result. I leave it to you to liaise with your contacts as to the date that this is implemented, but all UOP distributors must apply the increase as of the same date. I would suggest that this should either be the 5th February, or if this is not possible, the 5th March.[61]

Subsequently, Scullion telephoned UKae, Thermoseal, and DQS to set an implementation date of February 5. However, on January 8, Derek Aucott of DGS sent Scullion a fax informing him that, for administrative reasons, DGS would not be able to increase retail prices to its customers until March 1. Scullion quickly passed on this information to the three other distributors and asked them to also hold off until that date. Direct communication between the managing directors of UKae, Thermoseal, and DQS ensued. On

January 12, Garry Ealing of UKae replied to Scullion, "Further to your fax of the 11th January 2001 in connection with the above [price increase] I confirm that this is absolutely out of the question. I have spoken to DQS and Thermoseal who will be putting their prices up on the 1st February 2001."[62] Finally, Scullion faxed Aucott and sought to discourage DGS from taking advantage of the situation: "I have advised the other distributors that you cannot increase prices until 1st March. They have responded that they have no option but to go ahead from 1st February. I would therefore request that DGS respect the position of the other distributors and do not take advantage of the delay."[63]

Presumably, this meant that DGS not actively try to gain customers during the month in which it would have lower prices. There is no evidence of further communication regarding the retail price increase. It appears that UKae, Thermoseal, and DQS implemented the price increase as planned, with DGS following suit in March.

As noted, UKae, Thermoseal, and DQS communicated directly at the meeting with UOP in early November 2000 and then did so without UOP's participation in January 2001. In contrast, DGS only communicated with UOP. Nevertheless, the OFT viewed DGS as just as culpable, because its communications with UOP allowed it to coordinate its prices with those of the three other distributors:

> The OFT accepts that DGS did not have any direct contact with the other three distributors. . . . However, the OFT concludes that DGS knew, or ought to have known, that its views and decisions would be communicated to the other distributors through UOP, and that its views and decisions would have an impact on the other distributors. The OFT concludes that the material outlined above provides strong and compelling evidence that DGS was also party to an agreement and/or concerted practice with UOP to implement the 2001 price increase and was party through its communications with UOP to the discussions with the other distributors concerning the co-ordinated implementation of the 2001 price increase.[64]

Let us now turn to the 2002 price increase. At the start of 2002, Scullion wrote to the four distributors, proposing an increase in the wholesale prices charged to distributors and the retail prices charged by distributors. The communication began with a fax on January 4, 2002, in which he stated, "We are recommending a 4.5 per cent price increase for our products as shown in the accompanying letter. Our price to you will be increasing by less than 4 per cent, so there will hopefully be an opportunity for you to increase your margin at the same time."[65] This was followed by a letter on January 7 saying, "Please note that due to significant increases in the cost of primary raw materials used in the production of molecular sieves UOP will be increasing the price of our XL-8, HM2000 and DS2000 product ranges by approximately 4.5 per cent. This increase will take effect as of 4th March 2002."[66]

Again, the plan was for the increase to be used by distributors to falsely justify the increase in retail prices to their customers. Furthermore, in a subsequent fax sent by Scullion to the four distributors, he made clear that he was keen to coordinate the retail price increase, stating that, "Further to my letter of 4 January 2002, I would like, if possible, to coordinate the timing of your price increase. I suggest everybody advises their customers that prices for UOP desiccant will be increasing by 4.5 per cent as of 4th March. Whilst I obviously cannot impose this on you, doing so would avoid the usual round of 'tit for tat' exchanges that take place at the time of price increase."[67] From the text of the fax, it would appear that all four distributors were made aware that they were all recipients of the same fax, thereby promoting mutual understanding among them.

With regard to this proposed price increase, there was no further evidence of communication between UOP and the distributors and, in contrast to the first price rise, no evidence of direct communication between the distributors. Nevertheless, the wholesale and retail price increases were implemented exactly as planned. The OFT concluded that additional communication was unnecessary because of the mutual understanding established through the implementation of the 2001 price increase. This is hinted at in the following statement by Tony Scullion to the OFT: "As per [the] 2001 increase, however, I provided the distributors with a letter indicating that UOP prices would go up by 4.5 per cent, therefore giving our distributors this opportunity to increase their prices by more than 4 per cent and therefore increase their margins. This was provided on my initiative based on the previous example, but was again in response to comments from the distributors about unsatisfactory margins."[68]

The preceding discussion demonstrates that UOP was instrumental in coordinating price increases by the distributor-spokes. It was comparably crucial when it came to monitoring compliance with those price increases. As conveyed by Garry Ealing, the managing director of UKae, to the OFT, "The general policy of UOP was that UOP Distributors would not undercut other UOP Distributors. UOP Distributors were initially encouraged to resolve any issues they may have with other UOP Distributors on the sale of UOP desiccant between themselves. However, this often led to 'tit for tat' retaliation between the UOP Distributors. . . . Due to this retaliation between distributors, UOP advised that distributors should contact Tony Scullion at UOP to act almost as mediator in relation to any such disputes."[69]

A distributor might learn from a customer that another distributor's prices were not in compliance, and that would be conveyed to UOP. For example, an area sales manager for Thermoseal wrote to Scullion of UOP that, "In our efforts to successfully sell UOP DS 2000, I have come up against opposition to your product from both DQS and DGS, meaning that we have [x number of] pallets of DS 2000 that we cannot sell. The account in question is [name deleted]. They were buying [x number of] pallet per month at [x amount] per [x quantity], but have told me that we are no longer competitive in comparison to these two competitors. . . . Please can you help us with this issue."[70]

Consider also UKae's report of price undercutting by DGS to Scullion: "It would appear [name deleted] of DGS has had another moment of amnesia regarding policy. Please find enclosed a copy of a quotation dated 6 December 2001 together with a copy invoice confirming that product has been supplied in March of this year without a price increase! . . . May I point out that this is the second time that [name deleted] has totally ignored the rules of engagement with this particular customer."[71] Scullion described to the OFT the general protocol upon receiving such complaints: "The distributor would then complain to me and [send] me the 'undercutting' quote and ask me to investigate whether the quote was genuine . . . ; I would raise the complaint with the other distributor and advise the first distributor as to whether there was in fact genuine undercutting taking place."[72] Scullion also described how in response to a complaint he would seek to verify it: "DGS were convinced that UKae were undercutting them at an account called [name deleted]. I was trying to referee this, and had been told by UKae that they were adamant that all they had done was to match a package price. UKae said . . . there was an early settlement discount to take into account, plus some price deferrals that were complicating matters."[73]

If genuine undercutting was found to have occurred, UOP would ask the distributor to remove the quote or raise the price it was charging. However, the Policy also developed potential punishment mechanisms for undercutting distributors, which we review next.

For the November 3, 2001, meeting, Scullion's notes outlined a proposed solution to the recent episodes of cheating on the Policy. The plan was "to introduce a penalty for the company who have undercut. This would take the form of them having to pay a higher price to UOP for the amount of desiccant involved, which UOP would then pass back to the other distributor by means of selling the same quantity at a lower price, effectively subsidising the loss of earnings at that account."[74] UOP was then suggesting that it would enforce side payments from the deviating distributor to the harmed distributor. There is no evidence of this punishment mechanism being discussed at the meeting or that it was enacted. However, as we describe next, UOP put in place a more severe punishment mechanism in 2002.

Since 1998, the Policy had provided price supports, in the form of rebates, to distributors that were either trying to win new customers or defending their existing customers from sellers of non-UOP products. Thus, the Policy was intended both to facilitate interbrand competition and grow the cartel's market share and to discourage intrabrand competition within the cartel. Consistent with the latter objective, UOP would not provide price support when several of its distributors were competing for the same customer. However, by 2002 this had become untenable, as revealed in a letter sent by Scullion of UOP to Jason Williams, who was sales manager at UKae: "The area we discussed was that relating to how a distributor could compete for business at customers where UOP were supporting the desiccant business at that customer through another distributor. At the moment this is unclear, and to date I have shied away from supporting two distributors at any one account, simply because of the complications that would arise. However, this is clearly unacceptable and anti-competitive as current desiccant prices often prohibit another distributor from supplying at these accounts."[75]

While UOP was suggesting that it would be willing to provide price supports to several distributors for the same customer, Scullion also stressed in the letter his desire to avoid retail price competition: "While I cannot dictate that there should be no undercutting of prices I am sure you can understand the logic of not doing so."[76] The letter also made clear that in order to avoid price supports that promoted intrabrand competition, UOP would closely monitor the provision of support. A distributor requesting support was required to provide UOP with the customer's name, location, the quantity to be supplied, and the retail price it would charge.[77] However, Scullion noted that disputes continued to arise: "In late 2002, the disputes between distributors increased and I was constantly being asked to either offer price support for particular accounts (. . . some which were already UOP accounts), and to monitor whether UOP distributors had undercut prices (by, inter alia, using price support)."[78]

In response, on November 8, 2002, Scullion sent a fax to UOP's distributors stating that it would remove a distributor's price support if it did not adhere to the "common sense" approach of the Policy:

> We are often asked what controls UOP can exercise in the event that the "common sense" approach is unintentionally undermined. The answer is that until now we have always tried to get the transgressor to amend the situation, but this is always hard to do, and inevitably all that happens is that prices continue to erode. The only way to avoid this is to ensure that we don't get our facts wrong. We therefore need to ask all of you to re-emphasise the need for your sales team to be diligent when it comes to the price of desiccant. In future if we get proven examples where one supplier has had their price undercut by another UOP distributor we will need to look at addressing the loss by removing the appropriate amount of support from the transgressor . . . and supporting the aggrieved party's customer to the same extent.[79]

This threatened punishment elicited an expression of support by UKae. After reading the fax, Williams of UKae wrote to Scullion "regarding our obligations" and stated, "I trust this provides you with peace of mind that UKae are still as always acting in the best interests of all concerned."[80]

Although there is no evidence that price supports were pulled for this reason, the OFT viewed the punishment as having played a key role in enforcing the Policy. Gwain Paterson, managing director at Thermoseal, raised concerns regarding its legality, saying, "Whilst I applaud your efforts to try and bring some sense into the market place. There are some aspects of your fax that give rise to some concern. I have run it past my solicitors who advise me not to accept this policy."[81]

The evidence is compelling that UOP and its four distributors participated in a hub-and-spoke cartel. What is less clear is who initiated the Policy:

> Mr Scullion of UOP . . . has stated that he believes the Policy was driven and maintained by the distributors: "There was an understanding between UOP distributors. . . . This understanding was that they could match each other's price of UOP desiccant but that they did not need to undercut each other." However, the distributors indicated that they thought the Policy was maintained at the behest of UOP. Mr Ealing, Managing Director of UKae, stated: "The general policy of UOP was that UOP distributors would not undercut other UOP distributors. UOP

Distributors were initially encouraged to resolve any issues they may have with other UOP Distributors on the sale of UOP desiccant between themselves. However, this often led to 'tit for tat' retaliation between the UOP Distributors. . . . Due to this retaliation between distributors, UOP advised that distributors should contact Tony Scullion at UOP to act almost as mediator in relation to any such disputes."[82]

The documentary evidence reviewed here makes clear that UOP played a key role in coordinating, monitoring, and enforcing a collusive arrangement. Furthermore, despite UOP's claim that it could have achieved the same objectives by simply raising wholesale prices, it seems that the agreement helped to counteract the bargaining power of the distributors. In particular, UOP's original intention for the meeting during which the 2001 price increase was instigated was to impose a wholesale price increase on its distributors. However, this was strongly resisted by the distributors, who instead demanded an increase in their retail margins and a wholesale price reduction. It is clear that the distributors had substantive bargaining power, and that was relevant to the operations of the hub-and-spoke cartel.

There are two other reasons why UOP appears to have been prepared to accept increased retail margins. First, UOP was keen to have its distributors sourcing the product solely from them. This was a requirement to get the price support. Initially, DQS only promised to single source in the future. DQS's wholesale price was increased in line with the 2002 retail price increase, while, in contrast, the other distributors benefited from a margin increase because their wholesale prices were unchanged. DQS relented in 2003 and became a single-source distributor. This episode suggests that UOP used the Policy to get its distributors to make UOP their exclusive supplier of desiccant. Thus, not only was the cartel preventing intrabrand competition, it also had potential exclusionary effects through shifting demand away from the products of other manufacturers.

Second, UOP hoped that the increased retail margins resulting from the 2001 price rise would provide retailers with a further incentive to sell more of its products.[83] While the OFT did not specify the mechanism, it could have meant encouraging salespeople to direct customers to UOP products or even deciding to single source with UOP.

The OFT accepted that there was limited evidence on the effect of the cartel and for this reason reduced the starting point for calculating fines.[84] The OFT imposed penalties of £1.23 million on UOP, £230,000 on DGS,

£140,000 on Thermoseal, and £110,000 on DQS (which was reduced to £36,210 on appeal).[85] Full leniency was granted to UKae and partial leniency to Thermoseal (50%) and UOP (20%).[86]

3.2.3   Paints and Varnishes (Poland)

Just after 2000, the do-it-yourself (DIY) market grew in Poland, and with it came increased competition among DIY retail chains.[87] Of particular relevance was a decline in the retail prices of paint and varnishes. The reduced retail price margins were a concern for the retail chains but also for the upstream manufacturers. With rising prices for raw materials, the upstream manufacturers wanted to raise the wholesale prices of paints and varnishes but were finding resistance from the downstream retailers, who were concerned that it might mean yet smaller margins.

In response to this situation, paint and varnish manufacturer Polifarb Cieszyn Wrocław (PCW) created a program to induce retailers to set higher retail prices, referred to as a "price stabilizing system." PCW put forth recommended retail prices for its 10 best-selling products and encouraged retailers to price no lower than the recommended level. To induce compliance, PCW created the following rebate system: "Stores that maintain PCW suggested prices as their retail prices will be receiving an additional stabilizing rebate in their invoice as a bonus for price compliance. If a given store does not comply with the prices suggested by PCW, all supplies of all products will be stopped and the stabilizing rebate will be put on hold until prices are brought back to the suggested level."[88] A chain would be considered out of compliance if just one store priced below the recommended price.

If PCW had independently negotiated such a policy with each chain, there would not have been collusion. However, that may not have alleviated a retail chain's concern that rival chains would not comply and instead charge prices below PCW's recommended prices. Were that to occur, a retailer in compliance would lose market share. In light of the recent history of aggressive pricing, it was natural for the retailers to be skeptical about compliance: "The compliance by all major DIY chains . . . with the prices set by the suppliers was the key to the success of the price stabilization program. A deviation by one of the retailers generally caused an immediate reaction from other DIY store chains—the latter would either lower or threaten to lower their retail price so as to remain competitive with each other."[89]

The Polish competition authority—the Office of Competition and Consumer Protection (Urząd Ochrony Konkurencji i Konsumentów, or UOKIK)—found no evidence of any communications between the downstream retail chains. What they did find was a very engaged upstream manufacturer intent on assuring that all retailers adopt the policy. The UOKIK determined that "PCW had played the role of a 'mediator' who would 'appease disputes', explain price differences, and inform retailers about how quickly would the prices of their competitors return to the agreed level. The manufacturer would notify retailers of all price changes of their competitors (most often increases), no matter how small, so as to prevent price changes by other trading partners."[90] It was PCW's efforts in support of a *coordinated* adoption of its price stabilizing program among retailers that turned the program into hub-and-spoke collusion.

In addition to monitoring current prices for compliance, there were at least two other avenues through which an upstream manufacturer could learn about a retail chain's future prices:

> 1) Price information associated with . . . joint marketing campaigns organised by the supplier and its retailers. . . . The campaign would be commissioned by the given DIY chain but the manufacturer would usually participate in its costs. . . . When sending the draft for a supplier's approval, retailers would often disclose at the same time that product's intended retail price. If the price shown on the draft was lower than the price recommended by the supplier, the latter would try to persuade the DIY chain to raise it, for example by threatening to withdraw the co-financing of the campaign. 2) Suppliers would obtain information from retailers on their intended retail prices in the course of standard conversations or e-mail contacts.[91]

PCW's success was not lost on other paint and varnish manufacturers, who were also finding resistance to wholesale price increases because of shrinking retail margins. Soon, manufacturers Akzo Nobel and Tikkurila formed their own hub-and-spoke cartels in order to raise the retail prices for their paints and varnishes. As the UOKIK noted, "Akzo Nobel was transmitting to its retailers information on price changes intended by their competitors. As shown by the collected evidence, the company was not doing that at the request of the chains but rather to convince them that the given participant in the agreement would indeed comply with the arrangements. Such assurances would give the supplier more certainty as far as the compliance with the arrangements by those participating in the agreement."[92]

The UOKIK found no evidence of any communication among the three upstream manufacturers. Though these were therefore three separate hub-and-spoke conspiracies, they were not independent occurrences. Instead, Akzo Nobel and Tikkurila appeared to be imitating the success of PCW's hub-and-spoke cartel.

3.2.4 Drugstore, Perfumery, and Hygiene Products (Belgium)

From 2002 to 2007, a hub-and-spoke cartel raised prices for drugstore, perfumery, and hygiene (DPH) products in supermarkets throughout Belgium. Seven retailers were involved (Carrefour, Colruyt, Cora, Delhaize, Intermarché, Makro, and Mestdagh) and 11 suppliers (Beiersdorf, Belgium Retail Trading, Bolton, Colgate, DE HBC, GSK, Henkel, L'Oreal, Procter & Gamble, Reckitt, and Unilever). The cartel was discovered because Colgate applied for leniency. All 18 companies settled, and the Belgian Authority of Competition imposed an aggregate fine of 174 million euros.[93]

According to the Belgian Authority of Competition, the objective of the cartel was "to increase and stabilize the selling prices of domestically produced DPH products to consumers at similar or near similar levels at the [retailer] level."[94] Each upstream supplier, such as Unilever, ran its own hub-and-spoke cartel with its downstream suppliers. While there was no evidence of any communication among suppliers, the simultaneity of these hub-and-spoke cartels and the similarity of their practices suggest otherwise.[95] The documented communications between a supplier's account manager and a retailer's purchasing agent or department manager took the form of emails, telephone calls, and conversations in stores. There was no evidence of communications between retailers.

Presumably with the cooperation of its leniency awardee, Colgate, the Belgian Authority of Competition provided a detailed description of how a round of collusive price setting was conducted.[96] It had four stages, labeled initial, negotiation and consultation, implementation, and control. The initial phase had either the supplier (hub) or a retailer (spoke) contact the other to propose a price increase for certain products. The hub then informed all its spokes that a coordinated price increase was in the works. During the negotiation and consultation phase, the supplier would discuss with its retailers what the magnitude of the price increase should be, the date on which it should be implemented, and which retailers were to participate. The information that a supplier received from a retailer was then conveyed to the other retailers. Once an agreement had been reached, the supplier informed each retailer of the products, the new retail prices, the implementation dates, and the participating retailers.

The communications conducted by a supplier during the negotiation and consultation phase served to achieve a common understanding among the retailers regarding the price increases for certain products. The implementation phase was also crucial for dispelling retailers' concerns that other retailers would not comply. It was during the implementation phase that retailers were to adopt the new prices, which might take a week for all retailers to do. Some retailers would not raise their prices until the supplier showed them transaction receipts from rival retailers documenting that they were indeed charging the new prices. Also critical to ensuring continued compliance was the control phase, which had the supplier monitor the stores to check that the new prices were in place. The supplier would share the information acquired through store inspections with the participating stores. Retailers would also monitor and then share with the supplier any evidence of noncompliance and ask them to intervene with the deviant retailer.

The Belgian Authority of Competition concluded that the hub-and-spoke cartel had mixed success in that some agreed price increases were implemented whereas others were not.

3.2.5 Replica Football Kits

Replica football (soccer) kits, and especially replica shirts, are worn by fans to express support for a particular team. Football clubs and national team governing bodies, such as the Football Association (FA) in England, grant sportswear manufacturers the exclusive right to manufacture and supply their replica kit. The highest-selling replica kits in the UK at the time of this infringement were those of Manchester United Football Club and England's national team. These were manufactured by Umbro, which was one of the smaller sportswear manufacturers.

In 1999, there were estimated to be around 3,500 sports retail outlets in the UK, of which over 1,000 were part of large multiple chains, such as the market leader JJB, as well as AllSports, Blacks, JD, and Sports Soccer.[97] These chains accounted for the majority of replica kit sales, since smaller independent stores typically did not stock them. The football clubs were also involved at the retail level through their official club shops and online.

Similarly, the FA had granted Sportsetail the exclusive right to operate the FA's "England Direct" online and mail order retail operations.

As a matter of standard practice, Umbro sought to control the retail pricing of its replica football kits by setting a recommended retail price (RRP). Starting in 1998, Sports Soccer became more aggressive in its pricing in order to establish itself as a major sports retailer. Its business model was to price below Umbro's RRP and sell large volumes: "Mr. Attfield [Sports Soccer's account manager] states: 'Retailers have always complained about Sports Soccer. The complaints, however, became particular[ly] intense from around 1999, when Sports Soccer started to develop as a credible and important competitor to established major retailers, such as JJB."[98]

Initially, the response of the incumbent market-leading retailer, JJB, was to implement discounts of its own. At the same time, JJB and some other retailers, along with Manchester United, placed significant pressure on Umbro to lower its wholesale prices. JJB and Manchester United had significant bargaining power because JJB was Umbro's single biggest customer and Manchester United had the option to license its kits through a different sportswear manufacturer.

In April 2000, JJB moved away from offering heavy discounts. This coincided with JJB and Manchester United applying pressure on Umbro to make sure that all retailers maintained high retail prices. Consequently, a hub-and-spoke cartel was formed. The hub was the replica kit manufacturer Umbro, and the spokes were various sports retail outlets. The cartel covered a series of agreements related to England and/or Manchester United replica shirts.[99] Although not solely restricted to them, the cartel focused on key selling periods, such as when a new kit was launched or during the Euro 2000 international tournament.

A lifting of retail prices would also suit the licensors Manchester United and the FA because the royalty payments they received from Umbro (and Sportsetail) were tied to retail prices; lower retail prices meant lower royalty payments. Because of its presence in the retail market, Manchester United was particularly keen to maintain retail margins, especially given that it was about to launch a range of new kits. At the time, Umbro was under financial pressure, and lifting retail prices would enable it to charge higher wholesale prices. Furthermore, Umbro had concerns (subsequently realized) that it might lose its license for Manchester United, and the club used this threat to put pressure on Umbro to prevent discounting.

As the initial step of a plan to induce retailers to price at RRPs, Umbro lowered RRPs in April 2000: "Umbro made it clear that it wished retailers to adhere to its RRPs or 'high street' prices for the resale of its Replica Kit and that discounting of its key products was detrimental to its brand. For example, JD and First Sport have confirmed that Umbro pursued policies designed to persuade retailers to adhere to its RRPs or 'high street' prices and that their own respective policies of generally pricing at Umbro's RRPs were well known to Umbro."[100]

To consummate this plan, Umbro conducted bilateral communications with each retailer. The message was not just that it should price at the RRP but that other retailers were planning to do so. Such communications could deliver the assurances needed for a retailer to price at the RRP without the risk of another retailer undercutting it: "Mr Ashley of Sports Soccer has said that during May and/or June 2000 Mr Ronnie of Umbro contacted Mr Ashley, Mr Hughes of Allsports, Mr Knight of Blacks, Mr Sharpe of JJB and possibly Mr Makin of JD. The contact was by telephone to seek agreement that each retailer would price the England home Replica Shirt for the duration of England's participation in Euro 2000 at £39.99. Sports Soccer had agreed to this and had understood from Umbro that Allsports, Blacks, JJB and possibly JD had made similar agreements with Umbro (Umbro states that Mr Ashley's agreement was conditional upon this)."[101]

Representative of these communications, consider the following exchanges between Umbro and JJB, then between Umbro and Sports Soccer, and then again between Umbro and JJB. These bilateral exchanges of pricing intentions were designed to achieve a mutual understanding between JJB and Sports Soccer:

> Mr. Ronnie [of Umbro] spoke to Mr. Sharpe [of JJB] about JJB's pricing intentions, in response to which Mr. Sharpe told him that JJB would sell at High Street prices unless others discounted. . . . It must have been apparent to Mr. Sharpe, even if there was no express reference to Sports Soccer, that Mr. Ronnie wanted the information in the context of taking steps to guard against discounting. Mr. Sharpe was among those who had spoken to Umbro staff about the Sports Soccer discounting policy. It would be extraordinary to suppose that, when Mr. Ronnie asked him about JJB's own attitude to pricing England replica kit during Euro 2000, it did not occur to Mr. Sharpe that this was connected with the question of discounting by Sports Soccer and attempts to prevent it occurring, which Mr. Sharpe and others at JJB had been asking for over some time past.[102]

Given JJB's declared pricing intention, Umbro then spoke with Sports Soccer:

> The second stage in the process was Mr. Ronnie's [of Umbro] call to Mr. Ashley [of Sports Soccer], to persuade him that he should raise Sports Soccer's prices for the England shirt. It is evident that Mr. Ashley was very reluctant to do so. It required pressure from Umbro by way of veiled or not so veiled threats as regards supplies. It also required an assurance that other retailers would not be discounting the shirts. Mr. Ronnie gave him that assurance. He did not mention any retailer by name, but because JJB was so dominant in the field, any assurance as to retailers must have been taken, and intended to be taken, as including JJB. Mr. Ashley agreed to raise Sports Soccer's prices on that basis, conditionally on the others also raising or maintaining their prices to or at the same level. It seems to us that, in turn, he must have recognised that others concerned would be told of his agreement. He knew, from what Mr. Ronnie told him about other retailers, that Umbro had been in touch with the other retailers about their pricing intentions, and that these had been passed on to him. He must have realised that what he told Mr. Ronnie about Sports Soccer's intentions would, correspondingly, be passed back to the others, including, necessarily, JJB.[103]

Finally, Umbro returned to speaking with JJB in order to assure them about Sports Soccer's pricing:

> Then at the third stage, Mr. Ronnie telephoned Mr. Sharpe again and told him that Sports Soccer had agreed to raise their prices and to sell at High Street prices. He did so in order to make it known to JJB that Umbro had, as asked, "done something" about Sports Soccer's discounting, by securing an agreement that it would come to an end as regards this product. He also needed to make sure that JJB knew of this because of Mr. Sharpe having mentioned that JJB might discount if others did, so that JJB should be aware that, at any rate if Sports Soccer kept to their agreement, JJB would not need to discount.[104]

However, this was not a pure hub-and-spoke cartel, for there were also some direct communications between retailers:

> On 8 June 2000 at about 13.00 hours, Mr Hughes of Allsports, Mr Whelan and Mr Sharpe of JJB and Mr Ashley of Sports Soccer met in Mr Hughes' house. . . . The purpose of the meeting was to discuss "the state of the market for replica kit including the crippling price war between" Allsports, JJB and Sports Soccer. Allsports denies that any agreement was reached at the meeting and states that the JJB representatives merely restated JJB's public pricing policy on Replica Kit and that Sports Soccer refused to give an indication as to its future pricing policy. However, Sports Soccer has stated that, at this meeting, it agreed with Allsports and JJB that it would price the MU [Manchester United] home adult Replica Shirts at £39.99 at launch and for an unspecified period thereafter.[105]

It is also clear that Umbro promoted direct communications among the spokes:

> A letter dated 13 July 2000 from Mr Prothero of Umbro to Mr Richards of MU [Manchester United] says: "As you know Umbro have worked very hard in agreeing a consensus to the price of the new Manchester United jersey. At one stage we even managed to get Messrs Hughes [of Allsports], Ashley [of Sports Soccer] and Whelan [of JJB] in the same room to agree this issue."[106]
>
> Mr Ashley of Sports Soccer has also confirmed that Umbro had requested it to attend a meeting with Allsports and JJB to discuss retail pricing on the MU [Manchester United] home Replica Kit as Sports Soccer's assurances to Umbro regarding its pricing intentions were not sufficient for the other retailers.[107]

This episode suggests that Umbro was not convinced that bilateral communications between a hub and a spoke would be sufficient to deliver the mutual understanding among retailers that they would price at Umbro's RRPs. Sports Soccer confirmed that "at meetings of this sort it requested and received assurances over the pricing intentions of other retailers,"[108] and the OFT opined that "Sports Soccer would require such information in order to ensure that agreements reached with Umbro on retail pricing did not put it at a disadvantage."[109]

With this understanding in place, Umbro monitored retail prices at key stores operated by the largest retailers: "JJB retailed the England home Replica Shirt at High Street Prices, although there was a local exception to this in JJB's Carlisle store. Mr Bryan and Mr Fellone of Umbro contacted Mr Russell of JJB several times, raising Umbro's concerns in relation to JJB's Carlisle branch which was offering a 25 per cent discount off the new England Replica Kit on the day of its launch."[110]

In addition, the retailers and licensors, especially Manchester United, England, and JJB, would complain to Umbro if rival retailers were discounting. From Manchester United this would often be within a day, and if the discounting happened on the day a kit was launched, Manchester United would complain to Umbro within an hour.[111] Furthermore, Manchester United even requested information from Umbro on what they understood Sports Soccer's pricing intentions for non-Umbro kits would be. Manchester United believed this information would give an indication of how Sports Soccer would price their kits.[112] Hence, the information exchange may have also reduced interbrand competition on other products sold by the retailers.

The cartel members did not make explicit threats of a price war to enforce the agreement (though such an implicit understanding may have been present). Instead, Umbro threatened the spokes that their supplies would be delayed or denied if they did not price at RRP, and (licensor and spoke) Manchester United suggested they do this. Furthermore, such threats were realized on a number of occasions. For example, in April 2000, Umbro knew that if Sports Soccer continued to discount England replica kits, JJB in particular would be disgruntled. Therefore, Ronnie from Umbro spoke to Sports Soccer's owner, Mike Ashley, who initially refused to stop discounting. Consequently, a delivery of shirts to Sports Soccer was stopped and only reinstated once Sports Soccer agreed to price at the RRP: "I spoke to Mike Ashley to ask him not to discount the socks and shorts. I cannot remember the date when I spoke to Mike Ashley. Initially he refused. I stopped a delivery of [. . .][C] or [. . .][C] shirts to Sports Soccer. Mike Ashley then agreed to put the prices of the socks, shorts and infant kits back to full recommended retail price. The delivery of shirts was then reinstated."[113]

The spokes would also threaten the hub to ensure that it enforced the agreement. For example, prior to the launch of a new Manchester United kit in the summer of 2001, JJB was concerned that Sports Soccer would be selling the kit at a discount. JJB threatened to cancel orders of this kit and subsequently did so. The order was subsequently reinstated, with JJB claiming that this was because Umbro had offered better wholesale prices.[114] On the other hand, Umbro claimed that this was because of their assurances that Sports Soccer would not discount the kit at the time of its launch.[115] Similar pressure was placed on Umbro by Manchester United, and in 1999 Manchester United canceled an order for 5,000 shirts as a result of failing to resolve pricing issues with Umbro. Pressure from Manchester United was also applied to make sure Umbro refused to supply supermarket chains in order to protect the brand and prevent its shirts from being sold as "loss leaders."[116]

According to Umbro's internal documents, all these efforts to raise retail prices were successful. Its May 2000 monthly management report stated, "There has been a major step forward in the retail price of England [and] the launch of Manchester United. JJB, Sports Soccer, First Sports, JD Sports and Allsports have all agreed to retail their adults shirts at £39.99. This is following England being sold at various retail prices through April and May ranging from £24.99 to £29.99, £32.99 or £32.99 with a free £9.99 cap at JD Sports."[117]

Pricing data obtained by the OFT showed that the retailers involved in the agreements set remarkably similar prices while the agreements were in place.[118] For example, from its launch in August 2000 through December 2000, all retailers surveyed (JJB, AllSports, JD, and Blacks) priced the Manchester United replica shirt at £40 (when the RRP was £43). The only exception was Sports Soccer, which at times priced as low as £30.

The OFT first became aware of possible collusion in 1999, when they received complaints from retailers that they were being prevented from discounting. Subsequently, Umbro, the FA, and English clubs in the Premier League gave assurances to the OFT that discounting would not be prevented. However, in August 2000, the OFT received another complaint from Sports Soccer, claiming that price fixing had become even more prevalent than previously. This is yet more evidence of limited compliance with the collusive arrangement by Sports Soccer. The OFT then launched a formal investigation and concluded that the parties had engaged in unlawful agreements from April 2000 to August 2001,[119] explaining that "RRPs are not unlawful when they simply operate as recommended prices. In this case, however, the OFT is satisfied that RRPs and 'high street' prices during the period of the infringement operated as focal points for concerted behaviour. Umbro applied pressure to certain retailers for them to adhere to RRPs or 'high street' prices."[120] In aggregate, the cartel members were fined £18.6 million, with full leniency granted to Sportsetail and partial leniency (20%) to the FA.

The UK Competition Appeal Tribunal supported the OFT's decision, which was then affirmed in court following an appeal by JJB. In its decision, the Court of Appeal succinctly expressed the hub-and-spoke communications that were the basis for JJB and Sports Soccer having a "meeting of minds" that they would both raise their prices:

> The Tribunal was entitled to find that (1) JJB provided confidential price information to Umbro in circumstances in which it was obvious that it would or might be passed on to Sports Soccer in support of Umbro's attempt to persuade Sports Soccer to raise its prices (thereby adopting the pricing policy which JJB explicitly wanted adopted by all significant retailers), (2) Umbro did use the information in relation to Sports Soccer in that way, (3) Sports Soccer did agree to raise its prices in reliance on this information, and foreseeing that others including JJB would be told of its agreement, and later did raise its prices as it had agreed to do, and (4) Umbro did tell JJB of this, thereby making it clear to JJB that it would be able to maintain its prices at their current level, as it did.[121]

The replica football kits case has a number of features similar to the UK toy case. In response to intense retail price competition and complaints from at least one retailer, an upstream manufacturer sought to raise retail prices by engaging in bilateral communications with retailers in order to achieve a common understanding to set prices at the manufacturer's recommended level. The replica football kits case differs in that the hub also orchestrated a meeting of the spokes for them to engage in direct communications. Apparently, the hub was not sufficiently convinced that indirect communications would deliver an exchange of assurances among the spokes.

3.2.6 Pharmaceutical Products (US)

Parke, Davis & Company (hereafter Parke Davis) manufactured and sold pharmaceutical products to retailers and drug wholesalers (who would then sell them to retailers).[122] The particular retail market of interest was the Washington, D.C., metropolitan area. It had been Parke Davis's policy to have a suggested minimum retail price (SMRP). In early 1956, some drug store chains in the D.C. area started pricing below the SMRP and one retailer—Dart Drug Company—engaged in deep, well-advertised price cuts.

Frustrated with the retail pricing situation, the manager in charge of the D.C. area devised a strategy after learning he could legally refuse to sell to retailers who priced below the SMRP. He informed retailers that he would start doing this in July 1956, and he also told wholesalers that they would be denied supply should they supply retailers who did not respect the SMRP. Nevertheless, five retailers continued with their low prices. Parke Davis cut off their supplies, though some retailers were still pricing below the SMRP and selling out of their inventories. In July, Parke Davis consequently modified its policy. It would only cut off sales to the retailer (and to the wholesaler who sold to it) if the retailer *advertised* a price below the SMRP. Dart Drug initially respected the advertising policy, in response to which Parke Davis resumed supplies. However, by September, Dart Drug (along with other retailers) had returned to advertising prices below the SMRP. At that point, Parke Davis stopped refusing to sell to them because an investigation by the Antitrust Division of the US Department of Justice (DOJ) had been launched in response to a complaint from Dart Drug.

As thus far described, the actions of Parke Davis could well be nothing more than the exercise of its legal right to refuse to supply wholesalers and retailers. Furthermore, the communications it had with them were bilateral: either with a single wholesaler or a single retailer. However, the DOJ argued that there was a violation of Section 1 of the Sherman Act. As summarized by the US Supreme Court:

> The Government introduced evidence showing that appellee had (1) announced a policy of refusing to deal with retailers who failed to observe appellee's suggested minimum resale prices or who advertised discount prices on appellee's products, (2) discontinued direct sales to those retailers who failed to abide by the announced policy, (3) induced wholesale distributors to stop selling appellee's products to the offending retailers, (4) secured unanimous adherence by informing a number of the retailers that, if each of them would adhere to the announced policy, one of their principal competitors would also do so, and (5) permitted the retailers to resume purchasing its products after they had indicated willingness to observe the policy.[123]

It is item (4) that shifted Parke Davis's actions into unlawful territory.

The credibility of Parke Davis's threat to cut off a retailer's supply for having priced below the SMRP relied on having enough retailers comply. If many were charging below the SMRP, implementation of the threat would mean shutting off the supplies of many retailers, and that would significantly harm Parke Davis's sales. However, if a retailer expected other retailers to price at the SMRP, then if it priced below the SMRP, it became far more believable that Parke Davis would go through with the threat and refuse to supply it. To achieve those expectations, Parke Davis not only communicated its plan to wholesalers and retailers but also indicated that it was communicating with other wholesalers and retailers:

> In order to insure that retailers who did not comply would be cut off from sources of supply, representatives of Parke Davis visited the wholesalers and told them, in effect, that not only would Parke Davis refuse to sell to wholesalers who did not adhere to the policy announced in its catalogue, but also that it would refuse to sell to wholesalers who sold Parke Davis products to retailers who did not observe the suggested minimum retail prices. Each wholesaler was interviewed individually, but each was informed that his competitors were also being apprised of this. The wholesalers, without exception, indicated a willingness to go along. Representatives called contemporaneously upon the retailers involved, individually, and told each that, if he did not observe the suggested minimum retail prices, Parke Davis would refuse to deal with him, and that, furthermore, he would be unable to purchase any Parke Davis products from the wholesalers. Each of the retailers was also told that his competitors were being similarly informed.[124]

Of particular concern to retailers was that Dart Drug comply, for it had been pricing well below the SMRP. That it advertised its prices would have heightened this concern among other retailers, for a well-advertised discount to the SMRP price could attract many customers from retailers who were charging the SMRP:

> When interviewed, the president of Dart Drug Company indicated that he might be willing to stop advertising, although continuing to sell at discount prices, if shipments to him were resumed. Each of the other retailers was then told individually by Parke Davis representatives that Dart was ready to discontinue advertising. Each thereupon said that, if Dart stopped advertising, he would also. On August 28, Parke Davis reported this reaction to Dart. Thereafter, all of the retailers discontinued advertising of Parke Davis vitamins at less than suggested minimum retail prices.[125]

The district court dismissed the DOJ's complaint on the grounds that "there is no evidence that . . . Parke, Davis ever conferred or discussed its sales policies with more than one wholesaler or more than one retailer at a time, nor that it made the enforcement of its policies as to any one wholesaler or retailer dependent upon the action of any other wholesaler or retailer."[126] It is true that Parke Davis's communications were always one-on-one with a retailer or wholesaler. It never convened a meeting of retailers and wholesalers at which it encouraged collective adoption of prices that respected the SMRP or an agreement not to advertise prices below the SMRP. However, coordinated adoption of a plan can be achieved through a hub-and-spoke arrangement whereby the hub (Parke Davis) communicates with each of the spokes (retailers, like Dart Drug, and wholesalers) and conveys a plan to price at the SMRP *and* the hub is meeting with other spokes to achieve joint adoption of this plan. That is how the Supreme Court viewed the matter when it reversed the district court's judgment. It accepted the DOJ's argument that "what Parke Davis did here by entwining the wholesalers and retailers in a program to promote general compliance with its price maintenance policy went beyond mere customer selection, and created combinations or conspiracies to enforce resale price maintenance in violation of §§ 1 and 3 of the Sherman Act."[127] Furthermore, the Supreme Court noted that Parke Davis acted in this manner because "only by actively bringing about substantial unanimity among the competitors was Parke Davis able to gain adherence to its policy."[128]

3.2.7 Dairy (UK)

During the period from 2000 to 2003, UK farmers wanted retailers of dairy products to subsidize an increase in the farmgate price (which is the price paid by dairy processors).[129] At the time, the farmgate price for raw milk had reached very low levels, while the retail profit margins of dairy products had increased substantially since deregulation in 1994. To achieve their objective, the National Farmers' Union (NFU) and Farmers for Action (FFA) began to apply political pressure in 2000. They lobbied Parliament and protested at (even blockading) the depots of dairy processors and supermarkets. Toward the end of this period, a hub-and-spoke cartel was formed to coordinate retail price increases on cheese and milk on the grounds that a cartel could support a higher wholesale price from the dairy processors, which could then pay higher farmgate prices for raw milk. While the initial impetus for raising retail prices came from the farmers, the case is about collusion between the dairy processors and supermarkets.

The UK dairy industry consists of three stages of production. At the retail level, most consumers purchased their dairy products from "national multiples," which supply a range of grocery products in stores nationwide. Among others, this included the "big four" UK supermarkets: Asda, Safeway, Sainsbury's, and Tesco.

At the dairy processor level, there were four comparably sized suppliers of fresh milk—Arla, Express, Wiseman, and Dairy Crest—to the big four supermarkets.[130] The three main cheese processors were Dairy Crest, Glanbia, and McLelland. Each supplied the big four supermarkets, with the exception that Glanbia did not supply Tesco. Dairy Crest was the only processor of both milk and cheese. While milk is a homogeneous product and perishable, cheese products are branded and to some extent storable. This meant that cheese processors also faced interbrand competition from imports, whereas the milk processors did not.

At the farm level, there were a large number of small dairy farms that supplied raw milk to the dairy processors. This number was decreasing over the period because of a steep fall in the farmgate price in 1997.

The OFT started an investigation into price fixing when Arla applied for leniency in July 2003. The OFT initially alleged that there were five "initiatives" in which prices of various dairy products were fixed over 2002–2003, but ultimately it only prosecuted the following three:

- the 2002 Cheese Initiative, in which there were three hubs (Dairy Crest, Glanbia, and McLelland) and four spokes (Asda, Safeway, Sainsbury's, and Tesco);

- the 2003 Fresh Liquid Milk (FLM) Initiative, in which there were three hubs (Arla, Dairy Crest, and Wiseman) and three spokes (Asda, Safeway, and Sainsbury's);[131] and

- the 2003 Cheese Initiative, in which the sole hub was McLelland and the spokes were Asda, Sainsbury's, and Tesco.

All but Tesco admitted their guilt. Tesco appealed the OFT's decision to the Competition Appeal Tribunal, which overturned the judgment regarding conduct in 2002 but affirmed Tesco's guilt in the 2003 Cheese Initiative. The two alleged initiatives that were not prosecuted by the OFT were the 2002 Liquid Milk Initiative and the 2003 Butter Initiative.

The three prosecuted initiatives aimed for "2ppl [pence per litre] price increases (or £200pmt [per metric tonne] as the equivalent measure in the case of cheese) in the retail prices of cheddar and British territorial cheeses in 2002 and 2003 and FLM in 2003. These retail price increases were accompanied by corresponding wholesale price increases which were either implemented before or after the retail price increase had taken place."[132] The 2002 Cheese Initiative was to raise retail prices "through staggered increases over three weeks starting on 20 October 2002,"[133] and the 2003 Cheese Initiative planned to implement the increases beginning September 29, 2003.[134] In the 2003 FLM Initiative, Asda's FLM retail price increases on July 1, 2003, were "quickly followed by Safeway, Sainsbury's and [a retailer], who all increased their FLM retail prices by identical amounts on 2 July 2003."[135]

The purpose of both the 2002 Cheese and 2003 FLM Initiatives was "to financially assist U.K. dairy farmers by subsidising an increase in the farmgate price."[136] In contrast, the purpose of the 2003 Cheese Initiative was less noble in that its main aim was "to 'stabilise' McLelland's margins."[137] McLelland at that time was experiencing "cost increases which it was finding increasingly difficult to absorb given that it had not benefited from an increase in wholesale prices for the previous five years."[138] While there was some evidence that the supermarkets requested that the margins be passed on to farmers, this was not a requirement.[139]

The idea of aiding the plight of farmers through a coordinated increase in retail prices dates back to 2000, when the pressure group FFA "actively attempted to co-ordinate a FLM retail price increase to subsidise a farmgate price increase. As part of this plan FFA sought written statements from retailers confirming their willingness to increase FLM retail prices. These written commitments were usually provided on the basis that other retailers would take similar action. FFA then disclosed these letters to other retailers to facilitate further commitments to increase prices."[140]

This initiative was abandoned in April 2000, when Tesco, Safeway, and another retailer received confirmation from the OFT that it would likely breach UK competition law. However, following increased pressure from farmers' groups during summer 2002, a similar plan to coordinate retail price increases was instigated that autumn. Its difference from the FFA plan was that verbal commitments of the supermarkets (spokes) regarding their future retail pricing intentions were exchanged, most commonly via the cheese and milk processors (the hubs). A supermarket would often communicate a proposed increase via the processors, who would relay it to the other supermarkets, in response to which they might convey an intent to follow. Because of concerns about the veracity of the leader's plan to raise prices, a follower might wait for the leader to raise its retail prices before doing so itself. If followers failed to raise their prices, then the leader would lower its prices.

This process is illustrated by an internal email on June 27, 2003, from Sainsbury's dairy trading manager to a senior manager at Sainsbury's just four days prior to the price increase that was part of the 2003 FLM Initiative:

> Thought I'd drop you a quick update on the latest situation on milk retails. The industry believes that Asda will be increasing milk retails by the equivalent of 2 pence per litre from 01/07 (tuesday). The[y] have made it clear through their processors, the NFU and FFA that they expect the competition to follow within 48 hrs or they will revert back. Their biggest worry is that [a retailer] will not follow. From JS's [Sainsbury's] perspective, I have given assurance to the industry that we will be watching prices from monday of next week, and that we will "remain competitive in the market place" if we see a change. Realistically we will implement the increase from weds 2nd [July] if Asda move.[141]

While there were no direct communications between the retailers to help them coordinate price increases, there were multiple channels through which information flowed between them indirectly, as is evident in the preceding quotation. It is useful to summarize these channels before we present examples. First, there was a meeting between a supermarket and several of the processors supplying it. In that meeting, a supermarket expressed a desire to raise its cheese prices but that it was essential that other retailers do so as well. Second, there were bilateral communications between a processor and a supermarket, with a processor trying to convince a supermarket that other supermarkets were going to increase prices. Furthermore, to ensure consistency of messages from the processors (hubs) to the supermarkets (spokes), there were also direct communications between the processors. Third, there were bilateral communications between a supermarket and the pressure groups (i.e., the FFA or NFU), whereby the former expressed the need for a collective price increase and the latter shared information about other retailers' price intentions.

As is clear from the documentary evidence we will provide here, critical to the implementation of the retail price increases was that retailers jointly consummate them. As both the upstream processors and downstream supermarkets had been approached by the FFA to increase wholesale and retail prices, the thought of raising prices was on their minds even prior to the communications between processors and supermarkets.

The first documented channel was between a supermarket and several of its suppliers. A meeting on September 13, 2002, involved Tesco and a number of the cheese processors, including Tesco's two suppliers, Dairy Crest and McLelland, as well as a dairy processor that did not supply Tesco at that time.[142] In the OFT's statement of objections, it described this meeting as the "catalyst" for the 2002 Cheese Initiative.[143] At the meeting, there was discussion of how to raise the farmgate price "through extending the scope of the recent cost and retail price increases that had been achieved for milk to include other dairy products, in particular cheese."[144] Based on a processor employee's notes from the meeting,

> it is also evident that [Tesco's category manager for dairy] gave a clear and direct indication that Tesco was contemplating increasing its cheese retail prices as part of any price initiative with the note recording him as stating that: "Cheese and spread values have crashed over the last 3 years and Tesco has been selling them at a loss. Cautiously optimistic that Tesco can now start to move retail prices forward in this area but . . . very difficult to move out of line with other competitors . . . [Tesco's manager] senses there is a mood to move some of these prices forward."[145]

Regarding that meeting, the OFT commented, "In disclosing that it was prepared to increase its cheese retail prices . . . to its supplying processors in the context of discussions which had as their purpose the co-ordination of a market-wide cheese retail price increase, Tesco may be taken to have intended and did, in fact, foresee that its supplying processors would make use of that information to influence conditions on the cheese retail market by passing it to other retailers in order to facilitate further and wider retail price increases."[146]

Following this meeting, and consistent with a standard hub-and-spoke cartel, processors (hubs) disseminated pricing intentions of supermarkets (spokes) in order to provide assurances to each supermarket that it could raise prices, knowing that its competitors would do likewise. An example of this occurred about one month prior to the first retail price increases of the 2002 Cheese Initiative, when Dairy Crest's senior account manager for supermarket Asda met with Asda's category manager for dairy on September 17, 2002. At that meeting, Dairy Crest's manager provided a slide presentation titled "Asda Briefing Document Raw Milk Pricing," which demonstrated "that Dairy Crest proposed to Asda that it should participate in an initiative to subsidise a farmgate price increase through retail price increases on dairy products in addition to milk."[147] One slide stated, "Move Cheese Prices at retail up by £200 per tonne," and another stated, "Action—Move the whole market forward,"[148] which the OFT appropriately interpreted as Dairy Crest informing Asda "that it was not being expected to increase its cheese retail prices unilaterally, but as part of a wider market move which also involved the implementation of retail price increases by its competitors."[149] On the same day, Dairy Crest made a "virtually identical presentation" to another retailer.[150] These communications are consistent with an upstream processor promoting an increase in retail cheese prices with each of its customers while conveying to those customers that it was part of a plan for all supermarkets to raise prices. This was clearly expressed in a note by Dairy Crest's commercial director for its Tesco account, which stated that Dairy Crest "proposed to Asda that by early November all accounts would have followed the market moves . . . Asda—Tesco—Sainsbury's—Safeway—[a retailer]—[a retailer]."[151] If Asda were to raise its retail prices, it was assured that it would not be alone.

There were also several other documented communications in which a processor conveyed the explicit pricing intentions of one supermarket to another supermarket, which would have facilitated mutual understanding among the supermarkets regarding price increases. In one such example, "On 4 November 2002, [Dairy Crest's category manager (cheese and spreads) for its Tesco account] sent an e-mail and attached spreadsheet entitled 'Suggested RSP' to [Tesco's senior cheese buyer]. The e-mail reads as follows: 'I have attached a spreadsheet which shows the suggested rsp's [retail selling prices] of cheese lines that we supply Asda following the price increase. My understanding is that Asda will be applying £200 per tonne.'"[152] In an interview with the OFT, that Dairy Crest employee explained, "By sending this email, I was showing [Tesco's senior cheese buyer] that the suggested price of cheese was the same across the board and not specific to Tesco. The prices mentioned were only suggested prices and not guaranteed prices. In my view it was not a definitive statement that Asda's prices would go up by the amount listed; I stated that it was 'My understanding' that they would do so rather than stating that they definitely would."[153] Thus, Dairy Crest was not sharing the actual prices of Asda but rather its intended prices, and presumably doing so with the goal of affecting Tesco's prices.

Given that there was more than one hub in two of the pricing initiatives, the OFT found that there was also "a degree of direct co-ordination and contact between the processors themselves with the aim of implementing a market wide cheese retail price increase."[154] Such communications would ensure that there was a close degree of commonality of information provided by the processors (hubs) to the supermarkets (spokes). In particular, during the 2002 Cheese Initiative, a senior manager at Glanbia (hub)—who did not supply Tesco with cheese at that time—prepared an internal communication stating that he had been informed of Tesco's (spoke) pricing intentions by a senior manager at McLelland (hub): "I had a further lengthy discussion with [a senior manager at McLelland] on the same subject. He tells me that Tesco will go. if one other major player moves. He also told me that DC [Dairy Crest] are seeing Asda this afternoon. I have asked [an employee at Glanbia] to call [Asda's category manager for dairy] later this afternoon to elicit information on what Asda may now do on cheese pricing. [An employee at Glanbia] will feed this back into the system once we have made contact."[155]

The OFT concluded that "it is evident from the summary of this discussion that this was not the first time that [a senior manager at McLelland] and [a senior manager at Glanbia] had discussed the price initiative and that information was being passed between processors concerning retailers' cheese retail pricing intentions."[156] Such communications between the processors would facilitate having processors deliver consistent messages to the supermarkets.

Though the FFA and NFU were not prosecuted by the OFT, they also engaged in communications to promote common expectations among retailers about higher cheese and milk prices. For example, two weeks before the first price increases of the 2002 Cheese Initiative, when the FFA was lobbying supermarkets for a price hike, some supermarkets clearly expressed that there needed to be a marketwide movement in prices:

> On 4 October 2002, [Sainsbury's general manager for dairy and cheese] wrote to [an official at FFA] and informed him of the status of discussions between Sainsbury's and its processors regarding a cheese price increase. The letter reads as follows: "With regards to cheese we are still discussing the implementation of cost price increases with all our processors. It is intended that we will pass on an increase in our buying prices by £200/tonne in approx 3 weeks, for all our standard cheese range, provided other retailers also accept this. I must stress that if others do not generally support this initiative, I will have to withdraw my support for cheese, if I find I am uncompetitive in the wider market place."[157]

While there is no evidence that the FFA passed this information to other supermarkets, it would be in line with their involvement in the abandoned initiative in April 2000 to have done so. Indeed, in its decision, the OFT noted during the 2003 FLM Initiative "that FFA was seeking to promote an initiative to secure a farmgate price increase through increased FLM retail prices during June 2003 and held discussions with several major retailers concerning this."[158] Similarly, there are some documented communications where the NFU passed on the pricing intentions of supermarkets during the 2003 FLM Initiative: "On 25 June 2003, [a senior manager at Sainsbury's] e-mailed [a senior manager at Sainsbury's], together with other Sainsbury's employees, to inform them of the discussions he had had with [an official at NFU] in relation to 'the next milk round': 'He [an official at NFU] said that ASDA were prepared to move if others were. He also said that he was very upset about the amount of margin being absorbed by the processors and he felt that they were taking too much of the margin.'"[159]

In addition to the bilateral communications the supermarkets had with the processors and pressure groups, the media was also used to promote a common understanding among retailers. For example, on September 24, 2003, just five days before the retail first price increases of the 2003 Cheese Initiative, an article in the *Dairy Industry Newsletter* stated:

SUPERMARKETS AGREE £200/tonne PRICE INCREASE

Apparently, as of this week, all the major UK supermarkets are to implement an across-the-board £200/tonne increase in cheese prices as from next month. Asda were the last of the major chains to 'come on board'. Sainsbury led the initiative, followed by [a retailer], [a retailer] and [a retailer]. Tesco, initially reluctant, have agreed to a price increase. It is understood that Sainsbury are putting retail prices up this week, the others will follow.[160]

McLelland shared this article with Sainsbury's, which would have helped shore up Sainsbury's belief that other supermarkets would be raising prices. In addition, McLelland may have provided the information for the article:

On 24 September 2003, [McLelland's national account manager for its Sainsbury's account] e-mailed a copy of an article taken from the Dairy Industry Newsletter website of the same date to [Sainsbury's senior cheese buyer]. . . . [The] covering e-mail suggests that McLelland may have played a role in providing information for the article: "Please read the below feature on the retail move. As you can see, we have positioned you favourably in terms of moving the price forward, and as the Dairy Industry News is the 'Bible' of the dairy farming community, this has been viewed as a very favourable move by Sainsbury's."[161]

Similarly, the FFA also used the print media to promote a consensus of an imminent price increase only three weeks before the price increases of the 2003 FLM Initiative:

In an article in the Western Daily Press, dated 10 June 2003, [an official at FFA] was quoted as claiming he had secured Asda's support for an FLM price increase and that his aim was to secure "another across-the-board price rise" in order to subsidise a farmgate price increase: "[An official at] Farmers For Action says he has secured the backing of the first major supermarket chain for an increase in the milk price. Now there are hopes that another across-the-board price rise can be introduced this summer, with the margin passed back to producers. [An official at FFA] emerged from weekend talks with Asda in buoyant mood after setting out the farmers' case to directors. 'I think they now fully understand the predicament of the British dairy farmer and the likely outcome if nothing is done to get the price up,' she said."

Such public announcements of marketwide increases in retail prices could have gone a long way toward providing the assurances that the supermarkets needed.

The message from these communications is clear: A supermarket is willing to raise its retail prices as long as competing supermarkets are planning to do so. In order to achieve that common course of action, there were various forms of communication utilized to deliver the required common understanding among supermarkets. By conveying its pricing intentions to a processor like Dairy Crest and to the FFA, a processor and FFA could share those pricing intentions with other supermarkets. If a supermarket anticipated such sharing, which is reasonable given that other supermarkets' pricing intentions were being shared with them, then these retailers could have achieved the exchange of assurances necessary to consummate a rise in retail cheese prices. As the OFT summarized, "The type of information disclosed by retailers chiefly consisted of expressions of willingness to increase retail prices on condition that their competitors either led or followed the retail price increase and information concerning future retail price increases (such as the levels of the retail price increases and the dates on which those increases would be implemented)."[162]

In addition to communications regarding pricing intentions, these messages conveyed threats regarding the consequences if retailers did not follow the planned retail price increases. Perhaps the main concern of the supermarkets was the prospect of further protests by the farmers' pressure groups. These are evident in the preceding quotation by the FFA official at the end of the *Western Daily Press* article of June 10, 2003, and Asda's dairy category manager stating that increasing prices to support farmers "would make direct action by farmers, in the form of blockades, 'far less likely.'"[163]

The possibility of action by the pressure groups would have added to the threat of returning to the original prices, which could have made it unnecessary for supermarkets to threaten a price war. For instance, in the 2003 FLM Initiative, an internal email on June 27, 2003, from Sainsbury's dairy trading manager to a senior manager at Sainsbury's stated that Asda had "made it clear through their processors, the NFU and FFA that they expect the competition to follow [*their FLM retail price increase*] within 48hrs or they will revert back."[164]

Similarly, in the 2002 Cheese Initiative, Asda's buyer of milk, cream, and cheese sent an internal email to other colleagues within Asda on November 13, 2002, stating, "Stilton cheese—Asda not yet applied any increase— All have moved up except—[a retailer], will submit proposal to move up 25 Nov subject to [a retailer]. nb all Christmas line pricing will not change, nb—others have indicated will move back down unless we [*Asda*] follow due to moving 2 weeks ago."[165]

While there is no evidence that the supermarkets that led the price increases did revert to the original prices, in the 2003 Cheese Initiative price increases were delayed because of retailers not acting as expected. As in a contemporaneous internal report written by (hub) McLelland's national accounts manager for Tesco in October 2003,

> On Tuesday [September 30, 2003] morning I had a discussion with [Tesco's senior cheese buyer] and told her that Asda had not moved retail prices as expected but that [a retailer] and JS [Sainsbury's] had started to move and that I still believed Asda would move. At this time [Tesco's senior cheese buyer] told me that she would not enter her new case costs without evidence of Asda moving on retail prices. On Tuesday [September 30, 2003] afternoon I spoke to [Tesco's senior cheese buyer] to ask her to increase her costs and to help start the ball rolling on retail prices. It was at this time that [Tesco's senior cheese buyer] said she had not agreed to the £200 cost increase and that further justification was needed before Tesco would consider accepting the increase.[166]

Shortly after a meeting on October 6, 2003, and having received more information related to Asda's retail pricing intentions in the interim, Tesco began to implement the agreed retail price increases.

The decision also highlights that both the supermarkets and the dairy processors committed resources to monitoring the implementation of the price rises, which included bilateral communications between a processor and a supermarket. As we document, the approach to monitoring differed depending on the product.

In the 2003 FLM Initiative, monitoring of the price increase happened on the day of the expected price increase. For example, as documented by the OFT in its decision, "Between 09:00 and 09:30 on 1 July 2003, [Wiseman's national accounts manager for its Safeway and Sainsbury's accounts] sent e-mails to relevant contacts within [a retailer], Safeway, Sainsbury's and [a retailer], attaching a till receipt from an Asda store in Hamilton [Scotland] for purchases of various container sizes of FLM at 08:24 on 1 July 2003, thus confirming Asda's new FLM retail price levels. Wiseman sent similar e-mails to a number of other retailers."[167]

However, other processors outside Scotland had to commit resources to monitoring the price increase throughout that morning because while prices had increased as expected in Asda stores in Scotland, there was a delay in the price increases in Asda stores in England and possibly Wales. These delays resulted from "some breakdown in communication within the

ASDA organisation and not all prices in all their stores had moved at the same time":[168] "At 09.35 on 1 July 2003, [a national account controller at a processor] e-mailed [a trading director for supermarket accounts at a processor] to inform him that '[the dairy trading manager] from J.S. [Sainsbury's] . . . spoke to [an employee at a processor] this morning regarding RSP changes in Asda, we have visited 2 stores this morning and there was no change in RSPs. [Sainsbury's dairy trading manager] has been in a[n] Asda in Scotland and they have changed RSPs: . . . We will send more bods out during this morning to visit Asda.'"[169]

Subsequently, a national account controller at a processor sent an internal email stating that "Asda 'have moved RSPs on fresh milk' 'south of Scotland' 'as of 10.00 am.'"[170] This information, along with proof of the price increase in the form of a receipt, was provided to Sainsbury's dairy trading manager.[171]

In contrast, during the 2002 and 2003 Cheese Initiatives, there was not always a need to monitor the retail prices of cheese on the day of the increases, because the cheese processors (hubs) could provide evidence of the retail price increases to the supermarkets (spokes) before the cheese was in the supermarkets' refrigerators. This was because the supplying cheese processor was required to print the prices on the packages for the cheese that was prepackaged with random weight. Consequently, the processors could send evidence of the price increases to the spokes before the prices were in the public domain. For example, an internal email on September 29, 2003, from (hub) McLelland's sales support manager to McLelland's Mauchline packing station manager stated, "To confirm earlier telephone call in which I asked for your assistance to provide photocopy examples of all pre-pack labels that have been packed with the new retail prices as advised by [McLelland's quality control manager] and [McLelland's logistics manager] late last week. This information is to send to the buyers this afternoon so that they can be encouraged with proof that retails have moved and expedite price increases across the board."[172] This information would have helped to coordinate price rises for random-weight cheese, which was more difficult because "retailers need to sell their existing priced marked cheese stock before they are able to place stock with a revised price on the shelf."[173] Consequently, "there could be a gap between the implementation of a retail price increase by the first retailer and the increase implemented by the retailer following, while it used up price marked cheese."[174] Thus, such communications were important in avoiding any problems related to this gap.

The OFT noted that the printing of labels by processors provided a legitimate commercial reason for a retailer to inform that supplier of its retail pricing intentions for prepackaged cheese. However, it correctly concluded that the weight of evidence "clearly demonstrates that retailers disclosed information regarding their cheese retail pricing intentions to their supplying processors in circumstances where they clearly understood that the retail price increases were part of a coordinated plan to increase cheese prices across the grocery retail sector."[175]

In contrast to the typical hub-and-spoke cartel, the financial rewards from collusion may not have been the primary driving force for either the supermarkets (spokes) or the processors (hubs), or at least may not have been the original cause for collusion. Indeed, at the outset of these initiatives, it was considered that the supermarkets and the processors should not be perceived as profiteering from the price rises. This is outlined in the witness evidence provided to the OFT by Dairy Crest's commercial director for its Tesco account: "At Dairy Crest we wanted to be whiter than white and so we suggested to the retailers that the principle of cash margin maintenance rather than percentage margin maintenance should be adopted so as to reduce the risk of the accusation of profiteering. These suggestions were simply that, suggestions, as retailers have the power to decide what they want, but we thought it was important to set out Dairy Crest's position clearly."[176] This position is also backed up in the "briefing document" that Dairy Crest's senior account manager for its Asda account emailed to various employees of Asda, Safeway, Sainsbury's, and Tesco when trying to instigate the 2002 Cheese Initiative, which stated, "It should be noted that in the current climate cash margin maintenance should, in our view, be the rule. Percentage margin maintenance will only create accusations of profiteering."

However, there is evidence that processors may have tried to benefit financially from the cartel in the 2003 initiatives. Recall that the purpose of the 2003 Cheese Initiative was to improve the profit margins of McLelland (hub), yet even in the 2003 FLM Initiative there was talk of shared benefits between the processors and supermarkets:

> [A senior manager at Dairy Crest] then stated that he believed he had two objectives arising from the internal meeting of 4 June 2003. The first objective was to contact retailers to establish if they were prepared to engage in an initiative to subsidise a

farmgate price increase through increased wholesale and retail prices in respect of FLM; the second was to establish whether retailers were prepared to share possible surplus benefits of any retail price increase with the processors: "Whilst our first objective was to test if the retailers would consider an increase I was also asked to see if the principle of sharing benefit was acceptable."

Another way in which the supermarkets (spokes) could have benefited financially from the 2002 and 2003 Cheese Initiatives was through an increase in the retail prices of imported cheese products (which were not part of the cartel). The UK cheese processors were concerned about losing sales because of interbrand competition and requested that the supermarkets mitigate this by raising the prices of imported cheese. For example, the interview notes of a senior manager at Dairy Crest submitted to the OFT revealed the following insight: "We also knew that . . . [implementing a cheese price initiative] would put up the price of British cheese but not imported cheese. This was a difficult problem because we knew consumers would switch. . . . Therefore, it helped if the retail price of all cheese increased."[177] Furthermore, in Dairy Crest's briefing document that it emailed to Asda, Safeway, Sainsbury's, and Tesco, the following passage was included: "We are seeking to address an immediate problem in farming today. If however we jointly change the competitive set of British dairy products versus imports, damage would be done to this initiative. We ask that you bear this in mind when considering your retail pricing decisions."[178]

Unfortunately, we do not know the extent to which supermarkets adjusted the prices of imported cheese, as there is no documented evidence of these prices. However, given the increase in prices of British cheese, the supermarkets would have had a unilateral incentive to take advantage of the reduced interbrand competition by raising the prices of imported cheese.

That said, it does seem that the main benefits of the cartel were to reduce the bad publicity of the farmers' protests and to limit the disruption to supply chains. The coordinated action ensured that this could be achieved without lowering the supermarkets' and dairy processors' own profit margins, as the burden would fall on the consumer through increased retail and wholesale prices.

There seem to be two main reasons why farmgate prices could not rise without coordinated action. These are consistent with the theoretical factors under which a supplier would want to limit intrabrand competition. First, while wholesale prices for dairy products tended to be set by negotiation between processors and their individual customers, more bargaining power likely rested with the national multiples, in part because of their recently acquired dominant position in the market.[179] Second, retail competition for dairy products among supermarkets was particularly intense because dairy products were considered "known-value items," products for which consumers are likely to remember the retail prices, so they were considered to influence a consumer's perception of how expensive a particular super-market was relative to its competitors. Given the perceived importance of such products, supermarkets were reluctant to have retail prices out of line with their rivals', so they could not afford to be unilaterally charitable with their wholesale prices.

The OFT concluded that the cartel was successful in raising retail prices by 2 pence per liter for certain categories of cheese in autumn 2002 and autumn 2003 and FLM in July 2003. However, there is no statement as to how long the price increases were sustained. The OFT argued that it was less clear that there was a corresponding increase in farmgate prices. This con-clusion differed from that of the House of Commons Environment, Food and Rural Affairs Committee, which found that some proportion of the retail price increases had been passed back to farmers but that "some farm-ers benefited more than others" and that "it took some time for increases in retail prices to reach farmers."[180] The decision includes no discussion of the effect on wholesale prices.

3.2.8 Bread (Canada)

The setting for this case is the Canadian market for fresh commercial bread.[181] The two largest suppliers were Canada Bread and Weston Bakeries, with national market shares of 40% and 38%, respectively, in 2016. They supplied retailers across Canada with branded bread as well as related prod-ucts such as buns, rolls, bagels, wraps, tortillas, and naan bread. The main retailers of fresh commercial bread were the three largest grocers, Loblaws, Sobeys, and Metro, and two discounters, Wal-Mart and Giant Tiger. While each of the three largest grocers multisourced from the two main bread sup-pliers, a larger proportion of Loblaws's sales were of Weston Bakeries brands, whereas Sobeys and Metro sold a larger proportion of Canada Bread brands (Clark, Horstmann, and Houde 2020). In addition to the brands of Canada Bread and Weston Bakeries, known as "conventional banners," the retailers also supplied their own brands, which were considered "discount banners."

On January 31, 2018, the Canadian Competition Bureau released documents claiming there was a hub-and-spoke cartel in the market for fresh commercial bread that had begun in or around November 2001 and lasted until December 2017.[182] The alleged cartel comprised the bread suppliers Canada Bread and Weston Bakeries and the retailers Loblaws, Sobeys, Metro, Wal-Mart, and Giant Tiger. This was no ordinary hub-and-spoke cartel, however, as it involved two horizontal agreements that were vertically related and dependent on each other's success. There was an upstream horizontal agreement between the suppliers that aimed "to increase their respective wholesale prices for the sale or supply of fresh commercial bread,"[183] and there was a downstream agreement that the upstream suppliers facilitated "by coordinating retail prices for their respective fresh commercial bread products and ensuring pricing alignment amongst the Retailers."[184]

Clark, Horstmann, and Houde (2020) described this alleged conspiracy as a *two-sided* hub-and-spoke cartel because a firm could be both a spoke in one agreement and a hub in the other. Given that this feature is singular in our collection of hub-and-spoke cartels, it is useful to begin by describing the communication channels through which information flowed between the firms. The downstream agreement most resembled a standard hub-and-spoke structure: the retailers were the spokes and exclusively communicated indirectly via the two suppliers, each of which played the role of the hub for their branded products. With regard to the upstream agreement, the suppliers acted on occasion like spokes communicating with each other indirectly via a retailer who was acting as a hub, but there is also evidence of direct communication between the suppliers, as would have occurred with a regular suppliers' cartel.

The Competition Bureau's investigation was triggered by a leniency application from Loblaws and Weston Bakeries on March 3, 2015. The leniency applicants were initially obliged to keep their application confidential while the bureau began its investigation. On January 4, 2016, the bureau was also contacted by the Canadian Federation of Independent Grocers (CFIG), which alleged collusion between the suppliers. The case is still ongoing at the time of writing. While Canada Bread released a media statement saying they were investigating the allegations related to "former Canada Bread Executives" dating back to when "Canada Bread was under previous ownership," they have not admitted involvement in the cartel.[185] Likewise, Sobeys, Metro, Wal-Mart, and Giant Tiger have denied the allegations.

The documentary and economic evidence is sufficiently strong to war-
rant inclusion of this alleged hub-and-spoke cartel in our study. First, there
are two leniency applicants and, to our knowledge, it is rare for there not to
be a cartel when there is a leniency applicant. As stated by a spokesperson
for Loblaws, "We have admitted our role, and you cannot price fix alone."[186]
The main question for this case is not whether the cartel existed but rather
which firms—and in particular which retailers beyond Loblaws—were
involved. Second, Clark, Horstmann, and Houde (2020) have economic evidence consistent with there having been a cartel in the bread market. They
show that retail price increases during the early years of the alleged cartel period exceeded competitive benchmarks. Retail bread prices in Canada
were 20% higher than in the US and 30% higher than prices in other Canadian food sectors, such as wheat flour, other bakery products, and cereals.
They also find that when the allegation of collusion by the CFIG became
public, retail prices reacted in a manner consistent with cartel collapse. For
instance, retail bread prices fell more sharply in markets that were more concentrated, which is consistent with retailers having achieved higher collusive markups in such markets. Clark, Horstmann, and Houde also find that
after the announcement price dispersion increased in markets with more
discount chains, which suggests a breakdown in coordination on a common
retail price. Given the compelling economic evidence at the retail level and
that Weston Bakeries and Loblaws have admitted to participating in a cartel,
there was very likely a hub-and-spoke cartel in the Canadian bread market.

Having provided an overview of the cartel's structure and its effects, let
us now consider how the cartel was formed and how it operated. In what
follows, we mainly use the evidence in the Competition Bureau's documents, which draws on interviews of two immunity applicants. To keep
the identities of the applicants private, their names have been redacted,
and it is clear from our reading of the text that their pronouns have been
redacted, too. Retaining these redactions as presented in the bureau's documents could make some of the passages included here difficult to read.
Furthermore, it is also likely to be less apparent than in the bureau's documents that a redaction refers to the immunity applicant. Consequently, we
have inserted our reading of the text in square brackets to assist the reader.
One of the immunity applicants worked for both a retailer and supplier
Weston Bakeries at separate times during the period of the cartel, and this is
signified in the bureau's documents by an (R) and an (S), respectively. Given

that the case is still ongoing and we lack access to defendants' documents, our coverage may only provide one side of the story.

The cartel was allegedly instigated by the upstream firms through direct communication with each other. According to an immunity applicant employed by Weston Bakeries, it was an employee of Canada Bread who first raised the prospect of a cartel at an industry event where "all the retailers and manufacturers/suppliers got together."[187] That employee had prepared a PowerPoint presentation to be taken "out to the retailer community to show them the power of pricing in bakery."[188] The objective of the presentation was to demonstrate that "the profitability of the fresh bakery shelf at retail was underperforming, and then the wholesale side, the manufacturers, were underperforming as well."[189] The Canada Bread employee also proposed a plan that had the suppliers "going to the retailers to get their buy-in for a price increase with the goal of orchestrating alignment through the retail community."[190] The immunity applicant recalled conveying that he or she was "willing on behalf of Weston Bakeries to comply with an increase."[191]

Turning to how the cartel coordinated on and implemented price increases, the documentary evidence suggests that the upstream firms were the main drivers in coordinating price rises. However, instead of relying on direct communication, as they did in forming the cartel, "Canada Bread and Weston Bakeries each used the Retailers as conduits of information"[192] to reach an initial broad agreement with the suppliers. When passing messages between the two bread suppliers, a retailer was acting as a hub for the upstream horizontal agreement. While working for one of the retailers, an immunity applicant recalls the first episode in which he or she performed this role:

> (R) recalled that during the first price increase in which [she or he] was involved, Weston Bakeries had approached [her or him] indicating that they wanted to take a price increase. (R) then recalls being instructed by [redacted] to have pricing conversations with Canada Bread to determine whether Canada Bread was also interested in taking a price increase.[193]
>
> (R) recalls being informed by [redacted] about how price increases in the fresh commercial bread industry work. Further, (R)'s [redacted] provided [her or him] with specifics about what to discuss with Canada Bread.[194]
>
> (R) then recalls acting upon instructions from [redacted] and calling Rory Lesperance of Canada Bread [redacted]. As part of that conversation, (R) stated that [she or he] would communicate Weston Bakeries' pricing intentions to Canada Bread along with the date of the proposed price increase.[195]

As part of (R)'s conversation with Canada Bread (R) asked if Canada Bread was also open to taking an increase. (R) stated that Lesperance would not respond right away but would provide a response a couple of days later.[196]

(R) believes the delay in a response was a result of Lesperance's need to consult his superiors within Canada Bread.[197]

While this evidence shows that, on at least some occasions, the suppliers used indirect communication to achieve mutual understanding, it is not clear that they always did so. For example, in its summary of the alleged conduct, the Competition Bureau states that the suppliers agreed to fix their wholesale prices "via direct communications between senior officers in [the suppliers'] respective organizations."[198] However, beyond the direct communication to instigate the cartel, there are no specific examples in the documentary evidence of direct communications between the suppliers concerning subsequent price rises. Yet, given that there was some direct communication between the suppliers in the formation of the cartel as well as in other aspects (as we describe later), it is not possible to rule it out here either.

Achieving a broad agreement between the suppliers was only the first step to successfully implement a coordinated price rise. The suppliers recognized that "for a price increase to be successful it required compliance right through the chain from Supplier to Retailer."[199] Presumably, this was because the retailers had enough bargaining power to reject higher wholesale prices that were sufficiently unprofitable for them. Consequently, the suppliers needed the retailers' cooperation, which was obtained by assisting in a retail price rise above that wholesale price increase. It is this expectation of higher retail markups that led retailers to facilitate communication between the suppliers. Raising prices at both levels would be mutually beneficial for the suppliers and the retailers, provided the market demand for fresh commercial bread was relatively price inelastic, as is usually the case for necessities such as bread.

To get all the retailers on board with a common price increase, it was the suppliers' turn to act as a hub. It is alleged that both suppliers conducted a series of bilateral discussions with their respective retail customers, not only to get the retailers to agree to the wholesale price increase but also to discuss the associated retail prices. An important part of these discussions was for a supplier to reassure its retailers that their rivals were also on board with the wholesale and retail price rises: "(R) explained that important considerations in whether or not to accept a wholesale price increase from Weston

Bakeries [were] whether Canada Bread was also increasing its [wholesale] price for the supply of bread to [rival] retailers and whether other retailers would increase their retail prices. (R) stated that it was not possible for only one retailer to increase its retail price and the only way the price increase would happen is if there was a retail price increase among other Retailers (i.e., not including the smaller retailers who were less likely to compete with the Retailers on price)."[200]

Consequently, the suppliers engaged in back-and-forth communications with the retailers to "discuss specific dates and price points with respect to the increase."[201] Furthermore, to provide the necessary reassurance, "The suppliers would be rather definitive in saying that they had spoken with competing Retailers (naming specific Retailers) and the Suppliers were fairly certain that the suggested retail prices would be reflected on the store shelves, market-wide, post-price increase."[202] The retailers also knew that once they had agreed to go along with the price rises, the suppliers would communicate their intended compliance to the other retailers.[203]

When the firms had achieved their goal of reaching an agreement through-out the supply chain, the suppliers would signal it by sending "price increase letters" to the retailers. Prior to the cartel, the purpose of these letters was to confirm to the retailers the magnitude of the wholesale price increase for each product, as well as the date on which the wholesale price increase was to become effective. However, the letters took on an extra role in achiev-ing mutual understanding of the agreement. For instance, given that the retailers sourced from both suppliers, they would receive two letters, so they were able to compare the two announced price rises and thereby confirm that the suppliers had reached an agreement along the lines that had been discussed. A long delay between receipt of the two letters was interpreted as a bad signal by the retailers: "The timing of the Suppliers' price increase letters had to be close together to provide certainty to the retailers that everyone was going to take a price increase at the same time."[204]

It is unclear from the documentary evidence whether the retailers obtained their rivals' price increase letters. It is possible that the letters were shared, as doing so would have been useful in removing retailers' uncertainty over whether their rivals were accepting the wholesale price increase. This con-trasts with the suppliers, where there is evidence that they obtained copies of their rival suppliers' letters: "The final confirmation that Weston Bakeries would look for was a copy of the Canada Bread price increase letter. Weston

Bakeries would usually obtain the letter from a customer (e.g. a Retailer) or, occasionally, from someone at Canada Bread."[205] This episode demonstrates that retailers would often act as a hub by facilitating information exchange between the suppliers, although this was not always necessary because of direct communication between the suppliers.

Given that price increase letters were circulated between the suppliers, it was crucial for successfully implementing the increase that the information within the letter reflected what had been agreed. For example, on one occasion around February or March 2012, an attempt to coordinate a price hike failed because the price increase letter of Weston Bakeries did not include the appropriate price rises for products that were close substitutes of Canada Bread brands that had been included in Canada Bread's letter: "Weston Bakeries did not announce a price increase on plain white bread (including Weston's Wonder and Gadoua brands) or private label bread."[206] Since Canada Bread was concerned about being undercut on some of its products, it responded by sending the retailers a letter "rescinding its price increase [for each of the products listed within its original letter] which, in turn, led to Weston Bakeries not implementing its price increase [for each of its products]."[207] As this episode attests, these letters were a valuable instrument for confirming the agreed price changes.

Having achieved an agreement on the terms and the effective date of the wholesale price increases, the next task for the cartel was to coordinate the retail price increases. The suppliers again assumed the role of the hubs for their products as the retailers looked to the suppliers for help in coordinating the price rises. This would have been a difficult task for the retailers to handle on their own, particularly without direct communication, because the retailers preferred to follow on price rather than lead. This was especially the case for the discount retailers, which meant that "retail coordination was particularly difficult to manage in the discount end of the market, featuring retailers such as Walmart, Giant Tiger, [Loblaw]'s No Frills banner, Sobeys' FreshCo banner and Metro's Food Basics banner."[208] Furthermore, it was in the suppliers' best interest to facilitate the downstream horizontal agreement because failure to implement the retail price rise at this stage could have had detrimental implications for the upstream horizontal agreement.

Similar to the suppliers' role in initially getting the retailers on board with the upstream horizontal agreement, the suppliers again acted as hubs when they passed messages between the retailers in order to achieve a common understanding as to which retailer would lead the price increase. This also involved reassuring the price leader that its rivals would quickly follow: "(S) stated that there was quite a bit of negotiation when [she or he] dealt with the aforementioned Retailers because none of them wanted to be the first to implement the price increase. Consequently, it was incumbent upon the Suppliers to provide assurances that a Retailer's competitors would follow quickly. As (S) stated, there was always a negotiation process going back and forth between the four parties [Retailers] where [the Supplier] was trying to coordinate it because somebody had to be the first to move."[209] Thus, these supplier-retailer discussions led to "precise future pricing intentions being communicated from Retailer to Retailer via the Supplier."[210]

It was common for the prices of the conventional banners to rise first, which served to reassure other firms that the retail price increase was going to be successful: "The movement in retail prices amongst the conventional banners was an indication that the market was moving. Further, if this happened before the effective date of the [wholesale] price increase, which was often the case according to [redacted], it provided everybody [all the Suppliers and Retailers] with a sense that 'it feels like what we all talked about is going to happen.'"[211] Given the apparent complexity of the coordination task, the cartel members built in a long lead time, with the details of a price increase being "discussed at least 3–4 months in advance."[212]

With regard to monitoring the downstream horizontal agreement, this would have been relatively easy, given that retail prices were freely observable to anybody who entered a store. As a consequence, retailers could quickly discover when a rival was not complying with the agreement. In such an event, the retailers looked to suppliers to take on the role of a hub to ensure that deviators returned to compliance: "Retailers expected the Suppliers to deal with market disturbances with respect to pricing. When discrepancies arose, the Retailers would inform the Suppliers and dictate to the Supplier that the Supplier needed to fix the problem or the price increase would be rejected."[213]

This process is explained further by an immunity applicant who had experienced it from both a retailer's and a supplier's perspective. For instance, when working for a retailer, "(R) would inquire as to whether specific Retailers would continue to aggressively price a Supplier's product. Further, (R) would ask the Supplier to go back to the Retailer who was pricing aggressively and explain to them that such prices were not in their best interest. (R) confirmed that the Suppliers would come back to [her or him] and tell [her or him] exactly what the competing Retailer has said."[214]

While it was the job of the upstream supplier to explain to the downstream deviator that pricing aggressively was not in their "best interest," there is no documentary evidence that the supplier was involved in punishing deviators. There is some suggestion that the threat of punishment for noncompliance came from other retailers, in the form of a possible retail price war. For example, when the same immunity applicant worked for supplier Weston Bakeries:

> (S) stated that the Retailers frequently complained to Weston Bakeries about prices, at their retailer competitors, that they did not like. In reviewing an example of one such complaint memorialized in an email dated 24 April 2015, (S) explained that "[Ken Kunkel (Metro)] is essentially asking 'why the hell are they [Giant Tiger] at $1.88? The price increase just happened. Why would they go this cheap? You're upsetting the market. One crazy retail will cause other[s] to [decrease their retail prices] and it'll get aggressive and therefore drive the overall retails down.'"[215]

The bureau alleges that between April 2002 and March 2016 there were at least 15 attempts to coordinate price rises in the manner just described. The details of the wholesale price rises are listed in table 3.1. The majority occurred early in the alleged cartel period, and there were two periods of intense price hikes: five coordinated price increases occurring from April 2005 to October 2007 and another five from April 2010 to October 2012 (although one of these was the failed price rise previously discussed). Most of the wholesale price rises were for $0.07 (or around 4%), because the coordinated price rises would often follow a pattern known as the "7/10 convention."[216] This convention had the suppliers raise the wholesale prices by 7 cents per unit (e.g., per loaf of bread) and the retailers raise their prices by at least 10 cents per unit. On at least two occasions (one in 2007 and another in 2011), the price rises were double this convention.

The change in retail prices during the cartel period is shown in figure 3.2. Figure 3.2(a) plots the average retail price of a loaf of bread (675 grams) across Canada over time, along with indicators of the effective dates of the 15 alleged wholesale price increases in table 3.1. It shows that the timing of the rise in the average retail price of bread was similar to that of the alleged

Table 3.1
Wholesale price increases

Canada Bread			Weston Bread		
Date of letter	Effective date	Amount of Increase	Date of letter	Effective date	Amount of increase
February 2002	April 2002	$0.07	February 20, 2002	April 29, 2002	$0.07
Unknown	November 3, 2003	$0.07	September 13, 2002	November 3, 2002	Unknown
Unknown	Unknown	Unknown	January 14, 2004	March 21, 2004	~$0.08
Unknown	Unknown	Unknown	February 3, 2005	April 17, 2005	Unknown
Unknown	Unknown	Unknown	November 8, 2005	February 5, 2006	Unknown
July 27, 2006	October 15, 2006	$0.06–0.07[a]	August 8, 2006	October 22, 2006	Unknown
Unknown	Unknown	Unknown	Unknown	October 21, 2007	$0.08
Unknown	Unknown	Unknown	September 10, 2007	October 21, 2007	$0.16
March 23, 2010	June 13, 2010	$0.07	April 9, 2010	June 20, 2010	~4%
December 2010	February 1, 2011	4%	January 10, 2011	Mar 27, 2011	~4%
Unknown	Unknown	Unknown	February 3, 2011	March 27, 2011	~8%
February 2012	April 29, 2012	$0.07[b]	March 1, 2012	May 6, 2012	Unknown[b]
October 24, 2012	January 27, 2013	~$0.07	October 16, 2012	January 27, 2013	~$0.07
January 15, 2015	April 19, 2015	~$0.07	January 21, 2015	April 12, 2015	~$0.07
December 2, 2015	February 28, 2016	$0.07	November 30, 2015	March 6, 2016	$0.07

[a] $0.07 for branded products and $0.06 for private label products.
[b] The price increase was rescinded by both Canada Bread and Weston Bakeries.

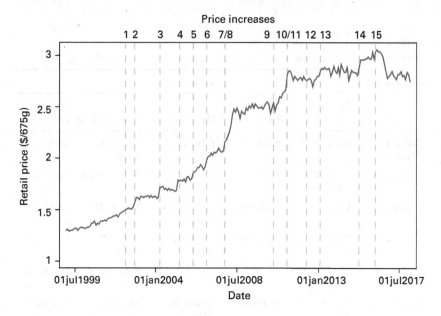

(a) The 7/10 convention

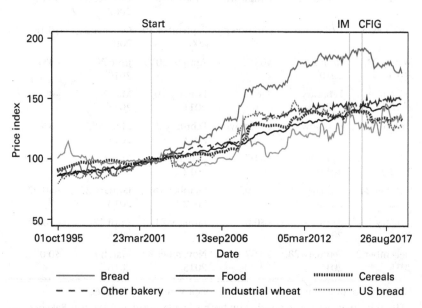

(b) Bread vs other products

Bread · · · Other bakery — Food — Industrial wheat ······· Cereals ·········· US bread

Figure 3.2
The change in retail prices during the cartel period. (a) The 7/10 convention; (b) bread
vs. other products. *Source*: Clark, Horstmann, and Houde (2020, 14).

wholesale price increase, which is consistent with successful implementation of the cartel's scheme. Figure 3.2(b) plots the consumer price indexes for bread and other related products from 1995 to 2018 (with 2002 = 100). Some important dates are also highlighted, including the reported date of the start of the alleged cartel (Start), the date of the immunity application (IM), and the date of the allegations of collusion by the Canadian Federation of Independent Grocers (CFIG). Figure 3.2(b) shows that the price index for bread in Canada followed a pattern similar to that of the price indexes for the other products prior to the alleged start date. It then increased more quickly than the prices for related products during the cartel period, and it fell sharply after the CFIG's allegations of collusion, with no noticeable change in the related products.[217]

To summarize, the alleged conspiracy in the Canadian bread market is unique within our collection of hub-and-spoke cartels because it is the only one in which there is explicit evidence of collusion both downstream and upstream. As is the case for the other hub-and-spoke cartels, an upstream firm primarily fulfilled the role of the hub to facilitate a downstream horizontal agreement among the retailers. These roles included instigating the downstream agreement, coordinating retail price rises, and sustaining the agreement by encouraging any deviators to return to compliance. Interestingly, the roles were reversed for the upstream agreement, where a retailer acted as a hub to the suppliers by passing messages between the suppliers to facilitate coordination on higher wholesale prices. Apparently, this indirect communication between the suppliers was not always sufficient. The suppliers also communicated with each other directly when the cartel was formed and later through price increase letters after having agreed to a common price. Finally, it is clear that the firms had incentives to facilitate the agreement at the other level of the supply chain, because the collapse of one agreement would most likely have meant the collapse of the other agreement.

3.2.9   Chicken (Chile)
The use of loss leaders is common among supermarkets. The strategy is to price a few popular items at a very low price to attract customers to the store, who are then likely to buy other items with higher profit margins. This case involved coordination among retailers to prevent a loss leader's price from being too low.[218]

In January 2016, the competition authority of Chile, Fiscalía Nacional Económica (FNE), filed a case with the Defensa de La Libre Competencia (Court of Defense of Free Competition) accusing the three major supermarket chains—Cencosud, SMU, and Wal-Mart—of agreeing to price fresh chicken at or above cost. It also accused the three major chicken suppliers—Agrosuper, Ariztía, and Don Pollo—of assisting them in the implementation of this collusive arrangement.[219] The FNE claimed that between 2008 and 2011, the "chains jointly executed an agreement or concerted practice that allowed them to set a minimum sale price in supermarkets for fresh chicken . . . given by the wholesale list price of the same (as we indicated, common to all supermarkets), plus VAT."[220] (In what follows, this minimum price is referred to as "cost.") In February 2019, the three supermarket chains were found guilty and received a fine of 8 billion pesos (approximately US$12 million).[221]

Our discussion will focus on the hub-and-spoke cartel that had Agrosuper as the hub and the three supermarket chains as spokes. Agrosuper was the largest supplier of fresh chicken in Chile, and Cencosud, SMU, and Wal-Mart controlled 91% of fresh chicken retail sales.[222] Emails among the parties indicate that there was an agreement going back to 2007 to price fresh chicken at or above cost:

> Email from SMU to Agrosuper September 29, 2009 15:19 PM—As per our conversation, it is very important to maintain our policy of not selling below costs in advertised sales or at the store, as it only generates disorder in the market. On our end, we will try to keep up with this policy as long as our competition does the same.

> Email from Cencosud to Agrosuper July 7, 2009 11:15—This is an agreement that we reached more than 2 years ago that was supposed to be implemented with the rest of the retailers.[223]

This mutual understanding to avoid below-cost pricing is also supported by the deposition of Victor Velasquez, who was Agrosuper's account manager for Cencosud:

FNE: Who knows about the existence of an implied rule to refrain from selling below cost?

Victor Velasquez: At Agrosuper, everyone.

FNE: Did all the clients, supermarkets, know about these rules?

Victor Velasquez: I'm not sure if they all did, but the clients that I dealt with did.[224]

The supermarkets actively engaged in monitoring compliance and would report any below-cost pricing episodes to Agrosuper. As the FNE noted, "The chains constantly monitored the sale prices to the public of the fresh chicken meat of its competitors, both through internal personnel and through external companies hired for that purpose."[225] In response to these complaints or other evidence of fresh chicken prices below cost, Agrosuper would contact a noncompliant supermarket to try to get them to raise the price:

> Email from Agrosuper to Cencosud September 25, 2009 9:08 AM—I know this is a small "figure" but regardless I sincerely request you comply with the tacit agreement of having prices above cost. This time you went out with a price of $13.8 below cost and Wal-Mart complained about it.

> Email from Agrosuper to Wal-Mart Tuesday, January 20[, 2008] 10:45—Please note that Cencosud left the price for whole chicken at 1490/kg, just as we talked about yesterday. I need you to match Cencosud so we do not carry on with this fight where everyone loses money. If you do not increase the price, they will match you and we will continue to lose money.[226]

Given that fresh chicken was a loss leader intended to attract customers to a chain's stores, prices were widely advertised, which meant that monitoring of the "no prices below cost" agreement was relatively easy. That there were still episodes of noncompliance suggests that the collusive arrangement was not particularly stable, in that a chain deviated in spite of knowing that it would be detected.

Agrosuper used threats of denying supply to incentivize compliance by supermarkets. The supermarkets expected Agrosuper to follow through on that threat, which they did on occasion:

> Email from Cencosud to Agrosuper February 25, 2010 20:34 PM—In case that the supermarkets . . . do not comply with the agreement . . . , the supplier will assure the retailer that it will not have the product in its shelf for the period of the promotion. Remember what we talked about, the sanction is to cut off supply, and additionally a second sanction could apply if the supermarket chain fails to comply with the agreement, namely, it shall not receive raw item promotions from Agrosuper during a 15-day period.

> Email from Agrosuper to Cencosud June 8, 2010 18:01 PM—As I told you, supply was cut off once the sale was made public, for the entire duration of the sale. . . . In the case of the SMU supermarket the same thing happened; the sale was yesterday and they received no supplies today. . . . The sanction for any supermarket that has a retail price below cost is cut off the supply of the product in question.[227]

This exclusionary threat was confirmed by the deposition of Francisco Noguera, who was an assistant account manager for national chains at Agrosuper:

FNE: Did the supermarkets call Agrosuper expecting it to carry out these proceedings, right? They wanted you to call the other supermarket and say "raise the price or I'll cut off your supply."

FN: Yes.

FNE: And avoid a price war. Is this correct?

FN: Yes.[228]

There is also reference to Agrosuper compensating those supermarkets that were harmed by a rival supermarket's low prices. If indeed compensation were provided, it would have enhanced the incentives for Agrosuper to both monitor and punish in order to avoid having to pay compensation.

The practices associated with this hub-and-spoke cartel are succinctly summarized in an expert report:

> This evidence taken as a whole indicates to me an agreement between the supermarket chains to set the retail price of poultry at or above cost, often referred to as wholesale price. This agreement was accomplished through the following acts and communications: 1) regular active monitoring by each supermarket chain of each competitor for the sale of loss leader (commercial hook) poultry items below cost or wholesale price; 2) regular complaints and communications to their common wholesale supplier Agrosuper . . . about the alleged violations of the pricing agreement by their competitors; 3) demands to Agrosuper either to cut off supplies to the offending competitor or for compensation from Agrosuper for any losses suffered by the failure of a competitor to adhere to the agreement; 4) a common understanding that each supermarket's continued compliance to the pricing agreement was conditioned on their competitors' compliance with the agreement; 5) Agrosuper promptly bringing these complaints to the attention of the company pricing below the agreed upon price and demanding that they cease violating the prices agreed upon by the supermarkets; 6) Agrosuper enforcing the supermarkets agreement by threats and occasional cutting off of supplies if the price reductions were not the result of some arithmetic error or similar extenuating circumstance; and 7) the supermarket that was the subject of the complaint promptly raising price or promising to do so on the condition or understanding that its competitors would continue to price in a similar manner.[229]

While our focus has been on a hub-and-spoke cartel with regard to the retail sale of fresh chicken, there is also evidence that it extended to other loss leaders, including beer and soft drinks: "In 2006, Walmart emailed its Coca Cola wholesaler stating: 'They sold everything below cost this weekend, the next time I will not warn you, but it will cost them dearly. Beware that everybody complies, or nobody does.' In 2007, Walmart emailed its beer and soft drink supplier demanding: 'Make the competition increase and we will too.'"[230]

Restraining price competition is clearly of value to supermarkets. The three chains dominated their markets, with the share of 2011 supermarket sales (for all products) equal to 36.4% for Wal-Mart, 28.4% for Cencosud, and 27.7% for SMU.[231] Aggressive pricing for loss leaders largely served to shift customers among those three chains, consequently lowering joint profit. Hence, an agreement to maintain prices at or above cost for fresh chicken would most likely prove profitable for them. The benefit to Agrosuper and the other chicken suppliers is less clear. There is no evidence that a higher retail price resulted in a higher wholesale price. Notably, Agrosuper, Ariztía, and Don Pollo were convicted of colluding in the wholesale fresh chicken market over this period.[232] As wholesale prices might then already have been relatively high, the incentive to engage in hub-and-spoke collusion in order to raise wholesale (and retail) prices would have been weak. This leaves one wondering why Agrosuper would have assisted the supermarkets in constraining price competition in the retail fresh chicken market. One possibility is that the supermarkets may limit their purchases of chicken if they incur a loss from every sale. Another possibility is that the supermarkets knew or suspected collusion in the wholesale market, and raising retail prices was a way for the chicken suppliers to share some of the rents and avoid having the supermarkets report their suspicions. Both explanations are speculative.

3.2.10 Automobile Retailing (US)

This private litigation case involved wholesale and retail markets for automobiles in several US states, including Delaware, Maryland, Pennsylvania, Virginia, and West Virginia.[233] The key player was the Frederick Weisman Holding Company and, more specifically, its corporate subsidiaries: Mid-Atlantic Toyota (MAT), which was a wholesale distributor, and Carecraft, whose subsidiary Crown Atlantic was MAT's port-handling agent.

When Toyota automobiles arrived in the port of Baltimore from Japan, Crown Atlantic received the cars and prepared them for distribution to local dealers through MAT. One available step in the preparation of a vehicle was the installation of a "protective package" that used Polyglycoat brand sealant products (such as rustproof shielding, paint sealant, interior sealant, and undercoating). CPC Distributors was a franchised distributor of Polyglycoat Corporation automotive products and was owned by Crown Atlantic (and thus by Weisman). CPC would pay $42 to Polyglycoat Corp. for each car having the protective package, then CPE would charge $78 to MAT, and MAT would charge $113 to a local Toyota dealer. Hence, Weisman earned $71 (113–42) for each protective package installed by Crown Atlantic and thus was interested in getting dealers to buy it.

The problem was that few dealers were demanding the protective package. Apparently, customers were not interested in it, which meant that a dealer whose vehicles had it would be at a competitive disadvantage with respect to other Toyota dealers, for they would be charging a higher price for a product that customers did not perceive to be of compensatingly higher quality. In response, MAT developed the Total Concept Protective Program (hereafter referred to as TCCP), which had the goal of getting dealers to install the protection package in their cars. If the protective package was installed, then a Toyota dealer could raise the suggested retail (or list) price by $533.90, which, under the Monroney Act of 1976, had to be listed on the "sticker" that was attached to all new vehicles: "The plaintiffs allege that by adding a set of accessories to a Toyota with a wholesale price of $113.00 but with a suggested retail price on the Monroney sticker of $533.90, MAT supposedly gave its dealers $420.90 worth of room to 'bargain' with. The dealer could discount from the suggested retail price and increase the 'deal' a buyer perceived he was receiving without reducing the dealer's original profit margin on the car."[234] According to this argument, a dealer could then earn a higher profit per vehicle sold. However, an individual retailer would still be at a competitive disadvantage if it was the only one to adopt the protective package, because prospective buyers would see a sticker price that was $533.90 higher than that of competitors.

Having devised the TCCP, the challenge faced by MAT was getting all, or enough, dealers to adopt it. If it succeeded, then all parties would be better off. MAT would earn money by selling more protective packages, while the retailers would receive higher transaction prices (exceeding the cost of the protective package) because of the higher sticker price. As long as buyers ended up paying more than $113 (and if market demand for Toyotas is not too price elastic, so the reduction in total sales is slight), MAT and its dealers would experience higher profits. However, it was critical that enough dealers adopt the protective package so those who did would not be at a competitive disadvantage compared to those who did not.

The anticompetitive dimension to the TCCP was that MAT was acting as an upstream hub to coordinate the industry-wide adoption of the protective package among downstream retailers:

> Supposedly unable to overcome this individualized dealer reluctance by forcing the Polyglycoat products on them, the Weisman defendants allegedly decided to attack the dealer's underlying competitive concerns directly by facilitating an interdealer conspiracy. In the late summer of 1979, . . . MAT convened a series of subregional dealer meetings which both Weisman and substantially all of the dealers attended. . . . The dealers received a direct appeal from William Abbott, MAT Vice-President for marketing, in support of the program. Abbott allegedly stressed the flexibility the protective package afforded the dealers, with the dealer keeping the full additional profit unless the customer balked. The additional profit margin attached to the package would then allow the dealer to "close the deal" without harming his original profit margin.[235]

Contrary to many of the other cases of hub-and-spoke collusion, initial communications between the upstream hub and a downstream spoke were not bilateral, for all the Toyota retailers were in the room when MAT made its announcement. Furthermore, the presence of the retailers in the same room created an opportunity for communication among them, though "controversy swirls over what happened after Abbott's presentation":[236] "The plaintiffs allege that the dealers 'milled around,' hovering over sign-up sheets which stated 'Yes, we want to participate in the Polyglycoat Total Concept Program' and discussing unrevealed subjects. It appears to be undisputed that significant numbers of dealers did in fact sign up at the meetings, that MAT conducted at least some followup on those dealers who did not sign up at the time, and that by January, 1980 all but three dealers either had signed up or were ordering the protective package on their vehicles."[237]

The postmeeting sign-up sheets gave dealers an opportunity to witness other dealers signing up, and possibly encouraged others to do so. The court saw such an argument as credible:

> Abbott raised the core element of the agreement—keeping the suggested price as the starting price—in a collective gathering of precisely those people who had the anti-competitive financial incentive to adopt it as a joint course of action. While meetings among competitors without more are not *per se* illegal, it certainly is not rank speculation to observe that a meeting provides an ideal device for facilitating horizontal agreements once the anti-competitive idea is jointly planted in

the minds of those competitors present at the meetings. The Weisman defendants then facilitated the dealers' adherence to the scheme by circulating sign up sheets. The use of these sheets allowed each dealer to observe which other dealers were joining the program. While the sign up sheets specifically dealt with ordering the protective package, and hence certainly are competent circumstantial evidence of a tacit agreement for uniform ordering, they also could have served as a facilitating mechanism for an agreement to raise the starting price, especially when viewed in the light of Abbott's comments about profit potential immediately prior to their circulation.[238]

MAT followed up this meeting with individual meetings with dealers to promote compliance. Less than six months after the original meeting in August 1979, many dealers were having their vehicles treated with the sealant products: "A marked change in dealer purchasing patterns occurred between August, 1979 and January, 1980. . . . Relatively few Toyotas were sold with Polyglycoat products in the years preceding the initiation of the protective package programs in September, 1979. . . . Polyglycoat-free Toyotas became almost impossible to obtain after the Total Concept Program took force. One consumer states that dealers told him they would have to wait for up to eight months to obtain a vehicle without the accessories."[239]

In assessing the profit impact of this scheme for the members of this hub-and-spoke cartel, it is immediately clear that MAT benefited from selling Polyglycoat products. However, it is the rise in the transaction price (by more than the cost of the protective package) that would make it profitable for dealers. Estimates of customer damages substantiate that dealers did indeed benefit. Recall that they paid $113 per vehicle for the protective package: "The plaintiffs have introduced economic evidence which suggests that Dealer defendants averaged $136 more in gross profit per Toyota as a result of the alleged conspiracy and that consumers paid between $172 and $249 (cost plus gross profit) more for their Toyotas as a result of the conspiracy."[240] After motions by the defendants for summary judgment were denied,[241] the two sides reached a settlement of approximately $5.1 million.[242]

In sum, Mid-Atlantic Toyota succeeded in getting dealers to coordinate in charging a higher list price through the common installation of the protective package. Though there was no discussion of actual transaction prices, the increase in the list price served to raise the prices that customers paid.[243] Key to this scheme's success was that individual dealers believed enough dealers overall would install the protective package for their vehicles. This mutual understanding was largely accomplished with

Mid-Atlantic Toyota's announcement of its Total Concept Protective Program at a meeting attended by all dealers, though some subsequent bilateral communications served to "close the deal." All parties benefited, as the dealers earned a higher profit margin on each automobile sold and Mid-Atlantic Toyota profited from more sales of the protective package.

3.3 General Lessons

Section 3.2 reviewed 10 hub-and-spoke cartels having a common structure and objective. The structure was described by at least one upstream manufacturer or wholesaler acting as the hub and downstream retailers or distributors acting as spokes. The objective was to produce a coordinated increase in prices among the downstream firms. Here we identify some general patterns of conduct but also ways in which the cartels differed.

3.3.1 Reasons for Cartel Formation

Given that the goal of the cartels was to raise downstream prices, it is not surprising that the original instigation for collusion often came from intense price competition in the downstream market. In the case involving the toy market in the UK (hereafter Toys-UK), retailers Argos and Littlewoods expressed displeasure regarding their margins to upstream manufacturer Hasbro. These complaints apparently led Hasbro to develop a strategy for Argos and Littlewoods to coordinate on adhering to the recommended retail price (RRP). In the UK market for desiccant (hereafter Desiccant-UK), it was also the downstream distributors who complained to upstream manufacturer UOP, a complaint that then led to the formation of a hub-and-spoke cartel.

In the UK market for replica football kits (hereafter Kits-UK) and in the drugstore market in a major US city (hereafter Drugs-US), it was again intense price competition, but this was largely, if not exclusively, attributed to one retailer: Sports Soccer in Kits-UK and Dart Drug in Drugs-US. Sports Soccer was explicit in its goal of expanding sales, which explained its tendency to undercut the prices of rival retailers. It is not clear who first expressed discontent with the low retail prices, but both retailer JJB and licensor Manchester United applied pressure to manufacturer Umbro to get retailers to comply with the recommended retail price. Similarly, Dart Drug was routinely pricing well below the suggested minimum retail price, which led manufacturer Parke Davis to approach retailers about coordinating on that price. Interestingly, the manager at Parke Davis initiated collusion only when he learned of an important lever for inducing compliance: Parke Davis had the right to refuse to supply a retailer.

In contrast, it appears that it was the upstream firm that was the instigator in the cases involving the retail markets for paints and varnishes in Poland (hereafter Paints-Poland), bread products in Canada (hereafter Bread-Canada), and automobiles in the US (hereafter Automobiles-US). In Paints-Poland and Bread-Canada, upstream firms wanted to raise wholesale prices to their buyers in response to higher input prices and perceived low wholesale profits, respectively. Given the apparent bargaining power of the downstream distributors, the upstream firms could not unilaterally impose higher wholesale prices and thought that coordinating a rise in downstream prices would facilitate higher wholesale prices. In Automobiles-US, upstream wholesaler Mid-Atlantic Toyota (MAT) sought to persuade its dealers to buy more of a package of add-ons for the cars sold to them by MAT. Orchestrating a rise in dealers' list prices, with a presumed rise in dealers' retail prices, was an inducement to get the dealers to buy more of the add-on.

Finally, the UK case involving processors and retailers of dairy products (hereafter Dairy-UK) showed that the motivation for the cartel need not be confined to a member of the cartel. The Dairy-UK cartel began with discontentment of farmers regarding the price of raw milk. Hub-and-spoke collusion was intended to raise the price of an input to the upstream milk and cheese processors, which would then be passed through as higher wholesale prices paid by downstream supermarkets, which would pass it through to final consumers. The lesson is that even if hub-and-spoke collusion raises downstream prices, it may have been initiated to raise prices elsewhere in the vertical chain.

3.3.2 Description of the Collusive Outcome
In Toys-UK, Kits-UK, Drugs-US, and Paints-Poland, the upstream hub set a recommended price and collusion took the form of downstream spokes coordinating on complying with that recommendation. In comparison, there was a targeted increase in retail prices in Dairy-UK (two pence per liter) and Desiccant-UK (4.5% rise). In the retail market for chicken in Chile (hereafter Chicken-Chile), the outcome took the form of maintaining the retail price at or above cost, thereby limiting the extent of competition in terms of loss leaders.

3.3.3 Benefits of Collusion to the Upstream Hub

The benefits from collusion are clear for a downstream retailer, for it produces a coordinated rise in retail prices. What is often not immediately clear is the benefit for the upstream supplier. However, as described in section 3.1, there are certain market conditions for which an increase in wholesale and retail prices can make all participants in a hub-and-spoke cartel better off. Those conditions include sufficient retailer bargaining power and sufficient substitutability among retailers and their products.

While in many of these cases there may be the ability to charge a higher wholesale price, it is explicit in Paints-Poland, Bread-Canada, and Desiccant-UK. Upstream PCW initiated hub-and-spoke collusion in order to be able to raise the wholesale price for paints and varnishes. Similarly, in Bread-Canada, bread manufacturers raised their wholesale prices by 7 cents and facilitated downstream collusion to raise retail prices by 10 cents. In Desiccant-UK, upstream UOP sought to raise its wholesale price but faced resistance and instead initially only raised retail prices. Subsequently, a 4% wholesale price increase was accepted when UOP coordinated the distributors to raise their prices by 4.5%.

Another potential benefit for the upstream hub is expanded sales. By creating a higher retail margin, UOP hoped that distributors would sell more of its product and perhaps sole source desiccant with UOP. In Toys-UK, the collusive outcome designed by hub Hasbro had two parts. First, retailers would price at the recommended level. Second, retailers would continue to stock some of Hasbro's products that were at risk of being dropped by the retailers. Thus, Hasbro might have benefited by selling more units of certain products. Similarly, in Automobiles-US, upstream MAT pursued hub-and-spoke collusion for the express purpose of selling more of its protective package to dealers. Aiding dealers in raising their margins was the tactic to get them to go along. In Kits-UK, the hub, Umbro, feared that it would lose the license to manufacture the replica kits of Manchester United (and hence future sales and profits) if it did not facilitate high retail prices, and Manchester United used this to pressure Umbro to keep prices high.

3.3.4 Communication to Achieve Mutual Understanding

Crucial to the effectiveness of any form of collusion is that each firm believes that its rivals will abide by the agreed collusive price. In some cases, there is rich documentation that downstream retailers were deeply concerned that not all retailers would comply. In Toys-UK, Littlewoods expressed skepticism that Argos would charge the recommended price. This concern was especially acute in that market because prices were set in catalogs, in which case a retailer whose price was undercut would be at a disadvantage for several months. In Kits-UK, JJB was concerned that Sports Soccer would undercut the recommended price, given that it had been doing so for some time in its effort to increase sales. Similarly, given Sports Soccer's focus on volume, it was concerned that raising its price would not only limit its sales growth but could cause a drop in sales if JJB undercut the recommended price. Given these concerns, upstream hub Umbro went back and forth between JJB and Sports Soccer, with each retailer agreeing to comply with the recommended price if other retailers did so. These bilateral communications were necessary to achieve mutual understanding between JJB and Sports Soccer and apparently were successful.

While bilateral communication between the hub and a spoke was the exclusive channel in most of the hub-and-spoke cartels, there were some isolated instances in which either the hub simultaneously communicated with multiple spokes or promoted some direct communication among the spokes. In Kits-UK, Umbro organized a meeting between retailers JJB, Sports Soccer, and Allsports. This move may have reflected retailers' doubts as to the veracity of Umbro's claims that the other retailers had actually agreed to higher prices. In Automobiles-US, upstream hub MAT initiated the communication process by announcing its plan at a meeting with downstream dealers. This setting provided the opportunity for dealers to communicate with each other and thereby achieve some level of mutual understanding. In Desiccant-UK, manufacturer UOP called a meeting of its distributors to discuss the downward spiral of retail prices, and they subsequently agreed to coordinate a price hike.

Another avenue for communication was through public announcements. In Dairy-UK, recall that hub-and-spoke collusion was a response to pressure from farmers to prop up the raw milk price. As a result, groups such as Farmers for Action (FFA) were involved in communications with the upstream processors and the downstream supermarkets. At one point, FFA had received assurances from supermarket Asda that it would raise its retail prices. FFA was then quoted in a regional newspaper as saying that Asda had agreed to this retail price increase and that it would aid in raising farmgate prices for milk. Such a public announcement served the cause of achieving a common belief among supermarkets that they would raise prices.

3.3.5 Monitoring Spokes for Compliance

Given a retailer's concern that rival retailers may not comply, it is not surprising that spokes were often active in monitoring. In Toys-UK, Desiccant-UK, and Kits-UK, spokes would monitor each other's prices and, upon observing that prices were too low, report that information to the upstream hub. There is no documentation of a spoke communicating directly with the noncompliant spoke. In Kits-UK, when a new kit was launched, failure to price at the recommended level would be detected and conveyed to Umbro the same day; hence, retailers were especially diligent in monitoring each other when demand was strong. In Desiccant-UK, there is evidence that a downstream distributor was informed by a customer that its prices were no longer competitive, which meant another distributor was pricing below the recommended level. That information was communicated to the upstream hub.

With Chicken-Chile, the downstream supermarkets not only used internal personnel but reportedly hired companies to keep track of rivals' prices (presumably not just for chicken). Monitoring might also involve a retailer sharing receipts with the upstream hub and thereby documenting that it was setting the agreed price. That practice occurred in Dairy-UK and the Belgian hub-and-spoke cartel involving drugstore, perfumery, and hygiene products (hereafter Drugstores-Belgium).

3.3.6 Exclusion as a Punishment

One of the most valuable instruments that an upstream hub can bring to a cartel of downstream retailers is the ability to deny or limit supply to a noncompliant retailer. In Chicken-Chile, upstream hub Agrosuper used the threat of denying supply to supermarkets that priced below cost. In Drugs-US, upstream manufacturer Parke Davis threatened to deny supply to a retailer whose price was below the recommended price (which was later changed to only when the *advertised* price was below the recommended price). Parke Davis went even further and threatened not to supply wholesalers who supplied noncompliant retailers. Because of continued aggressive pricing by retailers such as Dart Drug, Parke Davis did indeed cut off supplies for a limited time.

In Kits-UK, Umbro warned downstream retailers that they would not receive supply if they priced below the recommended price, and on a number of occasions the punishment was enacted. However, it appears that there was some issue regarding credibility of the punishment, because the spokes also threatened the hub if it did not follow through. JJB was particularly concerned with aggressive price cutting by its rival Sports Soccer and told upstream hub Umbro that it would cancel its order if Umbro did not curtail supply to Sports Soccer if it priced too low. On at least one occasion, this punishment was successful in persuading Sports Soccer to raise its price back to the collusive level.

Another exclusionary tactic was to raise the wholesale price to those downstream firms that did not abide by the agreed price. In Desiccant-UK, manufacturer UOP proposed to pursue such a tactic, though it is not clear that they went through with it. In both Desiccant-UK and Paints-Poland, they also threatened to raise the wholesale price for noncompliant retailers by withdrawing rebates or price supports.

Exclusion of deviators was not employed (or even threatened) in every cartel, however. Other cartels simply relied on the spokes' promise of a price war if some priced below agreed levels. In Toys-UK and Bread-Canada, it was threatened that noncompliance would be met by a period of intense price competition in the future. The hubs still played an important role in trying to convince deviators to return to compliance before any price war was initiated. In Dairy-UK, the spokes provided a time frame (usually a day or two) for rivals to comply; otherwise, the initiating spoke would reverse their price rise.

3.3.7 Multiple Hub-and-Spoke Cartels

Five of the 10 cases involved multiple hubs, each running its own hub-and-spoke cartel, often with spokes participating in more than one. In Drugstores-Belgium, 11 suppliers—including companies such as L'Oreal, Proctor & Gamble, and Unilever—coordinated various retail chains. There was no evidence of communication among the suppliers, so the retail chains would likely have encouraged their suppliers to assist them in coordinating on higher retail prices.

In the Paints-Poland case, manufacturer PCW was the first to organize a hub-and-spoke cartel. Later, two other manufacturers of paints and varnishes did the same, though there was no evidence of communication among them. One possibility is that the success of PCW's efforts became known throughout the industry—perhaps communicated by the downstream distributors—which led Akzo Nobel and Tikurila to imitate PCW's profitable enterprise.

The presence of multiple hub-and-spoke cartels in Dairy-UK is not surprising. Recall that the initial impetus for collusion came from farmers and their efforts to receive a higher price for raw milk. After farmers' groups pressured milk and cheese processors for a higher input price, each of the processors then went on to coordinate higher downstream retail prices so they could charge a higher wholesale price to cover the higher input price. With a common impetus for collusion, the simultaneous emergence of several hub-and-spoke cartels would not have required coordination among the processors.

In Chicken-Chile, each of the three major chicken suppliers ran a hub-and-spoke cartel with the three major supermarket chains. Supermarkets were concerned about their pricing below cost for this loss leader, so they could have complained to the three suppliers, all of which then made the same response: coordinate a price increase among the supermarkets. However, it is quite possible that the suppliers were communicating directly about raising retail prices since they were convicted of having colluded over wholesale chicken prices during that time.

Finally, the alleged conspiracy in Bread-Canada provides explicit evidence of collusion both downstream and upstream. While each bread supplier played the role of the hub to facilitate a downstream horizontal agreement among retailers that carried its products, the bread suppliers would also sometimes communicate indirectly via a retailer to facilitate the upstream horizontal agreement. However, the suppliers also supplemented this indirect communication with direct communication with each other when the cartel first formed and when they had reached agreement on the details of a price rise.

3.4 Appendix: Sugar (Canada)

The earliest documented case of a cartel among vertically related firms occurred in 1887 in the sugar markets of the Canadian provinces of Ontario and Quebec.[244] At the time, the refining of sugar was heavily concentrated among four refiners. The refiners largely sold their product to wholesalers, with some direct sales to grocery chains. The wholesale segment was highly competitive, with around 100 firms.

Displeased with their low margins, wholesalers formed the Dominion Grocers Guild. With nearly all wholesalers as members, the stated goal of the guild was to coordinate on a common wholesale price. To implement a collusive arrangement, they sought the assistance of the upstream refiners. A cartel was created, with the four upstream refiners collectively facilitating downstream collusion among the 100 or so downstream wholesalers. Given that all of this occurred prior to the introduction of Canada's competition law in 1889, communications between the wholesalers were unconstrained. Consequently, it is unlikely that the upstream firms acted as the nexus of the communication network, as was the case in the hub-and-spoke cartels reviewed in section 3.2.

The wholesalers' collusive price was set at the average price charged by refiners to wholesalers plus a markup of ⅜ cents per pound. For comparison, the overall wholesale price was around 7 cents per pound. Wholesalers who did not belong to the guild, and thus did not agree to this wholesale price, faced a surcharge of ¼ cent per pound from refiners. Given that grocery chains and other retailers did not belong to the guild, they would have to pay this surcharge. Thus, wholesalers benefited from the collusive markup and from the exclusion of retailers who had previously bought directly from the refiners and now would be more inclined to buy from a wholesaler.

The benefits to the refiners from facilitating downstream collusion are less clear. One potential benefit is that guild members did agree not to buy from foreign suppliers, which delivered some exclusionary benefit to refiners. Another benefit, based on statements at the time, is that "refiners may have feared ruinous competition among the wholesalers and the prospect of taking on the burden of distribution" (Asker and Hemphill 2020, 107). At the same time, there is evidence that refiners were concerned that the cartel might result in excessively high wholesale prices, which would adversely affect the demand for refined sugar. While the written agreement of the guild called for a minimum markup of ½ cent per pound, the refiners set the maximum at ⅜ cents per pound and thereby restricted the wholesale price to be below what the wholesalers would have liked.

In sum, this cartel exhibits the same setting as the ones analyzed throughout this chapter, where upstream firms assist downstream competitors to collude on higher downstream prices. However, given that communications among the downstream firms were unrestricted, there would be little benefit to them from exclusively communicating indirectly via the upstream firms, as in a standard hub-and-spoke cartel. Instead, the main benefit to the downstream firms came from the upstream firms partially excluding their downstream rivals who were not in the cartel by charging them higher input prices. In exchange, the downstream firms also excluded upstream rivals to the hubs.

3.5 Technical Appendix

This appendix develops and analyzes a theoretical model to show when vertically related firms will want to collude to set higher retail prices to maximize the profits of a supply chain and how the retailers can share the resultant collusive rents with the supplier by raising the wholesale price. We establish that downstream bargaining power and product substitutability are critical factors in determining when hub-and-spoke collusion is mutually profitable for the hub and spokes.

The structure of the appendix is as follows. After outlining the related theories, we present the assumptions of the model and derive the benchmark outcome when all firms are controlled by a vertically integrated monopolist. A hub-and-spoke cartel that seeks to maximize the profits of the supply chain would earn the same profits as an integrated monopolist. Then we solve for the equilibrium retail and wholesale prices when the firms are vertically separated and their conduct is noncollusive. Finally, we compare the profits of these two cases to find the conditions under which a hub-and-spoke cartel is able to both raise retail prices to the monopoly level—and thus increase total profits in the supply chain—and raise wholesale prices to pass some of the collusive rents to the supplier and thus satisfy the supplier's and retailers' participation constraints. All proofs are relegated to the end of this section.

3.5.1 Related Theories

The theories closest to ours are those of Van Cayseele and Miegielsen (2014), Sahuguet and Walckiers (2017), and Shamir (2017). As in our analysis, they aim to understand the conditions under which hub-and-spoke collusion is mutually beneficial for all participants in a market where retailers are supplied by a single upstream manufacturer. However, those analyses assume the colluding manufacturer and retailers do not take account of the vertical externalities their prices impose on each other, so the collusive retail prices are collectively inefficient for the cartel. In contrast, our cartel maximizes the profits of the supply chain, so the cartel is best able to satisfy each firm's participation constraint.

The main contribution of Van Cayseele and Miegielsen (2014) is to demonstrate when the manufacturer is willing to facilitate downstream collusion by denying supply to a deviating retailer. When products are differentiated, this can increase the severity of the punishment on the deviator and hence improve cartel stability compared to a standard horizontal cartel under the grim punishment (i.e., reversion to the stage game Nash equilibrium). Similar to the cases in our study, the manufacturer can benefit from downstream collusion because retailers have some bargaining power.

The approaches of Sahuguet and Walckiers (2017) and Shamir (2017) are different in that they consider the information exchanged by the cartel. In particular, they model situations where the manufacturer incentivizes retailers to reveal information about demand. In Sahuguet and Walckiers (2017), the state of demand is common knowledge among the retailers before prices are set. However, revealing this information to the manufacturer enables the manufacturer to vary the wholesale price with demand to increase its profits without making the retailers worse off compared to a standard horizontal cartel. In Shamir (2017), each retailer receives a noisy private signal about the market demand function. When direct communication between the retailers cannot be used to share this information, the retailers may instead reveal it to the manufacturer. The manufacturer can then aggregate the retailers' private signals and use its wholesale price to send a more precise signal to the retailers about the state of demand. Both the manufacturer and retailers benefit from better demand information, which can increase their profits compared with the competitive outcome.

3.5.2 Model

Suppose there is a monopoly supplier that sells its product to final consumers through two retailers. The retailers compete on prices, and their products are imperfect substitutes. Let q_i denote the quantity demanded of firm $i \in \{1, 2\}$. Following Shubik and Levitan (1980), the surplus function of a representative consumer is

$$U(q_1, q_2) = v(q_1 + q_2) - \frac{1}{(1+\mu)} \left[q_1^2 + q_2^2 + \frac{\mu}{2}(q_1 + q_2)^2 \right],$$

where $v>0$ and $\mu \in [0, \infty)$ controls the degree of substitutability between the products. The products are independent when $\mu=0$ and are increasingly substitutable as μ is raised; they are perfect substitutes when $\mu \to \infty$.

Maximizing net surplus (after subtracting expenditures from the surplus function), we can derive the inverse demand function for firm $i \neq j$:

$$p_i(q_i, q_j) = v - \frac{1}{1+\mu}(2q_i + \mu(q_i + q_j)). \tag{3.1}$$

Inverting the demand system yields the direct demand function of firm i:

$$q_i(p_i, p_j) = \max\left\{0, \left\{\min \frac{1}{2}\left[v - p_i - \frac{\mu}{2}(p_i - p_j)\right], \left(\frac{1+\mu}{2+\mu}\right)(v - p_i)\right\}\right\}.$$

An attractive feature of this specification is the absence of a market expansion effect (at equal retail prices) when changing the degree of product differentiation. For instance, if $p_i = p_j = p < v$, such that $q_i(p, p) = \frac{1}{2}(v - p)$, then the total market demand is $\Sigma_i\, q_i(p, p) = v - p$, which is independent of μ.[245] This property is attractive when performing comparative static solutions with respect to the degree of product differentiation, as then market size remains fixed.

Suppose the monopoly supplier uses linear pricing and sells its product to retailer i at a wholesale price of w_i for each unit bought by retailer i. For simplicity, we assume all other costs are zero, so retailer i's marginal cost is w_i and the supplier's marginal cost is zero. There are no fixed costs. Thus, the profit functions of retailer i and the supplier are, respectively,

$$\pi_{Ri}(p_i, p_j, w_i) = (p_i - w_i)q_i(p_i, p_j) \tag{3.2}$$

and

$$\pi_s(w_1, w_2, p_1, p_2) = w_1 q_1(p_1, p_2) + w_2 q_2(p_2, p_1). \tag{3.3}$$

We drop subscripts when there is no ambiguity, and when $w_1 = w_2 \equiv w$ and $p_1 = p_2 \equiv p$ we write $\pi_R(p, p, w) = \pi_R(p, w) = (p - w)q(p)$ and $\pi_s(w, w, p, p) = \pi_s(w, p) = w2q(p)$.

The timing of the game is as follows.

Stage 1 The supplier negotiates wholesale prices with retailers bilaterally and simultaneously.

Stage 2 Retailers observe the stage 1 outcome and simultaneously select their prices.

The game is solved using backward induction. We first find expressions for the equilibrium prices and quantities for any given pair of wholesale prices. Then the symmetric equilibrium wholesale prices are obtained using the two-player symmetric Nash bargaining solution. It will prove useful to first derive the outcome for an integrated monopolist, as it is a relevant benchmark.

3.5.3 Integrated Monopolist Benchmark

Suppose the actions of all firms are controlled by an integrated monopolist that seeks to maximize the profits of the supply chain. To do so, it would supply the input to its retailers at marginal cost, $w_1 = w_2 = 0$, and maximize the sum of its retailers' profits. When both demands are positive, the integrated monopolist's profit is

$$\frac{p_1}{2}\left[v - p_1 - \frac{\mu}{2}(p_1 - p_2)\right] + \frac{p_2}{2}\left[v - p_2 - \frac{\mu}{2}(p_2 - p_1)\right]. \tag{3.4}$$

Maximizing (3.4) with respect to p_1 and p_2 yields two first-order conditions of the form

$$\frac{1}{2}\left[v - p_i - \frac{\mu}{2}(p_i - p_j)\right] - \frac{p_i}{2}\left(1 + \frac{\mu}{2}\right) + \frac{p_j}{2}\frac{\mu}{2} = 0. \tag{3.5}$$

Solving (3.5) for $i = \{1, 2\}$ yields the (symmetric) monopoly price and quantity for each retailer,

$$p^m = \frac{v}{2} \text{ and } q(p^m) = \frac{v}{4},$$

and the integrated monopoly profits are $\Pi^m = p^m 2q(p^m) = \left(\frac{v}{2}\right)^2$.

3.5.4 Competitive Equilibrium

Next, we solve for the equilibrium when the firms are vertically separated and their conduct is noncollusive. We begin by providing a general characterization of the bargaining solution prior to deriving a closed-form solution.

3.5.4.1 Bargaining preliminaries
Given that negotiations in stage 1 are conducted bilaterally and simultaneously, each firm will treat the wholesale price from the other bargaining scenario as exogenous during their negotiations. Following Dobson and Waterson (1997, 2007), the symmetric equilibrium wholesale prices can then be obtained using the two-player symmetric Nash bargaining solution.[246] Denoting the resulting equilibrium retail prices

for retailers i and j as $p_i^N(w_i, w_j)$ and $p_j^N(w_j, w_i)$, respectively, the symmetric Nash bargaining solution between the supplier and retailer i over the wholesale price w_i is characterized by

$$w_i^* = \arg\max_{w_i}[\pi_S(w_i, w_j^*, p_i^N(w_i, w_j^*), p_j^N(w_j^*, w_i)) - D_S]^{1-\alpha}$$
$$\times [\pi_{Ri}(p_i^N(w_i, w_j^*), p_j^N(w_j^*, w_i), w_i) - D_R]^\alpha, \quad (3.6)$$

where D_S and D_R are the "disagreement" profits of the supplier and retailer i when they do not reach an agreement, respectively, and $\alpha \in [0, 1]$ represents the retailer's relative bargaining strength with respect to the supplier. When $\alpha = 1$, the retailer has all the bargaining power, and when $\alpha = 0$, the supplier has all the bargaining power. The first-order condition of (3.6) can be expressed as

$$\left(\frac{1-\alpha}{\pi_S - D_S}\right)\frac{d\pi_S}{dw_i} = -\left(\frac{\alpha}{\pi_{Ri} - D_R}\right)\frac{d\pi_{Ri}}{dw_i}, \quad (3.7)$$

where

$$\frac{d\pi_S}{dw_i} = \frac{\partial \pi_S}{\partial w_i} + \frac{\partial \pi_S}{\partial p_i}\frac{\partial p_i^N}{\partial w_i} + \frac{\partial \pi_S}{\partial p_j}\frac{\partial p_j^N}{\partial w_i},$$

$$\frac{d\pi_{Ri}}{dw_i} = \frac{\partial \pi_{Ri}}{\partial w_i} + \frac{\partial \pi_{Ri}}{\partial p_i}\frac{\partial p_i^N}{\partial w_i} + \frac{\partial \pi_{Ri}}{\partial p_j}\frac{\partial p_j^N}{\partial w_i}.$$

The left-hand side of (3.7) represents the supplier's weighted concession cost measured as a proportion of the gains from agreement, and the right-hand side is the equivalent expression for retailer i. The negotiated wholesale price balances the two costs. The intuition is that when, say, the left-hand side is smaller than the right-hand side, it is relatively less costly for the supplier to concede to a lower wholesale price than it is for the retailer to concede to a higher wholesale price. Consequently, the retailer will bargain more aggressively than the supplier, which will lead to a reduction in the wholesale price.

To solve for the symmetric equilibrium wholesale prices in stage 1, we must first find expressions for each of the terms in (3.7). That is, we must solve for the equilibrium retail prices and quantities in stage 2 when the supplier reaches agreement with both retailers and when it only reaches agreement with one retailer.

3.5.4.2 Equilibrium analysis First, we solve for the equilibrium retail prices and quantities in stage 2 assuming retailers 1 and 2 have negotiated wholesale prices of w_1 and w_2, respectively. When both retailers' demands are positive, maximizing (3.2) with respect to p_i gives us this first-order condition:

$$\frac{1}{2}\left[v - p_i - \frac{\mu}{2}(p_i - p_j)\right] + (p_i - w_i)\frac{1}{2}\left(1 + \frac{\mu}{2}\right) = 0. \tag{3.8}$$

Solving (3.8) for $i = \{1, 2\}$, the equilibrium retail prices and quantities are derived:

$$p_i^N(w_i, w_j; \mu) = w_j + \frac{2(v - w_j)}{4 + \mu} + (w_i - w_j)\frac{2(2 + \mu)^2}{(4 + \mu)(4 + 3\mu)}, \tag{3.9}$$

$$q_i(p_i^N(w_i, w_j; \mu), p_j^N(w_j, w_i; \mu)) = \frac{1}{2}\left(\frac{2 + \mu}{4 + \mu}\right)\left[(v - w_j) + (w_j - w_i)\frac{(8 + 8\mu + \mu^2)}{2(4 + 3\mu)}\right].$$

The Nash equilibrium profits of retailer i and the supplier are denoted by $\pi_{Ri}(p_i^N, p_j^N, w_i)$ and $\pi_S(w_1, w_2, p_1^N, p_2^N)$, respectively.

Next, consider the case where the supplier and retailer i fail to reach an agreement in stage 1. In this case, retailer i's disagreement profits are $D_R = 0$ because it has no outside option, given that the supplier is a monopolist. In contrast, if the supplier fails to reach an agreement with retailer i, it can still sell to retailer j at the negotiated wholesale price w_j. In such an event, it follows from (3.1) with $q_j > 0$ and $q_i = 0$ that firm j's demand function is

$$q_j(p_j; \mu) = (v - p_j)\left(\frac{1 + \mu}{2 + \mu}\right).$$

Retailer j's profits in stage 2 are then $\pi^* = (p_j - w_j)(v - p_j)\left(\frac{1 + \mu}{2 + \mu}\right)$ for any $p_j < v$ and are maximized with price $p^*(w_j) = \left(\frac{v + w_j}{2}\right)$. Thereby, the retailer sells $q(p^*(w_j); \mu) = \left(\frac{v - w_j}{2}\right)\left(\frac{1 + \mu}{2 + \mu}\right)$. Consequently, the supplier's disagreement profits are

$$D_S(w_j; \mu) = w_j q(p^*(w_j); \mu) = w_j\left(\frac{v - w_j}{2}\right)\left(\frac{1 + \mu}{2 + \mu}\right). \tag{3.10}$$

Even though only one product is available, these profits are a function of the degree of product substitutability, μ. That is because some consumers choose not to purchase product j when their preferred product i is not available, and the number that do so is determined by μ. For instance, when the products are perfect substitutes, $\mu \to \infty$, at a given price all consumers that purchase product i when it is available will switch to purchasing from firm j when product i is not available. In contrast, when the products are independent, $\mu=0$, no consumers will substitute product j for the unavailable product i. Consequently, the supplier's disagreement profits are higher when the products are closer substitutes.[247]

We are now in a position to solve for the symmetric equilibrium wholesale and retail prices under Nash bargaining.

Proposition 3.1 *The symmetric Nash bargaining solution results in a unique symmetric equilibrium wholesale price,*

$$w^N(\alpha, \mu) = \frac{v}{2 + \dfrac{\alpha}{1-\alpha} g(\mu)} \in \left[0, \frac{v}{2}\right],$$

where $g(\mu) \equiv 2 + \dfrac{\mu^2(4+\mu)(1+\mu)}{(2+\mu)^2(4+3\mu)} \in [2, \infty)$, *and there is a unique symmetric equilibrium retail price:*

$$p^N(w^N(\alpha, \mu); \mu) = w^N(\alpha, \mu) + \frac{2(v - w^N(\alpha, \mu))}{4+\mu} \in \left[\frac{2v}{4+\mu}, \frac{v(6+\mu)}{2(4+\mu)}\right].$$

The equilibrium wholesale and retail prices are both strictly decreasing in the retailers' bargaining power, α, and the degree of substitutability, μ.

As described in (3.7), the symmetric equilibrium wholesale price balances the supplier's and retailer i's weighted concession costs measured as a proportion of their gains from reaching agreement. Thus, when the supplier has all the bargaining power, so $\alpha=0$, the wholesale price maximizes the supplier's profit, so it is set at the monopoly wholesale level, $w^N(0, \mu) = \dfrac{v}{2}$. In contrast, when the retailers have all the bargaining power, so $\alpha=1$, the wholesale price maximizes the retailer's profit, so it is set to the supplier's marginal cost, $w^N(1, \mu)=0$. As retailers' bargaining power is increased relative to the supplier, they bargain more aggressively to negotiate a lower wholesale price. In terms of (3.7), as α rises from 0 toward 1, greater weight is placed on the right-hand side and less weight is placed on the left-hand side, so the equilibrium wholesale price strictly decreases to ensure that (3.7) is satisfied. Furthermore, given that the equilibrium retail price is increasing the wholesale price, the negative relationship between α and the equilibrium wholesale price also ensures that the equilibrium retail price strictly decreases with α.

Similarly, the wholesale and retail prices fall as the degree of substitutability increases, because it strengthens each retailer's overall bargaining power relative to the supplier's.[248] The driving force on the retailer's side is that each retailer has less to gain from reaching agreement, because greater substitutability intensifies competition between retailers (i.e., the denominator of the right-hand side of (3.7) is strictly decreasing in μ). This effect guarantees that the right-hand side of (3.7) strictly increases with μ, holding the wholesale price constant, even though the retailer can experience a lower cost by conceding a small cost disadvantage relative to its rival. This implies that the retailer bargains more aggressively than before. In contrast, as the degree of substitutability increases, the supplier always has more to gain from reaching agreement, because it sells more as a result of greater substitutability through two retailers than through one, but it also experiences a higher concession cost (i.e., both the numerator and the denominator of the left-hand side of (3.7) are strictly increasing in μ). The net effect of these counteracting forces increases the left-hand side of (3.7) when product substitutability is low and decreases it when it is high. Nevertheless, even when the net supplier effect works in the opposite direction, it is the net retailer effect that dominates, thus ensuring that the equilibrium wholesale prices are strictly decreasing in μ. This implies that the retailer's weighted concession cost measured as a proportion of the gains from agreement increases to such an extent that it is able to negotiate a lower wholesale price. Finally, given that equilibrium retail prices are decreasing in the wholesale price, the negative relationship between the equilibrium wholesale price and product substitutability guarantees that there is an indirect negative effect on equilibrium retail prices in addition to the standard negative direct effect of product substitutability on those prices.

3.5.5 Incentives
In this subsection, we consider the firms' incentives to form a hub-and-spoke cartel that has the objective of maximizing the profits of the supply chain. To do so, the cartel will want to set the same price as an integrated monopolist so the total profits of the supply chain equal the monopoly profit. We first find the conditions under which the hub-and-spoke cartel will need to raise retail prices to achieve such profits, and then we demonstrate that the retailers can share the collusive rents with the supplier by raising wholesale prices. It is well known that collusion can be sustained in an infinitely repeated game when firms are sufficiently patient (i.e., the discount factor is close enough to 1), so we do not explicitly model the stability (or incentive compatibility) constraint and instead focus on the participation constraints.

Proposition 3.2 provides conditions for a coordinated increase in retailers' prices to raise the total profits for the vertical chain.

Proposition 3.2 *For any $v > 0$ and $\mu \in [0, \infty)$, there exists a unique $\alpha^* \in (0,1)$ such that the symmetric equilibrium retail price is strictly less than the monopoly price, $p^N(w^N(\alpha, \mu); \mu) < p^m$, if and only if $\alpha > \alpha^*(\mu)$. This critical level of the bargaining power parameter is strictly decreasing in degree of substitutability, $\dfrac{\partial \alpha^*}{\partial \mu} < 0$.*

Intuitively, when the retailers have all the bargaining power, so $\alpha = 1$, the wholesale price is zero, $w^N(1, \mu) = 0$. Consequently, for any degree of substitutability, competition will ensure that the equilibrium retail price is below the monopoly level, $p^N(w^N(1, \mu); \mu) < p^m$. In contrast, when the supplier has all the bargaining power, so $\alpha = 0$, the wholesale price is already at the monopoly wholesale level, $w^N(0, \mu) = \dfrac{v}{2}$. There is then double marginalization whenever products are less than perfect substitutes, which implies that firms will not want to coordinate on raising retail prices. Given that equilibrium retail prices are decreasing in the level of α, it follows that the firms will want to form a hub-and-spoke cartel with the aim of raising retail prices when there is sufficient bargaining power at the retail level. As products become more substitutable, equilibrium retail prices move below the monopoly price for lower levels of α. That is because a greater degree of substitutability strengthens each retailer's overall bargaining power, which lowers both the equilibrium wholesale and retail prices, providing more scope to raise retail prices to the monopoly level through hub-and-spoke collusion.

Having shown in proposition 3.2 that the vertical chain can increase total profits by raising retail prices, we now show that retailers can share these collusive rents with the supplier by raising the wholesale price. A higher wholesale price will cause the supplier's participation constraint to be satisfied while still ensuring that retailers' participation constraint is satisfied.

Proposition 3.3 *If $\alpha \in (\alpha^*(\mu), 1)$, then there exists a unique $\underline{w} > w^N(\alpha, \mu)$ and a unique $\bar{w} \in (\underline{w}, p^m)$ such that the supplier's and the retailers' participation constraints are simultaneously satisfied if and only if $w \in (\underline{w}, \bar{w})$.*

Given that hub-and-spoke collusion raises retail prices for any $\alpha > \alpha^*(\mu)$, less of the supplier's product is demanded than before, $q(p^m) < q(p^N(w^N(\alpha, \mu); \mu))$. Thus, if collusion does not change the wholesale price from $w^N(\alpha, \mu)$, then the supplier's profit will decrease. Consequently, the supplier in a hub-and-spoke cartel must be compensated by a higher wholesale price. However, a higher wholesale price reduces the collusive profits of the retailers, holding retail prices fixed at the monopoly level. This implies that if the wholesale price is set too close to the monopoly retail price, p^m, then the retailers' collusive profits would be less than under competition. Thus, the wholesale price must be set high enough to make collusion profitable for the upstream firm but not so high that it makes collusion unprofitable for the downstream firms. Proposition 3.3 establishes that there is a range of wholesale prices for which the supplier's and retailers' participation constraints are both satisfied. For example, when products are close to perfect substitutes, this range is as wide as possible, with $\underline{w} = 0$ and $\bar{w} = p^m$. This is because neither the supplier nor a retailer places a markup on the product under competition. Therefore, the supplier's profit will increase even if the new wholesale price is positive yet very close to zero, and the retailers' profits will increase when the new wholesale price is below but very close to p^m. The range gets smaller as products become less substitutable. Finally, we would expect that a high level of downstream bargaining power will lead to a w close to $\underline{w}$ and that a low level will lead to a w close to $\bar{w}$.

To summarize, we have shown that collusively raising retail prices to the monopoly level increases the profits of the supply chain when retail prices are initially low, which will occur when downstream firms have sufficient bargaining power and products are sufficiently substitutable. Furthermore, we showed that the retailers can share the collusive rents with the upstream supplier by raising the wholesale price and that this will raise the profits of all firms in the vertical chain.

3.5.6 Proofs

Proof of Proposition 3.1 For any given $w_i = w_j = w < v$, Nash equilibrium profits of a retailer and its supplier are, respectively,

$$\pi_R(p^N(w, \mu), w) = \frac{(v - w)^2(2 + \mu)}{(4 + \mu)^2} \tag{3.11}$$

and $\pi_S(w, p^N(w, \mu)) = w(v - w)\dfrac{(2 + \mu)}{(4 + \mu)}$, such that

$$\pi_S(w, p^N(w, \mu)) - D_S(w; \mu) = \frac{w(v - w)(4 + 3\mu + \mu^2)}{2(2 + \mu)(4 + \mu)}. \tag{3.12}$$

Given

$$\frac{\partial \pi_{Ri}(p_i^N(\cdot), p_j^N(\cdot), w_i)}{\partial w_i}\bigg|_{w_i=w_j=w} = \frac{-(v-w)(2+\mu)(8+8\mu+\mu^2)}{(4+\mu)^2(4+3\mu)} \tag{3.13}$$

and

$$\frac{\partial \pi_S(w_i, w_j, p_i^N(\cdot), p_j^N(\cdot))}{\partial w_i}\bigg|_{w_i=w_j=w} = \frac{1}{2}\left(\frac{2+\mu}{4+\mu}\right)[v-2w], \tag{3.14}$$

and substituting (3.11), (3.12), (3.13), and (3.14) into (3.7), yields

$$\frac{(1-\alpha)(v-2w)}{w(v-w)}\frac{(2+\mu)^2}{(4+3\mu+\mu^2)} = \frac{\alpha}{(v-w)}\left(\frac{8+8\mu+\mu^2}{4+3\mu}\right). \tag{3.15}$$

It is straightforward to check that the right-hand side of (3.15) is strictly increasing in μ. This is because the denominator of the right-hand side of (3.7) is strictly decreasing in μ,

$$\frac{\partial \pi_R(p^N(w, \mu), w)}{\partial \mu} = \frac{-\mu(v-w)^2}{(4+\mu)^3} < 0 \text{ for all } w < v,$$

and this effect dominates even when μ is sufficiently small that the effect on the numerator of the right-hand side of (3.7) works in the opposite direction,

$$\frac{\partial^2 \pi_{Ri}(p_i^N(\cdot), p_j^N(\cdot), w_i)}{\partial w_i \partial \mu}\bigg|_{w_i=w_j=w} = \frac{2(v-w)[\mu(-40+(\mu-12)\mu)-32]}{(4+\mu)^3(4+3\mu)^2}.$$

It is straightforward to check that the left-hand side of (3.15) is strictly increasing in μ if $\mu<2$ and decreasing if $\mu>2$. This is because both the numerator and the denominator on the left-hand side of (3.7) are strictly increasing in μ,

$$\frac{\partial^2 \pi_S(w_i, w_j, p_i^N(\cdot), p_j^N(\cdot))}{\partial w_i \partial \mu}\bigg|_{w_i=w_j=w} = \frac{(v-2w)}{(4+\mu)^2} > 0,$$

and

$$\frac{\partial(\pi_S(w, p^N(w, \mu)) - D_S(w; \mu))}{\partial \mu} = \frac{w(v-w)\mu(8+3\mu)}{2(2+\mu)^2(4+\mu)^2} > 0 \ \forall \mu > 0,$$

where the effect on the numerator dominates if and only if μ is sufficiently small.

Rearranging (3.15) in terms of w shows that $w^N(\alpha, \mu)$ is as claimed, and substituting $w^N(\alpha, \mu)$ into (3.9) shows that $p^N(w^N(\alpha, \mu); \mu)$ is as claimed.

Differentiating $w^N(\alpha, \mu)$ with respect to α and μ yields

$$\frac{\partial w^N}{\partial \alpha} = -\frac{vg(\mu)}{(2 + \alpha(g(\mu) - 2))^2} < 0$$

and

$$\frac{\partial w^N}{\partial \mu} = -\frac{v(1 - \alpha)\dfrac{\partial g(\mu)}{\partial \mu}}{(2 + \alpha(g(\mu) - 2))^2} < 0$$

from $\dfrac{\partial g(\mu)}{\partial \mu} = \dfrac{64\mu + 144\mu^2 + 100\mu^3 + 26\mu^4 + 3\mu^5}{(2 + \mu)^3(4 + 3\mu)^2} > 0$, where $w^N(0, \mu) = \dfrac{v}{2}$ and

$w^N(1, \mu) = 0$. Furthermore, totally differentiating $p^N(w^N(\alpha, \mu); \mu)$ with respect to α and μ yields

$$\frac{dp^N}{d\alpha} = \frac{\partial p^N}{\partial \alpha} + \frac{\partial p^N}{\partial w}\frac{\partial w^N}{\partial \alpha} = \left(\frac{2 + \mu}{4 + \mu}\right)\frac{\partial w^N}{\partial \alpha} < 0$$

and

$$\frac{dp^N}{d\mu} = \frac{\partial p^N}{\partial \mu} + \frac{\partial p^N}{\partial w}\frac{\partial w^N}{\partial \mu} = -\frac{2(v - w^N)}{4 + \mu} + \left(\frac{2 + \mu}{4 + \mu}\right)\frac{\partial w^N}{\partial \mu} < 0,$$

respectively, where $p^N(w^N(0, \mu); \mu) = \dfrac{v(6 + \mu)}{2(4 + \mu)}$ and $p^N(w^N(1, \mu); \mu) = \dfrac{2v}{4 + \mu}$. ∎

Proof of proposition 3.2 It follows from $p^N(w^N(0, \mu); \mu) = \dfrac{v}{2} + \dfrac{v}{4 + \mu} >$

p^m, $p^N(w^N(1, \mu); \mu) = \dfrac{v}{2 + \dfrac{\mu}{2}} < p^m$, and $\dfrac{dp^N}{d\alpha} < 0$ for all $\mu < \infty$ that there exists

a unique level of α, denoted α^*, that results in $p^N(w^N(\alpha^*, \mu); \mu) = p^m$, and if $\alpha > \alpha^*$, then $p^N(w^N(\alpha, \mu); \mu) < p^m$. Using the implicit function theorem

on $p^m - p^N(w^N(\alpha^*, \mu); \mu) = 0$ shows that $\dfrac{\partial \alpha^*}{\partial \mu} = -\dfrac{dp^N}{d\mu}\dfrac{1}{\dfrac{dp^N}{d\alpha}} < 0$ from $\dfrac{dp^N}{d\alpha} < 0$

and $\dfrac{dp^N}{d\mu} < 0$ for all $\mu < \infty$, where $\lim\limits_{\mu \to \infty} p^N(w^N(0, \mu); \mu) = \dfrac{v}{2}$ implies $\lim\limits_{\mu \to \infty} \alpha^* = 0$

and $\lim\limits_{\mu \to 0} p^N(w^N(1, \mu); \mu) = \dfrac{v}{2}$ implies $\lim\limits_{\mu \to 0} \alpha^* = 1$. ∎

Proof of proposition 3.3 The supplier's participation constraint is $\pi_s(w, p^m) > \pi_s(w^N(\cdot), p^N(w^N(\cdot)))$. Substituting yields

$$w2q(p^m) > w^N(\alpha, \mu)2q(p^N(w^N(\alpha^*, \mu); \mu)).$$

Rearranging shows that $w > w^N(\alpha, \mu)\left(\dfrac{q(p^N(w^N(\alpha^*, \mu); \mu))}{q(p^m)}\right) \equiv \underline{w}$, where $\underline{w} >$

$w^N(\alpha, \mu)$ as $q(p^N(w^N(\alpha^*, \mu); \mu)) > q(p^m)$ for all $\alpha > \alpha^*(\mu)$.

The retailers' participation constraints are satisfied if $\pi_R(p^m, w) > \pi_R(p^N(\cdot), w^N(\cdot))$. Substituting yields

$$(p^m - w)\, q(p^m) > (p^N(w^N(\alpha^*, \mu); \mu) - w^N(\alpha, \mu))\, q(p^N(w^N(\alpha^*, \mu); \mu)).$$

Rearranging shows that

$$w < \underline{w} + \left[p^m - p^N(w^N(\alpha^*, \mu); \mu) \left(\frac{q(p^N(w^N(\alpha^*, \mu); \mu))}{q(p^m)} \right) \right] \equiv \bar{w}, \text{ where } \bar{w} > \underline{w} \text{ as}$$

$p^m q(p^m) > p^N(w^N(\alpha^*, \mu); \mu) q(p^N(w^N(\alpha^*, \mu); \mu))$ for all $\alpha \neq \alpha^*(\mu)$ and where $\bar{w} < p^m$

as $p^N(w^N(\alpha^*, \mu); \mu) > w^N(\alpha, \mu)$ for all $\mu < \infty$. ∎

4 Collusion to Raise Downstream Prices: Downstream Intermediary as Hub

As in chapter 3, we consider hub-and-spoke cartels created to raise downstream prices, but, unlike in that chapter, where the hub is not an upstream supplier. To properly understand the type of firm that is a hub in these cases, some background information on intermediaries will prove useful:

> An intermediary is an economic agent that purchases from suppliers for resale to buyers or that helps buyers and sellers meet and transact. Intermediaries seek out suppliers, find and encourage buyers, select buy and sell prices, define the terms of transactions, manage the payments and record keeping for transactions, and hold inventories to provide liquidity or availability of goods and services. (Spulber 1996, 135)

Intermediaries come in two types. There are intermediaries who buy from one set of agents and sell to a second set of agents. These intermediaries include, for example, wholesalers (who buy from manufacturers and sell to retailers), retailers (who buy from manufacturers or wholesalers and sell to consumers), and market makers on securities exchanges such as NASDAQ (who buy and sell shares). These intermediaries take ownership of the goods and assume the risk of buying a good at one price and reselling it at another price. An intermediary's compensation takes the form of a margin on the sale of the good; that is, the difference between the price at which it sells the good and the price at which it buys it, less any other costs incurred. For example, retailers earn a profit margin on the goods they sell, and market makers earn the bid-ask spread on stocks that they trade. The hub-and-spoke cartels in chapter 3 involved intermediaries of this type.

The other type of intermediary performs the functions just described but without buying and selling goods. Also included in this category are intermediaries who, while formally buying and selling goods, are acting on behalf of another party, and that party bears the risk coming from the prices at which the good is bought and sold.[1] Real estate brokers bring together property owners interested in selling and individuals or businesses interested in buying. In the US, the broker is hired by the seller for the purpose of finding prospective buyers and soliciting attractive offers. It is standard for the broker to receive a commission paid by the seller, which is a percentage of the selling price. Auction houses and online platforms—such as Christie's and eBay—are another class of intermediaries that bring together buyers and sellers. The owner of an object chooses the intermediary to sell that object. Auction houses such as Christie's and Sotheby's attract prospective buyers and manage the auction for the purpose of delivering a high winning bid. While the primary source of payment to the auction house is the commission earned from the seller on the selling price, there may be a commission paid by the buyer as well. Online auction sites such as eBay provide an auction program for sellers to use but otherwise are less involved in attracting bidders and managing the auction. Another class of intermediaries that neither buy nor sell are online platforms such as Uber, Airbnb, and Taskrabbit. They allow buyers and sellers to join and use the platform for the purpose of transacting. They are active in matching the right buyer with the right seller and are involved to varying degrees in determining the price of the transaction.

Turning to the topic at hand, we have only been able to find two cases involving a hub-and-spoke cartel designed to raise downstream prices and the hub was not an upstream supplier. In those two cases, the hub was an intermediary of the second type.[2] The Commercial Insurance case has an insurance broker as the hub and commercial insurance companies as the upstream spokes. The broker collected price quotes from the upstream insurance companies, and the buyer purchased insurance from one of those companies. The Specialty Pipe case has a pipe fabricator as the hub and pipe manufacturers as the upstream spokes. The pipe fabricator procured pipes for the downstream buyer and then fabricated those pipes for the buyer. The hub-and-spoke cartel only pertained to the pipe fabricator's role as a procurer of pipes. Though the pipe fabricator formally bought the pipes, it was part of the contract that the downstream buyer would pay for the cost of the pipes plus a fixed markup to the pipe fabricator. Thus, the downstream buyer incurred the risk associated with the purchase of the pipes, and the pipe fabricator was just acting as an agent on behalf of the downstream buyer.

In providing an economic framework for these two cases, we will then restrict our attention to when upstream suppliers are spokes, the hub is an intermediary lying between upstream suppliers and downstream buyers that is acting as an agent for a downstream buyer, and the goal of the cartel is to raise the prices charged by upstream suppliers to downstream buyers.

4.1 Economic Framework

The hub-and-spoke cartels to be examined concern markets for which an intermediary is contracted by the buyer to act on the buyer's behalf. Except when the intermediary conspires with the upstream suppliers, the intermediary's objective is to find the best deal for a buyer by identifying and attracting prospective upstream suppliers to bid on the buyer's business and getting the lowest prices out of those suppliers. For such markets, this section first examines what outcomes emerge under competition and then how collusion affects that outcome.

4.1.1 Competitive Benchmark

An intermediary can offer three services to a buyer: searching, matching, and dealing. The objective of searching is to identify possible upstream suppliers that can deliver this product or service to the buyer and are willing and able to bid for the buyer's business. The more upstream suppliers that are identified, the more options are available to the buyer and the more competition there will be for the buyer's business. When suppliers differ in the characteristics and quality of their product or service, an intermediary may engage in matching to find the most suitable supplier for a buyer. When the product or service is fairly homogeneous across suppliers, that activity is less important. Finally, dealing refers to getting the best deal for a buyer out of a set of suppliers. When suppliers offer heterogeneous products or services, an intermediary may evaluate the various options to identify the best one for a buyer in terms of price and traits. When the product or service is fairly standardized, dealing means getting the lowest price from the participating suppliers. That could involve negotiating with suppliers or conducting an auction.

In order to provide these services, an intermediary requires compensation, which could come from the buyer, the selected supplier, or both. It might be a flat fee, or a commission that is proportional to the supplier's price. If the payment to the intermediary is paid by the buyer, then the buyer's total expenditure is what it pays to the selected supplier plus that payment. If the payment is paid by the selected supplier, the buyer will still end up paying some or all of it because a supplier realizes that its cost is higher because of the payment it must make to the intermediary, and that will cause it to submit a higher price to the buyer. How much of the payment the buyer effectively pays depends on the cost pass-through for a supplier. In a highly competitive industry, the upstream suppliers will price close to cost, in which case they raise their prices by the amount of the payment to the intermediary. In that situation, the buyer pays for the intermediary whether the intermediary sends the bill to the selected supplier or the buyer. If the industry is less competitive then cost pass-through can be either below or above 100%, in which case the buyer pays less or more than the entire payment.

As the cases revolve around the intermediary conspiring with upstream suppliers to raise the price, let us examine in some detail the determination of price under competition. Suppose suppliers offer essentially identical products and services so the buyer is interested in minimizing the price it pays. For this purpose, consider the intermediary running a procurement auction while trying to attract as many suppliers as possible to submit bids. In some markets, procurement auctions are indeed used. In other markets, an intermediary may engage in a series of negotiations—using a low bid from one supplier to entice another supplier to lower its bid—which might prove to be comparable to running a procurement auction.

In order to participate in a procurement auction, a supplier typically incurs some expense that is distinct from the cost of actually providing the product or service should it win the contract. This participation expense includes providing documentation to the intermediary on its product or service, estimating the cost of providing the product or service, and deciding on the appropriate bid. For nontrivial projects, cost estimation in particular can be substantial. A supplier would participate at an auction only if the expected profit it would earn is positive; that is, the probability of winning the contract multiplied by the value of the contract (revenue earned less estimated cost) exceeds the participation expense. An intermediary will want to do what it can to lower the participation expense but, more importantly, to identify suppliers with a low cost of providing the product or service, as they will be more likely to participate. For example, that low cost could result from having ample capacity.

Having attracted some set of suppliers to participate in a procurement auction (and assuming they all provide the same product or service), the intermediary will need to decide on a particular auction format to determine the price.[3] One auction format is the oral English auction, which we'll describe in a form that departs slightly from how it is done in practice but delivers the same prediction regarding the winning bid. The auctioneer starts the bidding at some reasonably high level and invites any bidder to indicate their willingness to provide the service at that level. As long as there are two or more bidders active at the current bid, the bid is lowered. The bid continues to be reduced until only one active bidder remains, who is then awarded the contract at a price equal to the penultimate bid (i.e., the lowest bid at which there were two active bidders). Note that this auction results in the winning bid equaling the second-lowest cost among all bidders. As long as the bid is above the second-lowest cost, at least two bidders will be active. Once the bid falls below the second-lowest cost, only the lowest-cost bidder will be active, at which point the bidding stops. For example, suppose there are three upstream suppliers participating at the auction and their costs are 10, 15, and 18. Let the bidding start at 20, in which case all three bidders will indicate their willingness to contract. The bid is then lowered to 19, and again all three are active. At 18, the same is so (though now bidder 3 is indifferent about winning the contract). When the bid is lowered to 17, only bidders 1 and 2 remain active. The bid continues to fall until it reaches 14, at which time only bidder 1 is active. At that point, the contract is awarded to bidder 1 at a price of 15, which is the lowest bid for which there was more than one active bidder. The winning bid equals the second-lowest cost among the bidders.

A more common format for procurement auctions is the first-price sealed-bid auction, which yields, on average, the same result: the winning bid equals the second-lowest cost among the bidders. With this auction format, bidders simultaneously submit written bids, the contract is awarded to the bidder with the lowest bid, and that bidder receives a price equal to its bid. In such an auction, a bidder will submit a bid above its cost in order to leave some room to make money if it wins. In deciding how high to set that markup, it trades off a lower probability of winning against a higher profit in the event it wins. Under certain conditions, bidders select a markup such that, on average, the lowest bid equals the second-lowest cost among the bidders.

The critical property to take away from this discussion is that, under competition, the auction will result in the contract being awarded to the upstream supplier with the lowest cost, and the price it will charge the buyer approximately equals the bid with the second-lowest cost among the bidders. This presumes there is no payment made to the intermediary. As discussed previously, the buyer will cover some or all of that payment. Suppose the intermediary is paid by the selected supplier, in which case its all-inclusive cost is the sum of the cost of providing the product or service and the payment to the intermediary. The winning bid is the second-lowest all-inclusive cost, so the buyer will end up paying for the intermediary through a higher winning bid.

Increased competition in the form of more suppliers participating at the procurement auction lowers the price a buyer will pay in two ways. To explain them, let us note that each upstream supplier has a bidding rule that specifies how a bid depends on the supplier's cost; that is, the bidding rule prescribes how much margin to add to cost. Initially, suppose that each upstream supplier does not change its bidding rule in response to there being more suppliers participating at the auction. Because the lowest bid is submitted by the firm with the lowest cost, the lower the lowest cost among all bidders is, the lower the winning bid will be, and the lower the price that the buyer pays will be. By having more bidders, the lowest cost among them is likely to be lower. Thus, holding the bidding rules fixed, having more bidders at the auction will lower the winning bid.

In addition, for many auction formats, such as the first-price sealed-bid auction, the bidding rule will change with the number of bidders. When there are more bidders, a bidder realizes that the probability of winning is lower. As the markup trades off the probability of winning against the margin, a lower probability of winning will induce a bidder to reduce the margin. Thus, for a given cost, each bidder submits a lower bid when it anticipates that more bidders will participate in the auction.

In sum, having more bidders reduces the lowest cost among bidders and also lowers the bid submitted for a given cost. For these reasons, if an intermediary is trying to reduce the price that the buyer has to pay for this product or service, it will want to attract as many upstream suppliers as it can to bid for the buyer's business.

Having described what an intermediary does for a buyer, let us conclude by considering what goes into the buyer's selection of an intermediary. For example, a property owner chooses the real estate broker, and the owner of an object chooses the auction house. Intermediaries compete in terms of the price they charge for their services and the quality of their services. As already noted, a higher commission will mean a higher total price for a buyer, whether the commission is paid by the buyer or the selected supplier. Thus, holding all else the same, a buyer will prefer an intermediary that charges a lower commission or fee for its services. An intermediary's perceived quality in terms of attracting more upstream suppliers, especially those with higher quality and lower cost, is also relevant. Applicable to our ensuing cases, an intermediary that limits who is allowed to bid for a buyer's business will result in less attractive deals for buyers, which will eventually harm the intermediary's reputation and result in fewer buyers using its services.

Having described a market with intermediaries and how competition operates within it, let us turn to what happens when collusion is present. In doing so, we'll generally suppose that the intermediary performs its role using an auction, though much of the discussion pertains to other mechanisms that an intermediary might use.

4.1.2 Collusive Outcome

There are various forms by which collusion can arise in markets with intermediaries. First, the intermediaries themselves could collude. For example, from 1993 to 2000, the two leading fine art auction houses, Christie's and Sotheby's, colluded in raising the commission rates charged to sellers who used their services (Mason 2004). More common is when the bidders at an auction conspire against the auction house and the seller (when the auction is selling an object) or buyer (when it is a procurement auction seeking to award a contract) by forming a ring with the purpose of dampening competition among bidders.[4] Finally, collusion can involve both the bidders and the intermediary. A common example is a government procurement auction in which the government employee managing the auction is corrupt and aids the bidders in reducing competition (Lengwiler and Wolfstetter 2006). Collusion in which the intermediary assists the bidders is the form that will draw our interest from here on. More specifically, upstream suppliers (spokes) are bidding to provide a product or service to a buyer, and they coordinate their prices with the assistance of the intermediary (hub).

The collusive outcome in a hub-and-spoke cartel of this type has similarities to a standard bidding ring. An upstream supplier is designated by the cartel to win the auction, and it submits a bid that exceeds the level that it would have otherwise submitted under competition. (Recall that this is a procurement auction, so competition drives bids down and collusion raises them.) Some suppliers might be instructed not to submit a bid, while others are instructed to submit relatively high bids (known as "cover" bids), so the designated winner's bid is the most attractive but not so high that it creates the appearance that they are not trying to win. When there are no discernible differences between the product or service being offered, the contract is awarded to the bidder with the lowest bid, which means that as part of the collusive scheme the designated winner will submit the lowest bid. When quality varies across bidders, the designated winner will instead submit the lowest quality-adjusted bid so again its bid is the most attractive.

The cartel will vary the identity of the designated winner from tender to tender for the purpose of enhancing the cartel's profit and maintaining the cartel's stability. The former objective is best accomplished by always having the designated winner be the supplier with the lowest cost (at least when they all supply similar products or services). However, that could create challenges in satisfying the second objective. If some suppliers fail to win enough contracts, they may not be better off under collusion and thus choose to deviate by bidding below the bid of the designated winner. For collusion to be stable, all upstream suppliers that are part of the cartel must then receive a sufficient share of sales so they are better off under collusion. In both cartel cases that we examine in section 4.2, the intermediary determined which of the suppliers were to submit bids and restricted bidding to members of the cartel. Regarding the determination of the cartel supplier designated to win an auction, that responsibility can fall on the intermediary or the suppliers. In one case, the hub determined the allocation; in the other, the spokes determined it.

As compensation for their participation, the suppliers receive higher prices but may also benefit from higher sales, when they are allocated contracts that would otherwise have been won by suppliers outside the cartel. For our two cases, the intermediary's standard compensation is a commission based on the selling price, which is paid by the supplier awarded the contract. Thus, when collusion raises that selling price, the intermediary benefits from a higher commission. In addition, it can also receive side payments or kickbacks, which is a way for the upstream suppliers to shift some of the collusive profit back to the intermediary in order to incentivize its participation.

To understand the intermediary's participation and conduct, two questions need to be addressed. First, why would the intermediary want to raise suppliers' prices? If the intermediary were a monopolist, it would set the monopoly price for its services (to be paid by either the seller or the buyer) and would be worse off with the higher price that would come from collusion with upstream suppliers.[5] If it is not a monopolist and thereby faces competition from other intermediaries, the intermediary would seem likely to lose clients because it does not deliver as good a deal for buyers.

Supposing for the moment that there is an incentive for the intermediary to raise suppliers' prices, a second question arises: why would the intermediary seek to make more profit by coordinating a rise in upstream suppliers' bids when it could simply raise the price for its service as an intermediary? For the types of contracts in our cases, this second question can be posed in the context of a "cost-plus" contract. For these contracts, the final buyer pays the seller the price for its product or service as determined by their bid at the auction (the "cost") and pays to the intermediary a commission on that cost, either directly or indirectly when the commission is formally paid by the seller (which is the "plus"). Instead of colluding with the upstream suppliers to raise the cost component of the total price—which increases the magnitude of the commission the intermediary receives—the intermediary could raise the plus component (or commission rate), which also increases the magnitude of the commission. Either method would raise the payment received by the intermediary.

The answer to these two questions may lie in the manner in which buyers view the cost and plus components of the total price they pay. When comparing the services of different intermediaries, buyers are likely to assume that the cost component will be at a competitive level for all intermediaries, for that is the apparent purpose of using a mechanism like an auction. It would then seem reasonable for buyers to believe that the cost component is approximately the same across intermediaries, especially if intermediaries solicit bids from the same suppliers. Without knowing what the cost component will be when it is selecting an intermediary, and having no reason to think that the cost component will differ across intermediaries, a buyer is then likely to select the intermediary based on the plus component of the contract. This implies that the plus component would be constrained by competition but the cost component would not and thus be open to manipulation. Hence, collusion that affects the cost component will not cause any loss of business to rival intermediaries, because the higher cost it will generate is not known or anticipated by the buyer. In fact, the intermediary may be able to increase its sales despite a higher total price for the product or service because, in anticipation of making more than competitive profits as an intermediary, it will have an incentive to lower its commission rate (i.e., the plus component) in order to attract more business from rival intermediaries. In addition to the higher price, the resulting rise in sales would be an added benefit to the spoke-suppliers.

Regardless of the underlying reasons for the price rise, buyers will be harmed as a result of the hub-and-spoke cartel. This harm will result from paying higher prices to the colluding suppliers as well as higher payments to the intermediary. The latter may be paid directly in the form of a buyer commission or, when the commissions are paid by the sellers, indirectly passed through to the buyer from the higher prices paid to sellers. If, as described earlier, the colluding intermediary lowers the plus component in order to attract more business, that effect would partly mitigate the harm to the buyer, since the plus component would be lower while the cost component would be higher. However, the buyer will be worse off at the end as long as collusion is profitable for the intermediary and upstream suppliers.

The harm to buyers could be increased further if upstream suppliers that have lower costs or higher quality are not invited to participate in the tender by the intermediary. Under competition, an intermediary will want to be as inclusive as possible in order to find the best deal for a buyer. When there is a constraint on the number of participating bidders in any given tender, an intermediary may rotate the participants in order to continually assess who offers the best deal. In contrast, an intermediary orchestrating collusion will only solicit bids from those upstream suppliers that are part of the cartel, which could mean excluding noncolluding suppliers that otherwise would have offered the best deal. Consequently, the harm to buyers could be even greater than under a standard bid-rigging cartel that lacks a cooperating intermediary.

Assuming there is a collusive arrangement that is mutually beneficial to the intermediary and the upstream suppliers, there is the additional issue of how the arrangement is instigated. It is probably most natural for the intermediary to be the initiator. Generally, it would be risky for a supplier to ask the intermediary that runs an auction to assist it in the formation and operation of a bidding ring designed to circumvent the purpose of that auction. If that supplier receives a cold reception from the intermediary, it may no longer be invited to participate in tenders as well as risk litigation. It would be much safer for a supplier to form a standard bid-rigging cartel without the intermediary's participation. On the other hand, the intermediary brings certain advantages to running the bidding ring that could justify taking that risk. We now turn to discussing those advantages.

As always, the cartel will be looking for ways to facilitate coordination on a collusive allocation and to ensure its implementation by monitoring compliance and punishing when there is evidence of noncompliance. We begin by examining the role of the intermediary in coordinating and then move to discussing monitoring and punishing.

The first task of a bidding ring is to coordinate on allocating tenders. This involves deciding which bidder will be the designated winner, which bidders will submit cover bids (to give the appearance of competition), and which bidders will not participate. With a hub-and-spoke cartel, the intermediary-hub can assist in that task, which could involve bilateral communication between the hub and each bidder or multilateral communication. Regardless of the method of communication, there are at least three advantages to having the hub involved. The first is that the intermediary may have better information than the suppliers, and this may enable the cartel to acquire more of the surplus. For instance, in situations where the intermediary is supposed to work on behalf of the buyer, the buyer may divulge sensitive information to the intermediary, such as their willingness to pay. Once this information is in the hands of the colluding bidders, they are in a better position to set the winning bid to yield maximum profit.

The second advantage is that, as an independent party, the intermediary-hub may be more effective in determining the collusive allocation. Without a hub involved, the allocation would have to be determined by the bidders themselves, and this decision may often fall to the ringleaders of the cartel, with input coming from other colluding firms. In such cases, the ringleaders will have an incentive to allocate more tenders to themselves, which could cause tensions within the cartel. In contrast, when the intermediary-hub determines the collusive allocation, it is less biased, so the allocation it proposes may be more acceptable to the firms, which will serve to stabilize collusion. This issue is especially important in bidding rings, where cartel stability may be enhanced by allocating tenders equally among the suppliers, but such an equal allocation may run contrary to maximizing the cartel's profit. Furthermore, an equal allocation could look suspicious to buyers (especially when there is a recognizable pattern), which might result in the cartel's detection and prosecution. Enhancing profitability and avoiding detection could require an allocation whereby some firms are allocated few tenders over some window of time. For those firms to abide by that allocation, it is important that they perceive the allocation as not being biased in favor of certain firms, which is more likely to be the case if an unbiased intermediary is determining the allocation.

The third advantage of having an intermediary as a hub is that it can assist in implementing the collusive allocation. When nonprice factors matter in the bidding process, the designated winner may not be selected, because the buyer places more weight on them than anticipated by the cartel, and that can destabilize collusion. The intermediary can manage the process with the buyer to increase the likelihood that the designated winner is selected. Another reason the designated winner may not be selected is because non-cartel suppliers undercut the inflated bid of the designated winner. An intermediary can deal with that concern by excluding any unwelcome bids by noncartel members. Even if the procurer cannot exclude unwelcome bids, it may be able to distort the buyer's perception of nonprice differences and thereby ensure that the contract is awarded to the bidder designated by the cartel.

4.1.3 Monitoring

As well as assisting with the coordination and implementation of the collusive outcome, the hub can help monitor the colluding bidders for compliance with that outcome. In some auctions, the details of the winning bids are not made publicly available, in which case nonwinning firms will only observe which firm won the bid. This can pose a monitoring challenge when the winner is not the designated cartel member, for that supplier can claim to have submitted a cover bid and that it was chosen as a result of some nonprice preferences of the buyer. In such a situation, rival bidders will be uncertain whether there has been a deviation, which could undermine stable collusion.[6] When an intermediary is involved with the cartel, there will be no such uncertainty, because the intermediary collects and observes the bids. Consequently, even if such details are not publicly available, the cartel can always discover whether a firm did not submit the appropriate cover bid and sought to acquire the contract that the cartel had allocated to another of its members. In addition, if the hub were able to exclude unwelcome bids coming from noncartel suppliers, it would also be able to do the same for deviations from cartel suppliers. In particular, it could disqualify a deviator from the auction and request new bids from other cartel suppliers or from the deviator. In such a situation, the stability of the collusive agreement would be enhanced because the incentive to cheat would be diminished.

4.1.4 Punishment

Even when the hub is unable to suppress deviating bids, it may be able to disincentivize suppliers from submitting deviating bids by threatening a harsh punishment. In standard bid-rigging cartels, a detected deviation could lead to an episode of competitive bidding. An alternative punishment available to a bidding ring with an intermediary-hub is the exclusion of the deviant supplier from subsequent tenders. This could be implemented by not inviting the supplier to submit bids or, if the intermediary cannot restrict bidders, by suppressing the supplier's bid so it is not seen by the buyer. An advantage of this type of punishment is that it would avoid the need to have a temporary reversion to competitive bidding, which means the intermediary and the compliant suppliers would not forgo collusive profits during the punishment phase. While in principle such an exclusionary punishment is possible for a cartel involving only suppliers, it does require that the noncompliant supplier voluntarily exclude itself from participation for some period. Thus, the noncompliant supplier would have to be incentivized to participate in an exclusionary punishment, such as through the promise of being allocated future tenders. With involvement of the intermediary, exclusion could be forced on them.

4.1.5 Final Remarks

In concluding this section, let us address the rather interesting fact that there are no documented hub-and-spoke cartels whose goal is to raise upstream and downstream prices and for which the hub is a downstream intermediary of the type exemplified by a retailer (i.e., it takes ownership of goods, resells them, and assumes the price risk from buying and selling). We know from chapter 3 that there have been many hub-and-spoke cartels designed to raise prices where an upstream manufacturer acted as the hub (e.g., Hasbro) and downstream retailers (which are intermediaries that buy and sell goods) were spokes (e.g., Argos and Littlewoods). However, we have not found any hub-and-spoke cartels designed to raise prices where it is instead a downstream retailer that is the hub (e.g., Argos) and upstream suppliers are the spokes (e.g., Hasbro and Mattel). While it could be that these hub-and-spoke cartels exist and have not been discovered, we will argue that they do not exist because such hub-and-spoke cartels are not viable.

Recall from section 3.1 that hub-and-spoke collusion can be profitable for both the upstream manufacturer and downstream retailers when retailers have sufficient bargaining power and competition in the retail market is sufficiently intense. Under those two conditions, it is possible to increase upstream and downstream prices in order to raise the profits of both the upstream and downstream firms. When instead retail competition is weak or retailers do not have much bargaining power, such hub-and-spoke collusion is not viable because—having raised downstream firms' prices—the requisite rise in upstream prices to make the upstream supplier better off would make downstream firms worse off (and, similarly, given a rise in upstream prices, the requisite rise in downstream prices to make downstream firms better off would make the upstream supplier worse off).

With that understanding, consider a hub-and-spoke cartel that has upstream firms as spokes and a downstream firm as the hub. The downstream firm raising its price in response to higher upstream prices would find it profitable only if there was insufficient competition in the downstream market; otherwise, the downstream hub's higher price would cause it to lose considerable demand to downstream rivals. But, as just reviewed, if downstream competition is weak, then it is unlikely that both an upstream firm and a downstream firm could benefit from raising upstream and downstream prices. Put another way, hub-and-spoke collusion that raises downstream prices (and also upstream prices) is viable when retailers are aggressively competing and when enough of those retailers participate in the cartel; one retailer is not enough. Thus, downstream retailers can be spokes, but not the hub, in a cartel intended to raise downstream and upstream prices.[7]

In comparison, when the downstream hub is an intermediary that does not buy and sell goods (or, if it does buy and sell, it is compensated by the buyer under a cost-plus contract), it does not suffer from lower demand when it assists upstream suppliers in raising their prices even though downstream prices go up. Because the buyer is not suspecting that the intermediary is orchestrating collusion among upstream suppliers, it expects the intermediary to deliver the same selling price as other intermediaries. Therefore, the intermediary does not lose demand to other intermediaries even though the buyer ends up paying a higher price. Given that the intermediary earns higher commissions or markups from the rise in upstream firms' prices and does not lose demand to other intermediaries, the intermediary finds it profitable to be a hub.[8]

4.2 Cases

Though we have just two cases to offer, they are quite distinct in that one occurs in an insurance market and the other in a market for customized manufactured goods.

4.2.1 Commercial Insurance (US)

The setting is the market for commercial insurance, which pertains to policies covering a variety of commercial property and casualty risks, including fire, workers' compensation, product liability, and professional malpractice.[9] Insurance brokers acted as intermediaries that matched their business clients with commercial insurance companies. The four largest commercial insurance brokers were Marsh, Aon, Willis, and Gallagher, accounting for 55% of US commercial brokerage revenue. By comparison, the segment of commercial insurers was largely unconcentrated.

A broker provided a number of services to its business clients, including "analyzing the client's risk, assessing the type of insurance needed, comparing and interpreting policies [of the commercial insurance companies] and, importantly, providing unbiased, sound and accurate advice regarding the insurance marketplace and the insurers they recommend."[10] The brokers and their clients often formed close and long-lasting relationships, and this provided brokers with some influence and control over the placement of their clients' business.

Despite providing a service for their clients, the broker received payment from the insurer. Historically, such payments took the form of a commission, which was a fixed percentage of the written premium paid by the business client to the insurer. However, over time, brokers began to be paid "contingent commissions," where brokers earned additional bonuses from insurers if they fulfilled certain criteria. Such criteria included, for example, whether insurers retained a certain amount of renewal business or whether the volume of business allocated by the broker to the insurer exceeded some threshold. One study estimated that the additional compensation from these contingent commissions was 1%–2% of premiums, which is on top of the standard commission of around 10%–11% (Cummins and Doherty 2006).

Starting in the latter half of the 1990s, in response to the incentives provided by contingent commissions, each broker formed "strategic partnerships" with specific insurance companies. The brokers would then allocate most of their business clients to this small group of insurers, instead of using "30 or 40 different insurance companies or more"[11] as they previously did.

The legal case began in October 2004 with a public investigation into the effects of contingent commissions. New York State attorney general Eliot Spitzer filed a civil complaint alleging "that Marsh had solicited rigged bids for insurance contracts, and had received improper contingent commission payments in exchange for steering its clients to a select group of insurers."[12] Marsh settled this and a related lawsuit in January 2005 for $850 million. In subsequent lawsuits against other brokers, Aon settled for $190 million and Willis for $50 million in spring 2005.[13]

Shortly after Spitzer's civil complaint against Marsh, private parties began to file federal actions against Marsh and the other insurance brokers. These actions were consolidated into two dockets, referred to as the "Commercial case" and the "Employee Benefit case." Each complaint alleged violations of the Sherman Act and the Racketeer Influenced and Corrupt Organizations (RICO) Act.

Regarding the antitrust claims, the plaintiffs in both cases alleged that a number of the strategic partnerships developed into hub-and-spoke conspiracies, with a broker acting as a hub that coordinated an illegal horizontal agreement among the insurers, which were the spokes. As we will describe in more detail, the claimed agreement involved allocating buyers to insurers, which then charged supracompetitive prices. Of course, a broker that coordinated with its preferred insurers to charge buyers higher prices could lose those buyers to other brokers offering better deals. To avoid such customer poaching, the plaintiffs also alleged that some of the largest brokers participated in a "global conspiracy" that amounted to a "broader, common horizontal anticompetitive agreement,"[14] in which the hubs "expressly or tacitly agreed horizontally among themselves not to disclose their contingent commission agreements and resulting in supra-competitive premiums to rival brokers' customers."[15] They went on to claim that "although each broker . . . knew that the other brokers were using contingent commission arrangements to obtain outsized profits, each 'also knew that exposing another broker's contingent commission arrangements to the other broker's customers would lead to retaliation, thereby threatening the first broker's own contingent commission scheme and supra-competitive profits.'"[16]

The District Court of New Jersey dismissed both the Sherman Act and RICO claims. The Court of Appeals for the Third Circuit affirmed much of the district court's decision, including its dismissal of the "global conspiracy" among the brokers. However, it vacated the judgments in the Commercial case regarding the claimed hub-and-spoke cartel involving Marsh on the basis that "the complaint contains enough well-pled factual matter to suggest a plausible horizontal agreement among the insurers not to compete for renewal business."[17] The private actions concluded in August 2013, by which time all the defendants in the Marsh-centric conspiracy had settled out of court. As some indication of the strength of the plaintiffs' case, Marsh and several insurers (including AIG, Hartford, Fireman's Fund, Travelers, and Zurich) agreed to pay damages exceeding $270 million.[18]

In what follows, we focus on the alleged conspiracy led by Marsh, which operated from at least January 1, 1998, through December 31, 2004. This conspiracy included insurance broker Marsh and 13 commercial insurers, which were Marsh's "strategic partners" (also referred to as "preferred insurers"): AIG, ACE, CNA, Chubb, Crum & Forster, Hartford, Liberty Mutual, Travelers, Zurich, Fireman's Fund, Munich, XL, and Axis. Given that the conspiracy was never proved in court, we are reliant on the information provided within the plaintiff's complaint and the circuit court's judgment that the alleged conspiracy surpassed the *Twombly* standard that it is "plausible" that there was a violation of Section 1 of the Sherman Act.[19]

The main aim of the conspiracy, according to Marsh's managing director Kathryn Winter, was "to maximize Marsh's profits by controlling the market, and [by] protecting incumbent insurance carriers when their business was up for renewal."[20] The insurers' incumbent business was protected from competition coming "both from insurers inside and outside of the arrangement,"[21] which thereby allowed the incumbent insurer to raise its premiums for renewals. Thus, the benefit to the insurers was that the agreement led to "stabilization of market share and reduced pressure on the Insurers to compete based upon price."[22] Marsh used a variety of devices to protect incumbent insurers' renewal business, "including the solicitation of false bids"[23] from nonincumbent insurers. The insurers were willing to supply losing quotes because it was agreed that they would be protected from competition when their own business was up for renewal.[24]

In return for organizing—in the words of a Munich employee—this "incumbent protection racket,"[25] Marsh extracted its share of the profits by having their payments from insurers be in the form of a certain type of contingent commission, known as placement service agreements (PSAs). Such commissions were "based primarily on the volume of the business steered to the carriers."[26] If an insurer did not have a PSA with Marsh, then Marsh would stop steering business to the insurer and would not protect the insurer from competition.[27] For example, "When Liberty Mutual 'lost a renewal account after matching terms/conditions requested by the broker,' it questioned Marsh as to why, to which Marsh responded, 'no PSA.' Liberty was so unhappy with its 'dismal' 2002 results that it agreed to a PSA with Marsh for 2003. As soon as Liberty confirmed its intention to proceed with a 2003 PSA, Marsh made clear that Liberty Mutual was again a market Marsh would use."[28]

Marsh's role in coordinating the collusive arrangement involved rigging the bids of the insurers, whereby the incumbent firm would submit a collusive bid and some of the other conspiring insurers would be requested "to 'artificially' provide 'quotes . . . that were non-competitive.'"[29] The purpose of these cover bids was to mislead business clients into believing that they were renewing their insurance coverage at competitive rates, and they were "designed to make the incumbent's quote look attractive."[30] The cartel members often referred to the winning collusive bids as "A quotes" and the higher protective bids as "B quotes." The latter were also sometimes referred to as "backup quotes" and "bullshit quotes."

The terms of the collusive agreement were decided by Marsh's global broking coordinators (GBCs), who "held senior level, leadership roles within [Marsh] Global Broking and were responsible for groups of regional offices."[31] In particular, the GBCs were responsible for developing the "broking plan," which "assigned the business to a specific insurer at a target price and outlined the coverage" and "also included instructions as to which preferred Insurers would be asked to provide alternative [B] quotes."[32] If the incumbent insurer met the target price and had a PSA with Marsh, then it would be allocated the business.

It was left to the local broking coordinators (LBCs), who dealt directly with Marsh's strategic partners, to solicit B quotes from other members of the cartel.[33] When doing so, the LBCs would share detailed information with their conspiring insurers regarding upcoming renewals: "For example, on June 16, 2003, Greg Doherty, Marsh's LBC for ACE, sent an email to underwriters at Liberty Mutual and ACE, among others, attaching a chart entitled 'Doherty Account Assignments.' The chart included information concerning the accounts where ACE or Liberty Mutual will provide alternative [B] quotes. The chart also included the terms of the incumbent Insurer's lead [A] quote."[34] Furthermore, on at least two occasions in 2001 and 2002, Marsh requested quotes from CNA that were "reasonably competitive, but will not be a winner" and provided CNA with the quotes of ACE and Zurich.[35]

On other occasions, instead of requesting that nonincumbent insurers provide cover quotes, Marsh required that they decline to submit bids. For example, Marsh's senior vice president Joshua Bewlay emailed Kathy Drake, Marsh's LBC team leader for Chubb, stating: "Need Chubb to say no thank you on a lead basis and excess basis." Chubb declined a few hours later, and the client ended up purchasing from AIG. In return, Chubb won the renewal in the Basic American account after Marsh asked Liberty Mutual and Zurich to provide B quotes. Additionally, Chubb was rewarded with a protective quote from XL, which gave the appearance that Chubb's "pricing is comparable to the market."[36]

In addition to orchestrating the bid rigging, Marsh also shared other information with its preferred insurers: "Marsh told its preferred insurers who the other conspiring insurers were; details of the contingent commission arrangements that the other insurers had with Marsh; the amount of contingent commissions paid by other insurers; and the amount of premium volume delivered or expected to be delivered to other partner insurers."[37]

If a nonincumbent insurer did not comply with the broking plan and instead provided a competitive quote, Marsh was willing to retaliate. For example, the executive marketing director at Marsh's Global Broking Excess Casualty, Bill Gilman, stated, "If an alternative [i.e., a nonincumbent insurer from which Marsh has solicited a sham bid] quotes below [the incumbent insurer's target bid] then they have made a conscious decision to quote below [the incumbent insurer] and pull [the incumbent] down. If that happens, then , . . . we will put this guy in open competition on every acct. and CRUCIFY him. Further, we must make sure [the] incumbent [or another insurer] keep[s] this [account] and NOT give it to the alternative and reward them."[38]

Such a response from Marsh would provide little incentive for insurers to deviate from the broking plan for two reasons. First, it is uncertain whether a deviation would actually increase the deviant's profits even in the short term, because the deviation would be immediately observed by Marsh, which could then steer the business away from the noncompliant company to a different insurer. Second, as is standard for cartels, a deviation would subsequently trigger a punishment for the deviant, which would lower the insurer's profits in the future.

Despite these threats of punishment, there was evidence that insurers considered reverting to competitive behavior when Marsh was thought not to have provided the promised protection. For example, an email from an employee at Zurich stated:

> We need and expect to be protected on our renewals just like AIG is protected on theirs. . . . The only solution I see if we can not get protection against the AWAC's and ACE's of the world who have not been there for MMGB [Marsh] in the past when [they] needed favors, is to go after AIG leads which we are very prepared to do. If we can not get proper protection, we will go hard after AIG leads that we feel you are protecting. We will no longer provide you with protective quotes for AIG but will put out quotes that you will be forced to release, just like you tell me you are forced to release AWAC and ACE quotes. I do not think we are ask-ing for the moon. We just want the same protection given to AIG and MMGB is definitely not doing that for Zurich now.[39]

In assessing the effect of the cartel, the plaintiffs claimed that it "effec-tively reduced or eliminated competition for the bulk of Marsh's business"[40] and consequently it caused both Marsh's revenue from contingent commis-sions and its strategic partners' gross written premiums (from Marsh) to "sky-rocket."[41] Of course, these are unsubstantiated claims, and the precise claimed effect on Marsh's revenue is redacted from the complaint. However, regard-ing the increase in written premiums for insurers, Liberty Mutual's business with Marsh grew "by 73% from 2000 to 2002," which led an employee of Liberty Mutual to comment that "paying $1.45 million in contingent com-missions . . . was a 'small price for $80M in additional revenue!'"[42] ACE's gross written premiums with Marsh "grew from $3.95 million in the first half of 2002 to over $34 million in the same period in 2003."[43] Crum & Forster's gross written premiums with Marsh "more than quadrupled from 2000 to 2004, from $35 million to over $170 million."[44] Fireman's Fund's gross written premiums grew from $142,000 in 1997 to $2.6 million in 2001.[45]

If this rise in revenues is indeed attributable to the cartel, there are two possible sources. First, there would be the diversion of business from other insurers to strategic partners who participated in the cartel. That would surely be the dominant source of any significant rise in an insurer's revenue. Second, there would be the rise in insurance rates. Rates would be higher because of reduced competition but also the higher expenses associated with the increased commissions being paid to Marsh, which, according to one study, would be almost entirely passed through to the premiums paid by buyers (Cummins and Doherty 2006). This second source caused the primary harm to consumers.

In sum, the novelty of this hub-and-spoke conspiracy is that collusion among the spoke-insurers was facilitated by the intermediary Marsh, whose role in a competitive market would be to bring together the two sides of the market. Despite having close and long-lasting relationships with its clients, Marsh received payment from insurers, which incentivized it to facilitate collusion among the insurers at the expense of its clients.

4.2.2 Specialty Pipe (US)

Collusion in this case has the vertical dimension indicative of a hub-and-spoke cartel but with communications between competitors that are more in line with those of a standard cartel. As we will describe, this intermediate format for organizing a cartel exemplifies the richness of the arrangements that firms have deployed to suppress competition.[46]

The setting for this case is the US specialty pipe market in the early 1980s. Specialty steel or alloy pipe is used in oil refineries and power plants to transport materials that are corrosive or of extreme temperature. The end users of specialty pipe often need the pipes assembled, welded, and bent, and this work was commonly performed by a pipe fabricator. One of the largest pipe fabricators in the US at that time was Texas Pipe Bending Company (TPB). During the early 1980s, TPB was supplied by five to seven distributors of specialty pipe.

Typically, the contract between an end user and the fabricator required that the fabricator purchase the pipe on a "cost-plus" basis, where the end user paid "the fabricator the invoice price of the pipe ('cost'), plus a specific percentage of that price as the fabricator's mark-up ('plus')."[47] Such contracts were used when the precise quantities of pipe were unknown at the time of contract. A condition of such contracts was that fabricators must solicit bids from three or more distributors in order to assure the end user that the materials were bought at a competitive price. Fabricators sometimes carried their own specialty pipe inventory, so a fabricator could also submit a bid to supply the pipe.

In connection with our discussion in section 4.1, it is important to emphasize two features of this setting. First, while TPB provided fabrication services to the end user, our focus is exclusively on its role as a procurer of specialty pipe that was to be used as an input in providing that service. With a cost-plus contract for the purchase of specialty pipe, TPB was an intermediary of the second type when acting as a procuring agent for the end user. Second, the procurement of specialty pipe was conducted *after* TPB had the contract to provide fabrication services.[48] This meant that the price the end user paid for specialty pipe did not influence the demand for TPB's services, since the contract was already in place. In particular, an increase in the upstream price for specialty pipe (i.e., the price charged by a supplier of specialty pipe) would not reduce the demand for the downstream firm's services even though the downstream price (i.e., the cost-plus paid by the end user) was higher. Thus, if TPB assisted upstream suppliers in raising the prices they charged for specialty pipe, TPB would not be harmed through reduced demand for its services by end users. Furthermore, if some of the increase in profit realized by upstream suppliers from a coordinated increase in their prices was shared with TPB, then there would be a mutual basis for engaging in such collusion.

The conspiracy was described by the DOJ as a "classic bid rigging agreement among competing distributors."[49] Starting before 1981 and continuing into 1984, its aim was "to eliminate competition on bids to TPB on jobs in which TPB was purchasing pipe for its customers on a 'cost-plus' basis."[50] The distributors whose bids were rigged were All Star, Capitol, Guyon Alloys, Mannesmann International Alloys (MIA), Midco, and U.S. Metals.[51] Consistent with a hub-and-spoke cartel, "TPB and its head purchasing agent, Carlton Bartula, aided and abetted this conspiracy."[52] Thus, this was not actually a classic bid-rigging case at all, because "the usual 'victim' of the bid rigging . . . initiated, participated in, and directed the pricing arrangements."[53]

In addition to TPB's Carlton Bartula, other prominent individuals involved in the conspiracy included Richard Brazzale, who was vice president of sales at MIA, and Ronald Palma, who worked for Capitol during 1981–1982 (as executive vice president), then as an independent contractor for MIA in 1983, and finally for All Star during 1983–1984 (as vice president and sales director).

The objective of the conspiracy was to increase TPB's prices to end users by raising the cost component of the cost-plus contracts through bid rigging. The higher revenue collected would be distributed among TPB and the specialty pipe distributors involved in the cartel. In the usual manner associated with a bid-rigging scheme, all distributors would be instructed to raise their bids, with those designated to win the contract submitting the lowest bids. To share the rents with TPB, they added "five to 15 percent onto their bids and later rebated that money to TPB in the form of a 'credit memo' or check."[54] Such transfers were referred to as TPB's "volume discount program" by the cartel members. TPB also profited from the fabricator's markup being applied to a higher cost basis. Finally, TPB benefited on at least one occasion, when it used the materials in its inventory to "bid along with the distributors, and . . . bidding for these materials [was] rigged so that TPB would win."[55] The DOJ claimed that this bid-rigging scheme "resulted in prices that were generally 20 percent, and as much as 75 percent, higher than competitive prices."[56]

The manner in which the firms coordinated on the collusive outcomes differed from that of the canonical hub-and-spoke cartel, which has the hub take the lead in coordinating the spokes. In this case, the task was allocated by the hub to one of the spokes. When TPB was awarded a fabrication job on a cost-plus basis, "Carlton Bartula would decide which of the distributors who were part of the bid rigging conspiracy should submit bids."[57] Then "Bartula or another TPB employee would then ask Palma to 'quarterback' the job—that is, to act as a go-between among the distributors and TPB by discussing the prospective bids, allocating various material among the bidders, and working with the bidders to decide the prices each would submit to TPB."[58] Either Bartula or Palma would then call "to inform them that (1) they would be receiving a request for a quotation on a cost-plus job, (2) Palma would quarterback the job, and (3) the job was to be handled on a 'code 5', '10', or '15' basis—meaning that the job was to be rigged and TPB would receive either a five, ten, or fifteen percent kickback."[59]

Palma's main role as "quarterback" was to organize how the bids would be rigged, usually by participating in a number of bilateral discussions with the distributors: "As quarterback, Palma would discuss the bidders' preferences and agree on an allocation among them of the materials needed. The bidders who were designated winners would then determine their prices. . . . Palma would then pass these inflated prices onto the other bidders who would protect them by bidding higher. Work was usually awarded according to the allocation agreed upon by the distributors."[60]

In sum, there were bilateral communications between the downstream hub (Bartula of TPB) and one of the upstream spokes (Palma of Capital, MIA, or All Star, depending on the year), and that same upstream spoke would then engage in bilateral (and sometimes multilateral) communications with the other spokes. The hub's Bartula would decide on and convey the market allocation for a contract to Palma, Palma would coordinate with the other distributors to agree on bids, and then Palma would relay this information back to Bartula.

Although Palma was the one more involved in the operation of the cartel, the role of Bartula should not be understated. While there is little detail in the court documents regarding Bartula's role, other than that described here, they do state that Bartula "commanded"[61] the operation. Furthermore, according to Midco, "the orders came from the top down through Palma"[62] and "if Palma played the role of 'quarterback,' Bartula called the plays as coach."[63] Midco also claimed that omitting Bartula's role from the conspiracy's story would be "akin to telling the story of the Persian Gulf exercise without mentioning General Schwartzkopf."[64] Consistent with the claim that Bartula had a critical role, he received the most severe penalty by the court.

While the distributors generally did their bid-rigging negotiations, allocations, and price determinations through Palma, on occasion some of them would engage in face-to-face meetings. For example, in autumn 1981, Palma (who was then working for Capitol) and Brazzale of MIA met with James Dooner of Guyon in Dooner's office. The purpose of the meeting was "to decide how to allocate the materials for an unusually large American Natural Gas (ANG)/Lummus Engineering coal gasification project that TPB had been awarded. . . . They agreed that MIA would get the seamless grade 3 items, and Guyon and Capitol would split the remaining items. After a few more discussions by telephone, they decided that a more balanced allocation would allow Guyon and Capitol to furnish some of the grade 3 pipe as well. They then submitted quotes pursuant to that agreement and were awarded contracts based on that allocation."[65]

Though there were some expressions of disappointment over allocations of TPB contracts, there is no documented evidence of deviations or breakdowns in the agreement: "Steve Scott of US Metals complained directly to Jim Dooner [of Guyon] and Richard Brazzale [of MIA] that Palma was not allocating the TPB jobs evenly. But, while the others commiserated, no action was taken."[66]

That disappointment did not translate into deviation is unsurprising for two reasons. First, any such deviation would have been immediately observed by TPB. Thus, if a distributor sought to pick up unallocated business by submitting a low bid, TPB would have been able to deny supply by requesting a new set of bids from them or a different distributor. Second, if an upstream distributor did not do as directed, TPB could have reduced the amount of sales allocated to that distributor in the future. For example, Lorne Van Stone, a former executive vice president of MIA, testified that "Brazzale told him that MIA had to work with Ron Palma to set price levels if it wanted TPB's business."[67]

One explanation for the uneven allocation was that it was a deliberate effort to maintain the appearance of competitive bidding. As stated in the testimony of James Dooner of Guyon: "The percentage [sales of a rigged bid to each bidder] varied because being an equal percentage would look as if it was pre-done."[68] This deception also extended to the distributors that had not been selected as a winning bidder: "Even on contracts for items they knew they would not be getting because they were protecting the prices of other bidders, the distributors would 'develop' their prices by calling manufacturers to give them the impression that distributors were preparing competitive bids."[69]

In January 1988, a grand jury sitting in the Southern District of Texas formally charged six of the firms (TPB, All Star, Capitol, Midco, MIA, and U.S. Metals) and three individuals (Bartula, Palma, and Brazzale) with violating Section 1 of the Sherman Act. TPB, Capitol, and U.S. Metals entered into plea agreements. In April 1989, the charges against Capitol and U.S. Metals were dropped, and TPB was fined $1,000,000 following a guilty plea. The other defendants went to trial and were convicted in March 1990. The court fined each of the corporate defendants $250,000 and ordered them to make restitution of $859,935. Bartula was sentenced to three years imprisonment, with all but six months suspended. Palma and Brazzale were each sentenced to 300 hours of community service.[70]

Following the trial, MIA, Midco, and Brazzale appealed their convictions, arguing, among other things, that the court should not have applied the per se rule because the case was not a purely horizontal conspiracy. The government's position was that "horizontal price fixing conspiracy does not lose its *per se* illegal character simply because a noncompeting party on another distribution level joins the conspiracy."[71] In May 1992, the US Court of Appeals for the Fifth Circuit affirmed the convictions and restitution orders, stating, "We find that defendants cannot escape the *per se* rule simply because their conspiracy depended upon the participation of a 'middle-man', even if that middleman conceptualized the conspiracy, orchestrated it by bringing the distributors together around contracts it held with its buyers, and collected most of the booty."[72]

In conclusion, one can view the specialty pipe cartel as a standard supplier cartel modified by the participation of the downstream purchaser, which has a tolling contract with the end user. The gains from collusion were shared with that downstream purchaser through direct payments, as well as having a fixed markup to the end user applied to an inflated cost basis. Alternatively, one can view the cartel as a variant of a standard hub-and-spoke cartel in which the downstream hub and upstream spokes jointly ran operations, with extensive direct communications among the upstream spokes. Viewed from either perspective, the specialty pipe cartel adds to the rich set of collusive arrangements involving vertical relations.

4.3 General Lessons

Section 4.2 reviewed two cartels similar in structure and objective. Both had the feature that the hub acted like a broker that intermediated between suppliers and buyers. The main role of the intermediary was to solicit bids from the suppliers for the buyers. We now discuss some differences and similarities between the cartels.

4.3.1 Description of the Collusive Outcome
In both cases, instead of using the procurement process to promote competition among the suppliers, the intermediary-hub coordinated a bid-rigging scam for the supplier-spokes and allocated business among them. In the commercial insurance market (hereafter Insurance-US), the objective was

to raise the premiums of commercial insurance that intermediary Marsh procured for its clients. This was to be achieved by protecting the incumbent business of insurers. In the specialty pipe market (hereafter Pipes-US), the aim was to raise the cost of pipes that intermediary Texas Pipe Bending Company (TPB) would acquire from the suppliers on behalf of end users.

For the supplier-spokes, the main benefit of collusion was that they were able to charge higher prices. The intermediary-hub benefited in two ways. First, it received a payment that was proportional to the prices paid by their customers, so supracompetitive prices for the suppliers automatically implied higher payments to the hub. Second, the suppliers provided additional payments to the hubs through bonuses or kickbacks. Specifically, in Insurance-US, intermediary Marsh received commissions from the suppliers on the premiums paid by their clients, and Marsh was also paid bonuses from the suppliers related to how much business it allocated to them. In Pipes-US, the end user paid TPB a percentage markup over the costs TPB incurred in acquiring pipe from the supplier-spokes, and the suppliers paid TPB further kickbacks of 5%–15% of their revenue from the project.

Hub-and-spoke collusion may also have resulted in higher sales. In Insurance-US, the supplier-spokes' sales increased because the intermediary-hub allocated sales to them that would otherwise have been allocated to suppliers not part of the cartel. In both cases, there is also the possibility that the intermediary-hub could have attracted more buyers (and thereby more sales for the suppliers) despite final buyers receiving higher prices. To see how this could occur, first note that the intermediary-hub would not lose business to rival intermediaries from the higher prices it delivered for its clients because it secured their business *before* the suppliers' prices were revealed to them. As long as buyers assumed that the suppliers' prices were at competitive levels regardless of the intermediary used, the intermediary-hub could find it profitable to offer a lower commission rate than rival intermediaries in order to attract more business. That would be profitable because it would anticipate receiving higher profits via its share of the collusive increase in a supplier's price. Thus, hub-and-spoke collusion might have resulted in higher prices *and* higher sales!

4.3.2 Communication to Achieve Mutual Understanding

There was little documented evidence of communication related to how the collusive schemes were instigated, but there was a stark difference in how the firms communicated to reach agreement on the collusive outcomes;

that is, communication related to which supplier would win a bid and at what price, and which firms would submit cover bids.

In Insurance-US, the terms of the designated winner's bid were determined by senior-level management in the intermediary Marsh, and it was left to other staff at Marsh to inform the suppliers. This could involve bilateral communications between Marsh and the insurers, but it sometimes took the form of multilateral communications, such as emailing the details of the terms to the winning insurer and copying other insurers, who would be submitting cover bids.

In Pipes-US, the intermediary TPB decided which suppliers would be involved in the procurement process, but the specific details regarding who would win and at what price were left to the suppliers to determine. To facilitate coordination between them, the hub appointed an employee of the supplier-spokes (who worked for a number of them at different times during the cartel period) to act as the ringleader. In that role, he sought information from and disseminated information to other suppliers, as well as acting as a go-between for the hub and spokes.

In speculating on the reasons for the different approaches to determining the collusive allocation, note that the task of allocating specific contracts was easier in Insurance-US than in Pipes-US. In the former, the collusive arrangement was to protect incumbent business, so there was no controversy over the identity of the designated winner. All that had to be decided were the terms of the insurance provided by the incumbent supplier and which suppliers would protect that incumbent. In Pipes-US, the cartel had to decide how to allocate new business among the supplier-spokes (which was often spread across more than one supplier) as well as agree on the winning terms. Further complications arose because the suppliers would probably have had better information than the intermediary regarding how to maximize the cartel's profit. For instance, the suppliers would supply pipes from their inventories and naturally have better knowledge of those inventories, and they operated in a market where the wholesale price of pipes was volatile, about which they would be better informed. Consequently, the supplier-spokes were likely to have better information than the intermediary-hub regarding which of them was best able to fulfill the contract at the lowest cost. This difference in information could explain why the spokes were more heavily involved in deciding on the allocation of contracts in Pipes-US.

4.3.3 Hub Discouraged Deviations

It is generally the case that colluding firms will be tempted to deviate from the collusive agreement. Through organizing the procurement process, the intermediary-hub was able to ensure that any such deviation would be detected immediately, and it was in a position to punish the deviators. In Insurance-US, intermediary Marsh, upon observing a lower than expected bid, would try to prevent a deviator from winning the business, though it was not always able to do so. This inevitably caused tensions within the cartel, and other insurers threatened to retaliate by competing for rivals' incumbent business. In order to disincentivize such departures from the collusive allocation, Marsh threatened to put deviators in open competition when their business was up for renewal.

In Pipes-US, there was no documented evidence of deviations from the collusive arrangement. This may have been because the intermediary TPB was able to prevent a deviator from winning the project, as it was able to replace a deviant quote with a different cover bid before presenting the quote to the buyer. Alternatively, the suppliers may have understood that if they did not do as directed, TPB could reduce the amount of sales that were allocated to them in the future.

5 Collusion to Exclude Rival Firms

This chapter examines hub-and-spoke cartels when the hub is located downstream and coordinates upstream spokes to exclude a rival to the hub in the downstream market. There are two main avenues by which such exclusion could take place. First, there is naked exclusion, whereby upstream manufacturers cease to supply a downstream retailer to foreclose it from the downstream market. Second, exclusion can be partial in that the upstream spokes still supply the hub's downstream rivals but limit their ability to compete. This may be achieved by raising the wholesale price that a downstream rival pays, preventing it from pricing below other downstream firms (e.g., through minimum resale price maintenance), or reducing the quality of their offerings.

We have identified four cases involving a hub-and-spoke cartel for which the purpose was to exclude downstream firms. One case involved naked exclusion and the other cases partial exclusion. Section 5.1 provides an economic framework that will be useful for analyzing the four hub-and-spoke cartels examined in section 5.2. Section 5.3 distills some general lessons from those cases. To provide additional evidence of the ways in which vertical cartels are able to monitor for compliance and punish deviations, section 5.4 discusses a cartel among vertically related firms. This cartel has the same exclusionary objective as the hub-and-spoke cartels of this chapter but differs from the other cartels in our sample in that there was widespread multilateral communication among the spokes. The case serves to underscore some of the benefits from having an upstream supplier as a hub. Section 5.5 provides a technical appendix that delivers a formal analysis underlying some of the discussion in section 5.1.

5.1 Economic Framework

This section develops some economic insight relevant for analyzing cases of hub-and-spoke cartels with exclusionary intent. It identifies possible reasons for a downstream firm and upstream suppliers to coordinate in order to exclude rival downstream firms, examines some relevant factors affecting the profitability of such exclusion, and presents the challenges associated with forming and executing a collusive plan.

5.1.1 Competitive Benchmark

To keep things as simple as possible, much of our discussion will focus on a market with the following structure. Suppose there are two upstream suppliers (e.g., manufacturers) who offer possibly differentiated products; supplier 1 supplies product 1 and supplier 2 supplies product 2. There are two downstream firms (e.g., retailers), which we'll refer to as retailers A and B. Retailers may also be differentiated, and, absent exclusion, each carries both suppliers' products. Suppliers compete in terms of the wholesale prices they charge retailers for their products. Retailers choose the markup on those wholesale prices and compete in terms of the retail prices they charge final customers.

As reviewed in section 3.1, this vertical structure can generate an inefficiency from double marginalization. The supplier's wholesale price includes a markup on its cost and, as that wholesale price enters into the retailer's cost and the retailer's price includes a markup on its cost, the supplier's cost is marked up twice. Double marginalization can lead to inefficiently high retail prices, though competition can counteract this effect by compressing margins. Interbrand competition between suppliers 1 and 2 will reduce wholesale margins on products 1 and 2, and intrabrand competition between retailers A and B will reduce retail margins on those products.

Under competition, it is typically unprofitable for a supplier to nakedly exclude a retailer, because it cuts off a source of demand for a supplier. If a supplier wanted to affect retailers' prices for its product, it would generally do better by raising its wholesale prices rather than denying supply to a retailer. Thus, the competitive scenario is presumed to have suppliers 1 and 2 supplying their products to both retailers A and B.

5.1.2 Collusive Outcome

In the midst of that competition, let us consider hub-and-spoke collusion between retailer A and upstream suppliers 1 and 2 whereby those suppliers deny supply of their products to retailer B. By virtue of this naked exclusion, retailer A now has a monopoly, and this will benefit it for two reasons. First, as long as there is some substitutability across retailers, some of the consumers who previously bought from retailer B will now buy from retailer A. Thus, holding wholesale and retail prices fixed, retailer A's profit is higher because of greater demand. Second, the increase in its market power will induce retailer A to raise its prices. While this results in a reduction in demand, it is more than compensated by the increase in margins (which is the usual implication of moving from competitive prices toward monopoly prices) such that retailer A's profits increase further.[1] Turning to the impact on upstream suppliers, if wholesale prices are unchanged, then the exclusion of a retailer unambiguously harms them. Unless retailers A and B are perfect substitutes, there is some market demand lost from eliminating the preferred retailer for some consumers. That translates into lower sales and profits for upstream suppliers. When retailer A exercises its enhanced market power by raising its markup on wholesale prices, that will further reduce suppliers' sales and profits. Thus, holding upstream suppliers' prices fixed, the coordinated exclusion of a downstream firm by upstream suppliers will increase the profits of the nonexcluded downstream firm but decrease the profits of the upstream firms.

A downstream firm and upstream suppliers would jointly be interested in forming a cartel to exclude another downstream firm when doing so raises each of those firms' profits. The preceding discussion then leads us to ask two questions. First, can the rise in profits for the downstream hub exceed the decline in profits for the upstream spokes? If that is not the case, then collusion cannot benefit all members of the cartel. If the answer to the question is "yes," the next question is: what arrangement allows some of the higher profits received by the downstream hub to be transferred to the upstream spokes? Of course, a straight side payment would work, but that is not always implementable without creating suspicions about collusion. As we explain next, there are conditions under which coordinated exclusion of a downstream firm can raise aggregate profits of the hub and spokes and, by appropriately adjusting wholesale prices, increase the hub's profits and the profits earned by each of the spokes.

To see that there are conditions under which all firms benefit, consider the extreme case in which products are identical (or nearly identical) and retailers are identical (or nearly identical). This structure will lead to intense interbrand competition, which results in wholesale prices close to the marginal cost of the suppliers, and to intense intrabrand competition, so that retail markups are close to zero (i.e., retail prices approximately equal wholesale prices plus any additional marginal cost). All firms are then earning profits near zero. Now consider when suppliers 1 and 2 exclude retailer B so that retailer A is a monopolist in the retail market. At the initial wholesale prices, retailer A will set the monopoly price and earn higher profits. Furthermore, if the retailer pays slightly higher wholesale prices to the upstream suppliers, it will still earn higher profits, and the upstream suppliers will now make positive, and thus higher, profits. Retailers are highly substitutable, so there is little market demand loss from consumers no longer being able to buy products 1 and 2 from retailer B. While there is a reduction in demand from higher retail prices, that is more than compensated by the increase in margins. In sum, when intrabrand and interbrand competition are sufficiently intense, hub-and-spoke collusion can raise the profits of the downstream hub and the upstream spokes by enhancing market power in the downstream market. The spokes benefit through higher wholesale prices, and the hub benefits through a higher markup on those wholesale prices.

Thus far, we've shown that exclusion can be profitable for all members of the hub-and-spoke cartel when products and retailers are highly substitutable so both intrabrand and interbrand competition are severe. Let us now consider allowing for some differentiation in products and retailers. It will be argued that this reduces the additional profits to be earned by exclusion, though it remains profitable as long as differentiation is not too great.

To begin, consider the case where suppliers' products remain highly substitutable but retailers are now differentiated. Prior to collusion, retailers will then have substantive markups, which reflect, for example, different features of their stores or different locations, which gives them market power over consumers. Given that retailers are already pricing above wholesale prices, there will be a smaller incremental gain in retail markups experienced by the downstream hub that now has its rival excluded. In other words, the rise in market power from exclusion is less, which then makes the rise in markups and profits to the downstream hub smaller. In addition, there will be a reduction in market demand because some consumers prefer to buy from retailer B, perhaps because of a shorter travel distance. While some of those consumers will shift their demand to retailer A, some will choose not to buy at all. The demand loss lowers profits for the cartel. Both these effects would appear to make hub-and-spoke collusion less attractive when differentiation of retailers is increased.

Now suppose suppliers' products are differentiated and retailers are highly substitutable. Thus, there is market power upstream, which means wholesale prices exceed cost, but not downstream, so retail markups are slim. The market demand loss from excluding retailer B that arises in the previous case is absent here because retailer A is an excellent substitute for retailer B. The factor that may make collusion less attractive is double marginalization. Recall that double marginalization can reduce total vertical chain profits because a markup is imposed both upstream (on the inputs sold to the downstream firms) and downstream (on the product sold to final consumers). This sequence of markups can lead to an excessive final price from the joint perspective of upstream and downstream firms. Under competition, market power is exclusively upstream, so there is no double-marginalization problem because only the upstream firms are adding a markup. However, exclusion creates market power downstream, so the hub-and-spoke cartel will create a retail markup on top of the preexisting wholesale markup. With market power both upstream and downstream, if the firms do not take into account the effect of their prices on each other's profits, double marginalization becomes relevant and could reduce the profitability of collusion. Given that upstream suppliers will be worse off from exclusion if they hold their prices fixed—as they experience lower demand without a rise in margins— they must raise their wholesale prices for collusion to be profitable for them, but then double marginalization will be exacerbated if the retailer responds by raising its price. This discussion suggests that hub-and-spoke collusion is less attractive when there is more product differentiation.

The takeaway from the preceding discussion is that allowing for some differentiation between products or between retailers introduces other forces that appear to make hub-and-spoke collusion less profitable. Those takeaways seem intuitive but have not been formally proven. In section 5.4, we look at these forces more formally and consider the effect of simultaneously increasing the differentiation between products and retailers. Thus, the analysis combines the two changes discussed earlier.[2] There we show the existence of a critical threshold of substitutability such that if products and retailers are more substitutable than that threshold, then hub-and-spoke collusion is profitable. More specifically, exclusion of retailer B along with an appropriate increase in the prices of suppliers 1 and 2 and the price of retailer A will increase the profits of each of the three cartel members. However, if products and retailers are more differentiated than that threshold, then while exclusion could raise the profits of the downstream hub, it cannot do so without reducing the upstream suppliers' profits. Though retailer A benefits from the stronger demand coming from excluding retailer B, the requisite rise in wholesale prices to make upstream spokes better off would necessarily end up harming the downstream hub to the point where there would be no retail price it could charge that would make collusion profitable for it. Consistent with the earlier informal discussion, hub-and-spoke collusion designed to exclude a downstream firm will benefit all members if and only if, prior to exclusion, retailers and products are sufficiently substitutable that intrabrand and interbrand competition are sufficiently intense.

The preceding analysis has focused on when hub-and-spoke collusion can raise the profits of all cartel members compared to competition. That is a sufficient condition for them to find it optimal to participate, but it is not necessary. An upstream supplier will participate if its profits from doing so are higher than from not doing so, *given that the other upstream suppliers and downstream hub are participating*. That is, it is an equilibrium for all cartel members to participate. How might an upstream supplier find it optimal to exclude even though it would prefer competition to collusion? Suppose the downstream hub has a fair amount of market power and threatens to refuse to buy an upstream supplier's product if it does not exclude the hub's rival in the downstream market. In that case, it is possible that an upstream supplier's profits from excluding retailer B may exceed its profits from supplying retailer B and being excluded itself by retailer A. That is more likely to be the case when retailer A is more important to the upstream supplier than retailer B. While the upstream suppliers might earn higher profits under competition when they sell to both retailers, each of them might find it optimal to exclude retailer B when the alternative is to lose retailer A as an outlet for its product. As we'll see, this possibility is relevant to two of our cases.

Thus far, the discussion has focused on naked exclusion. Alternatively, a hub-and-spoke cartel could engage in partial exclusion. Partial exclusion can be achieved by having the excluded retailer pay a higher wholesale price—thereby incentivizing them to raise their retail price—or having a higher retail price directly imposed on them. With its rival induced to price higher, the downstream hub benefits. Such a strategy reduces the excluded retailer's sales but does not entirely eliminate them. Compared to naked exclusion, this is likely to be more desirable to upstream spokes— as the demand loss is less than under naked exclusion—and less desirable to the downstream hub, for it still faces competition. When naked exclusion does not benefit all cartel members, perhaps partial exclusion would.

An additional way of partially excluding a retailer is for the cartel to affect the quality of the excluded retailer's offerings. Reducing the quality of a retailer's product has an effect similar to raising its price, because it will encourage consumers to substitute away from the retailer. Upstream suppliers could reduce a downstream firm's quality by providing lower-quality inputs, or there could be restrictions on how the excluded retailer bundles suppliers' products, which arose in one of the cases to be discussed. Adversely affecting the excluded retailer's offerings could be complemented by a rise in the upstream suppliers' prices. While the downstream hub's demand would rise, the upstream spokes' sales would fall. Thus, as discussed earlier, there would need to be a rise in wholesale prices paid by the hub to the spokes if the latter were to realize higher profits under collusion.

In some of the cases, another form of retailer heterogeneity was present: the excluded firms were aggressive discount retailers that set lower prices than the downstream hub. They may have charged lower prices because of lower costs resulting from greater efficiency or offering fewer complementary services (such as the support of salespeople). Alternatively, they may simply have wanted to increase their market share (perhaps investing in future demand by building customer loyalty). Since such rivals reduce retail margins, it is clear why a retailer would be particularly keen to exclude them. In contrast, a supplier's incentives for excluding discounters will depend on how margins from supplying them compare to those from other retailers. If the margins are low compared to those of other retailers, the suppliers' profits may not fall if those discounters are partially or fully excluded. In contrast, if wholesale margins are similar to those earned from other retailers, upstream suppliers clearly benefit from the low retail margins set by discounters—as it is raising demand for the upstream firms' products—which then makes their exclusion less attractive to those suppliers.

Given that the downstream firm is the clear beneficiary of the exclusionary conduct, it is expected to be the one that instigates a collusive scheme. We will later discuss how this is done. Next, we examine how the downstream hub can coordinate the suppliers on a scheme to collectively exclude a retailer. As a supplier may be tempted to deviate from the exclusionary plan, we discuss how compliance can be monitored and punished.

A central challenge for the downstream hub will be to coordinate the collective exclusion of its downstream rivals by the upstream suppliers. Coordinating the suppliers is essential since if a supplier was the only one to exclude a retailer, consumers would just buy the other suppliers' products from this retailer. Thus, each supplier would be unlikely to agree to exclude a retailer unless it could expect its rival suppliers to do so as well. Therefore, the hub's role in coordinating exclusionary conduct encompasses establishing mutual understanding of the collusive agreement, as described in the general analysis of hub-and-spoke collusion in chapter 2. Given that no supplier will want to exclude on its own, a series of independent vertical agreements between each supplier and the downstream firm will be insufficient. Instead, the downstream firm must convey to each upstream supplier that it is entering into these agreements with other suppliers. The hub may also be required to stress to each of the suppliers that the plan will only work if all the suppliers are involved and use one supplier's acceptance of the plan to induce other suppliers to come on board. We will describe many examples of such communications when we turn to examining cases.

5.1.3 Monitoring

While the firms may be able to construct a collusive scheme in which they all do better than under competition, it may be yet more attractive for a supplier to deviate from that scheme. Therefore, next we consider the incentives to abide by the collusive arrangement and how the firms can monitor compliance.

Under naked exclusion, a single supplier that deviates from the exclusionary strategy will be a monopolist over the excluded retailer. Hence, it can set a high wholesale price to the excluded retailer and still receive all its demand. In contrast, under partial exclusion, a deviating supplier would not have a monopoly over the excluded retailer. This will reduce the incentive to deviate, though perhaps not eliminate it entirely. In a similar fashion, the incentive to deviate is lower if there is at least one rival supplier that is not involved in the exclusionary conduct. This is because such suppliers would provide competition for a deviating supplier to the excluded retailer. Consequently, as the number of suppliers outside the excluding group increases, the incentives to deviate will be diminished.

Given that suppliers may be tempted to deviate, it will be important for the firms to monitor compliance. The ease of detecting noncompliance is likely to depend on which form of exclusionary conduct is adopted. Starting with naked exclusion, monitoring should be straightforward when all suppliers are involved. Compliance implies that the excluded firms do not stock the suppliers' goods, so it should be easy to determine whether that is the case. Similarly, if the suppliers' brands are differentiated, it would not be difficult to detect which firm has deviated by taking account of the products available for sale at the targeted retailer. For example, if manufacturers are producing branded toys, observing which toys a retailer has available would provide a clear indication of which supplier has deviated. On the other hand, if the product is a homogeneous good, observing the targeted retailer with the product in stock would only inform the firms that at least one supplier has deviated; it would not be clear which of the suppliers was noncompliant. The hub and spokes will then have a role to play in monitoring to make sure that exclusion is being implemented. Furthermore, given that a supplier will be disadvantaged if rival suppliers do not comply, it has an incentive to monitor its rivals.

When a retailer is partially excluded by suppliers raising wholesale prices, monitoring is more difficult, because such prices are unlikely to be publicly available. Here there may be an enhanced role for suppliers to monitor each other, because their negotiations with downstream firms may reveal information on rivals' prices. In contrast, when a downstream firm is partially excluded by suppliers imposing higher retail prices, monitoring is easier, because these prices are more transparent than wholesale prices. Upstream spokes may, for example, be able to monitor other products' retail prices when they are at the stores making deliveries. Ease of monitoring may then be an advantage of exclusion through the imposition of higher retail prices as opposed to charging higher wholesale prices.

5.1.4 Punishment

If an upstream supplier is found not to be complying with the exclusionary plan, the provision of incentives for compliance requires imposing a punishment. If collusion is more profitable than competition, one obvious punishment is to return to competition for some length of time, which means discontinuing exclusion, with an associated fall in wholesale and retail prices. Alternatively, the downstream hub could seek to maintain exclusion but refuse to buy from the noncompliant supplier. Such a punishment would be necessary when upstream suppliers find that collusion is actually less profitable than competition, as otherwise they would be incentivized to cause cartel breakdown.

The credibility of a punishment in which the downstream hub refuses to buy from an uncooperative upstream spoke depends on whether most or all suppliers comply. If all other suppliers are complying, the hub might be fine with cutting off one supplier in order to establish the credibility of its threat and thereby keep other suppliers compliant moving forward. In contrast, if several suppliers are not complying, it becomes very costly for the hub not to buy from all of them. Thus, a supplier could well believe that the hub would punish it for a deviation only if most or all other suppliers were complying. This demonstrates that achieving mutual understanding among upstream suppliers that they will exclude is integral. They must not only coordinate on a common outcome of exclusion but also establish the credibility of a punishment that incentivizes upstream suppliers to implement that outcome.

5.2 Cases

Our four cases span from the 1930s, with the distribution of films to cinemas, to the 2010s and the market for electronic books.

5.2.1 Movie Exhibition (US)

This case concerns the distribution and exhibition of motion pictures in the mid-1930s.[3] At the time, the market for the exhibition of movies included first-run theaters, where newly released films were shown, and subsequent-run (or second-run) theaters, where those same films appeared at a later date for a lower admission price. Interstate Circuit operated 43 theaters and Texas Consolidated operated 66 theaters, both of which had a mix of first-run and subsequent-run movie houses. The two chains dominated the cities in which they had theaters, including having a monopoly position in many of them.[4]

The problem faced by Interstate was that the subsequent-run theaters not owned by Interstate or Texas Consolidated were aggressively competing.

While the first-run theaters were showing a single film for an admission price of 40 cents, many subsequent-run theaters were charging a significantly lower price and often showing two films: "In seventeen of the eighteen independent [subsequent-run] theatres . . . the admission price was less than 25 cents. . . . In most of them the admission was 15 cents or less. It was also the general practice in those theatres to provide double bills either on certain days of the week or with any feature picture which was weak in drawing power."[5]

This stiff competition was eating into admission sales at Interstate's first-run theaters, so it sought to coordinate the motion picture distributors on a plan to control these independent subsequent-run theaters. Hence, the movie exhibitor was acting as the hub to the movie distributors, who were the spokes. As a departure from the canonical hub-and-spoke cartel, Interstate was 50% owned by one of the distributors, Paramount. While this vertical relationship proved useful for Interstate (as we will describe), it did not alter the fundamental challenges faced by a hub in coordinating spokes.

The collusive plan that Interstate formulated was for distributors to require, as a condition of supplying their product, subsequent-run theaters to charge no less than 25 cents for admission and show only one film. If a distributor did not follow that policy, then Interstate threatened not to show the distributor's films in its first-run theaters. Clearly, this plan would benefit Interstate, as it would raise the price and lower the quality of rival exhibitors. It is less clear that it would benefit distributors. To begin, they would lose the additional demand delivered by those subsequent-run theaters selling tickets at lower prices, which appealed to certain consumers. On the other hand, by raising their prices, more demand would be generated for first-run theaters, which had a higher profit margin. While that is likely to raise total industry profits, it is not immediately clear that the distributors would end up with more profits. That would depend on the relative bargaining positions of the movie exhibitors and the movie distributors, for that determines how this profit gain is allocated among the parties. Even if the distributors were not made better off by this collusive arrangement, that is not necessary for their participation. It is sufficient that it is in the best interest of a movie distributor to participate if it believes that the other distributors will participate and find Interstate's threat of punishment for noncompliance credible. Given that the initial reaction of the distributors was to object to the plan,[6] it is quite likely that they saw it as making them worse off.

In considering a distributor's incentives to go along with the exclusionary plan, it would be unlikely to comply unless it thought that a sufficient number of other distributors were planning to comply, because suppose most distributors did allow subsequent-run theaters to show their films at an admission price less than 25 cents. If a distributor went along with Interstate's scheme and only licensed its films to subsequent-run theaters that charged at least 25 cents, subsequent-run theaters would choose to exhibit the films of other distributors in order to be able to charge a price that was competitive in the market. Hence, a compliant distributor could lose significant demand if the other distributors were noncompliant. Furthermore, the credibility of Interstate's threat of punishment for noncompliance—not showing the distributor's films in its theaters—would be put into question if many distributors did not go along. Interstate may be willing to go through with that threat against a few distributors, but it would be very costly for it to do so with many distributors, as then there would be many films it would not be showing in its theaters. Thus, the credibility of Interstate's punishment depended on a distributor believing many other distributors were intending to comply. In sum, a distributor probably would not comply if most other distributors did not comply, because it would lose significant demand, and Interstate's retaliatory threat would not be credible. However, if all other distributors complied, then a distributor would be at no competitive disadvantage from complying, and Interstate's threatened punishment for noncompliance could have been a credible deterrent to deviating from the collusive outcome.

For Interstate's scheme to work, it must then inform each distributor of its plan *and* have each distributor believe that the other distributors were planning to go along with it. Mr. O'Donnell, the manager of Interstate and Consolidated, began by sending each distributor a letter on April 25, 1934, which included the following passage: "We also want to go on record that we will expect certain clearance next season as regards our first run programs which are presented at a minimum price of 40 cents or more. In these situations, we are going to insist that subsequent run prices be held to a minimum scale of 25 cents."[7]

Taking advantage of its vertical integration with a distributor, Interstate discussed this proposal with Paramount, which led to a new proposal that included barring double features. A second letter was mailed on July 11, 1934, to each of the eight distributors with *all of them named as addressees*. Here are some relevant excerpts from that letter:

Interstate Circuit, Inc. will not agree to purchase product to be exhibited in its "A" theatres at a price of 40¢ or more for night admission, unless distributors agree that in selling their product to subsequent runs, that this "A" product will never be exhibited at any time or in any theatre at a smaller admission price than 25¢ for adults in the evening. In addition to this price restriction, we also request that on "A" pictures which are exhibited at a night admission price of 40¢ or more— they shall never be exhibited in conjunction with another feature picture under the so-called policy of double-features. . . . In the event that a distributor sees fit to sell his product to subsequent runs in violation of this request, it definitely means that we cannot negotiate for his product to be exhibited in our "A" theatres at top admission prices.[8]

The letter was followed by bilateral meetings between O'Donnell and each distributor.

The US Supreme Court considered the letter instrumental in achieving mutual understanding among distributors:

The O'Donnell letter named on its face as addressees the eight local representatives of the distributors, and so from the beginning each of the distributors knew that the proposals were under consideration by the others. Each was aware that all were in active competition and that without substantially unanimous action with respect to the restrictions for any given territory there was risk of a substantial loss of the business and good will of the subsequent-run and independent exhibitors, but that with it there was the prospect of increased profits. There was, therefore, strong motive for concerted action, full advantage of which was taken by Interstate and Consolidated in presenting their demands to all in a single document.[9]

The court concluded that there was an unlawful agreement in spite of the lack of direct communication among the movie distributors: "It was enough that, knowing that concerted action was contemplated and invited, the distributors gave their adherence to the scheme and participated in it. Each distributor was advised that the others were asked to participate; each knew that cooperation was essential to successful operation of the plan. They knew that the plan, if carried out, would result in a restraint of commerce, . . . and knowing it, all participated in the plan."[10]

In sum, *Interstate* was a case in which collusion was initiated by the downstream (exhibitor) firm in response to aggressive competition from rival downstream firms. The collusive plan was exclusionary in that it proposed that the upstream (distributor) firms require Interstate's rival firms to raise their prices and lower their quality as a condition of having the upstream firms' products. An upstream firm would find it optimal to go along only if it believed many other upstream firms would do so, which then required that the downstream firm achieve mutual understanding of compliance among the upstream firms. In the absence of direct communication between the upstream firms, the downstream firm sought to obtain mutual understanding by sending a letter with the collusive plan to all upstream firms while noting in the letter that it was sent to all upstream firms. The letter was supplemented by bilateral verbal communications in order to achieve enough confidence among upstream firms that other upstream firms were likely to comply.

The court found the conduct illegal because it went beyond a vertical contract between one upstream firm and one downstream firm. Rather, the downstream firm sought coordinated adoption of the collusive plan by the upstream firms. Informing each upstream firm that the other upstream firms were being asked to comply created a horizontal dimension to this conduct and was essential for Interstate's plan to succeed because it would not have been in the interest of an upstream firm to comply unless it thought enough other upstream firms would do so.

5.2.2   Toys (US)

The dominant US toy retailer in the early–mid-1990s was Toys "R" Us (hereafter TRU), with a 20% national market share.[11] In 18 metropolitan areas, its market share ranged between 35% and 49%, and it was over 50% in eight metropolitan areas and Puerto Rico. In the upstream market, the five leading toy manufacturers were Mattel, Hasbro, Fisher-Price, Tyco, and Little Tikes. Toys "R" Us was the most important customer for most of those manufacturers, making up 28% of Mattel's sales, 28% of Hasbro's, 31% of Little Tikes's, 35% of Fisher-Price's, and 48% of Tyco's.

At the time, the retail landscape had been disrupted by warehouse clubs, which sold at lower prices than TRU though in a sparse, less attractive selling environment. Clubs included Sam's Club (a division of Wal-Mart with 256 stores in 1992), Pace (a division of Kmart with 115 stores), Costco (100 stores), Price Club (94 stores), and BJ's Wholesale (39 stores). Though the clubs stocked fewer toy products than TRU, they were able to choose from the entire product line of a toy manufacturer when deciding which ones to sell. In addition to selling products that were also found in TRU stores, the clubs worked with toy manufacturers to create specially packaged products that sold at a higher total price but a lower unit price, so they provided better value.

With a gross margin of around 25%, TRU had entered the toy market as the low-price retailer when compared to department stores (with gross margins of 40%–50%) and small toy stores. It was forced to defend that status against discount department stores such as Wal-Mart and Kmart, but the clubs were a more serious threat, with gross margins of 9%–12%: "By 1989, TRU senior executives were concerned that the clubs presented a threat to TRU's low-price image and its profits. TRU knew that consumers form opinions about a store's relative prices based on a few visible items. TRU referred to these products as 'price image' or 'price sensitive' items. . . . TRU had already lowered the prices of these popular items to meet Wal-Mart's challenge, but the clubs' marketing strategies threatened to bring prices even lower."[12] As of mid-1992, TRU reported that a warehouse club was within a five-mile radius of 238 of its 497 US stores.

TRU's concern was that upon comparing the prices of TRU and a club for the same item, a customer would learn that TRU's price was higher, and consequently TRU would no longer be seen as the low-price outlet for toys. One strategic response would have been to lower prices, but that would have cut into profit margins and could have fueled a price war with the clubs. An alternative path was for TRU to avoid such price comparisons by preventing clubs from carrying any toy that TRU carried. Of course, implementation of that strategy required the participation of the toy manufacturers: "In a document drafted around Toy Fair 1993, Greg Staley from TRU's international division summarized TRU's policy as follows: 'Our buying is simple—we will not carry an identical item which is sold to a Warehouse Club. If we find an item in both our assortments and those of a Club, we will discontinue carrying that item immediately; and we reserve the right to take clearance markdowns to dramatically accelerate the rate of sale on that item. In summary, the vendor has to make a choice as to whom he sells an item—either us or them.'"[13] Thus, the strategy was one of exclusion: harm rival firms by limiting the products they are offered by manufacturers. TRU was going to have manufacturers sell to the clubs only those products that TRU did not stock, and it was going to induce the manufacturers to go along by threatening not to carry their products.

While TRU would clearly be better off with this collusive plan, what about the toy manufacturers? If clubs were paying a lower wholesale price than TRU and the increase in sales from the lower retail price at the clubs was insufficient to offset the lower margins being earned by manufacturers, then collusion could be more profitable for them. However, if the clubs paid approximately the same wholesale price as TRU and were willing to accept smaller margins with retail prices below that of TRU, the toy manufacturers would benefit from higher sales by selling to the clubs. In that case, collusion would harm the upstream manufacturer-spokes.

While we do not have the data to address the question of whether TRU's exclusionary plan made the toy manufacturers better or worse off, the documentary evidence reveals that the manufacturers argued against stopping sales to the clubs. Clubs were a growing source of sales, which meant exclusion would result in a reduction in demand for the toy manufacturers and would make them more dependent on TRU. Playskool's president noted "that his company could not stop doing business with the clubs, and that in view of the consolidation in the retail trade it was important for Playskool to have other customers than TRU."[14] If indeed the toy manufacturers liked having the clubs as an outlet for their products, that would pose a challenge for TRU in getting those manufacturers to exclude the clubs.

A second challenge for TRU was a toy manufacturer's concern that it would be at a disadvantage if it restricted its sales to the clubs when many other manufacturers did not: "The toy companies were afraid of yielding a potentially important new channel of distribution to their competitors. Small changes in sales volumes have a significant effect on toy manufacturers' overall profits, and no retail channel other than the clubs offered similar opportunities for rapid growth. For example, Mattel's sales volume to the clubs increased by 87% between 1989 and 1991. Much of this growth was a result of Sam's emergence as a toy buyer, but sales to BJ's, Costco and Pace also increased at a rapid rate. By comparison, Mattel's overall sales grew by approximately 10% during this period."[15]

Unilaterally restricting sales to clubs was not in the best interest of a toy manufacturer. Furthermore, as argued earlier, even a coordinated restriction of sales by toy manufacturers may have been harmful to them. What made it sensible for a toy manufacturer to comply with the collusive plan was TRU's threat of exclusion if it did not: "While most—if not all—of the toy companies disliked having to choose between what they saw as two bad options—(1) sell to TRU and restrict club sales, or (2) sell to the clubs and risk retaliation from TRU—the decision was made easier by the horizontal agreement which took the sting out of reducing sales to the clubs. From the manufacturers' point of view, the boycott was the second-best alternative."[16] An individual toy manufacturer found it better to comply than not, but only as long as other toy manufacturers complied.

Finally, TRU faced a third obstacle to getting the toy manufacturers on board; the credibility of TRU's threat to cut off purchases from a noncompliant toy manufacturer was unclear. Doing so would certainly harm TRU in the short run. The credibility of the threat also hinged on most or all toy manufacturers complying. If all other toy manufacturers complied, TRU might find it optimal to cut off one toy manufacturer in order to establish the credibility of its threat and keep other toy manufacturers from breaking ranks. However, if several toy manufacturers did not comply, it would be very costly for TRU not to stock their toys. Thus, a toy manufacturer could well believe that TRU would punish it for not complying only if most or all other toy manufacturers were complying.

For all these reasons, TRU's collusive plan would be implemented by the toy manufacturers only if each believed their rivals had bought into it. Only then would a toy manufacturer not be at a competitive disadvantage by restricting supply to the clubs, and only then would it find TRU's exclusionary threat credible. The toy manufacturers clearly conveyed the need for assurances that all would be participating: "Mattel, Hasbro, Tyco, Little Tikes, Fisher-Price and others all wanted to know how competitors were reacting to TRU. The manufacturers wanted assurances from TRU that their competitors were subject to the same rule. They informed TRU that they wanted a level playing field to avoid being placed at a competitive disadvantage."[17]

The challenge to TRU was clear: convince each toy manufacturer that the other manufacturers were going to restrict sales to the clubs. It met this challenge by using bilateral communications with each toy manufacturer and making each aware of its bilateral communications with rival toy manufacturers. There is no evidence that TRU ever communicated to them as a group: "[TRU] tried to obtain a coordinated response from manufacturers by assuring them that they would not be placed at a competitive disadvantage because TRU was applying its policy to their competitors. . . . The manufacturers all were aware that TRU was communicating its policy to everyone and that uniformity was contemplated. And everyone knew that without unanimity regular line product sales to the clubs would recommence."[18]

A key early contact was Hasbro, for whom TRU was its biggest US customer: "In fall 1990, TRU's CEO, Charles Lazarus, met with Hasbro's executives and told them that the clubs were a threat to TRU because of their low prices. He said that if Hasbro continued to aggressively supply the clubs . . . that this could affect their business at TRU."[19] TRU went to each major toy manufacturer with a similar pitch, and each was informed that their rivals were similarly being pressured to restrict sales to the clubs:

> During conversations with manufacturers, TRU did not merely announce that it would refuse to deal with manufacturers selling to the clubs, or inform manufacturers that all manufacturers would be treated equally. Instead, TRU communicated the quid pro quo (i.e., I'll stop if they stop) from manufacturer to manufacturer.[20]

> [TRU vice president Roger] Goddu clarified that TRU engaged in these conversations with all the key toy manufacturing firms. "We communicated to our vendors that we were communicating with all our key suppliers, and we did that I believe at Toy Fair 1992. We made a point to tell each of the vendors that we spoke to that we would be talking to our other key suppliers."[21]

Furthermore, TRU would use one toy manufacturer's acceptance to induce others to come on board with the policy:

> After Mattel agreed not to sell to the clubs the same products "based on the fact that competition does the same", TRU told Hasbro that Mattel had agreed. . . . Before committing not to sell certain products to the clubs, Little Tikes asked TRU what its main competitor in the clubs (Today's Kids) was going to do. Goddu informed Little Tikes that Today's Kids "was going to start doing less business with the warehouse clubs" whereupon Little Tikes committed to restrict its sales. . . . Lazarus and Goddu told Sega that TRU had convinced Nintendo to stop selling product to the clubs as part of TRU's effort to convince Sega to do the same. TRU argued that Sega should stop selling because TRU had convinced Nintendo to stop.[22]

> . . . Just before or at Toy Fair 1992, Hasbro's then western regional sales manager, James Inane, met with [Hasbro CEO] Verrecchia [who] said that he had just come from a meeting with TRU, that TRU had met with Hasbro's competitors, including Mattel and Fisher-Price, and that they had agreed not to sell promoted products to the clubs. Verrecchia said that because Hasbro's competitors had agreed not to sell promoted products, Hasbro would go along with the agreement. Verrecchia told his staff that Hasbro would not sell promoted products to the clubs and that Hasbro would watch other manufacturers' sales to the clubs. Hasbro would refrain from selling to the clubs until another manufacturer broke the agreement.[23]

As the FTC referred to it, TRU engaged in "shuttle diplomacy" to reassure manufacturers.

> It was only after assurances were exchanged that the toy manufacturers, overcoming their natural inclination to sell through all potential outlets, became willing

to discriminate against the clubs. At that point, a "conscious commitment to a common scheme" was perfected, and a uniform, clearly interdependent, course of conduct came into being.[24]

TRU worked for over a year and surmounted many obstacles to convince the large toy manufacturers to discriminate against the clubs by selling to them on less favorable terms and conditions. The biggest hindrance TRU had to overcome was the major toy companies' reluctance to give up a new, fast-growing, and profitable channel of distribution, and their concern that any of their rivals who sold to the clubs might gain sales at their expense. TRU's solution was to build a horizontal understanding—essentially an agreement to boycott the clubs—among its key suppliers.[25]

While there was some direct communication between the toy manufacturers,[26] it was rare. The nearly exclusive channel for communication between toy manufacturers was through TRU, which proved sufficient to achieve the needed mutual understanding among the spokes. The FTC concluded that many of the toy manufacturers "required assurances that rivals would sell on discriminatory terms to the clubs, and . . . were satisfied with TRU's assurances that such uniform policies would be adopted. Evidence of that exchange of commitments—not necessarily direct communications among the toy manufacturers but clearly through the intermediation of TRU—is present with respect to Mattel, Hasbro, Fisher Price, Tyco, Little Tykes, Today's Kids, and Tiger Electronics."[27]

However, the job was not done. Even though many toy manufacturers had agreed to TRU's plan, they were continuously concerned with possible deviations by rival firms. In response, TRU actively monitored the toy manufacturers for compliance, and the toy manufacturers themselves were instrumental in reporting a rival that supplied clubs outside the agreement. Table 5.1 provides a list of infractions that was part of a memo to the CEO of TRU. It states the noncompliant toy manufacturer and the product that was sold to the clubs, and often offers an explanation for the apparent infraction and a plan to rectify the situation.

The toy manufacturers had strong incentives to monitor and share any infractions with TRU so that rival firms would be brought into compliance:

When Mattel heard rumors that Hasbro and Tyco might be selling regular line to the clubs, the president of Mattel's Toy Division instructed that the clubs be shopped and the information sent to TRU.[28]

. . . TRU promised to "take care of it" after Fisher-Price representatives complained about Playskool product they found in Price Club.[29]

Table 5.1

List of noncompliance episodes reported to Toys "R" Us

Manufacturer	Description	Comments
Hasbro	Puppy Surprise	Shipped early. No more will be shipped to warehouses.
Binney & Smith	[various]	Per Brent Blaine: Understood our concern. Going forward they will offer special packs only for '93. Commitments already made for '92.
Mattel	Barbie Dream House	Sold LY mdse. Will not sell again.
Huffy Sports	Graphite Ultra Pak	Per Dave Allen, VP Sales: They admit their mistake. Effective immediately only special Backboards will be sold to clubs.
Playtime (Div. of Tyco)	Super Saturator	Per Howard Abrams, SVP Sales: Pleaded ignorance. He's now aware and other than some prior commitment, they will only sell club "special" items or items we don't carry.
Today's Kids	Activity Rocker Little Golfer All Star Baseball	Per Jim Stephens: They needed the business but fully understand our position. They will sell special items going forward.
Tyco	123 Firehouse Blocks Deluxe Set Magnadoodle DB Nursery/ Playground	Per Ken Shumaker: These are goods shipped last year—prior to their new "no ship" policy on current goods we carry.
Century	Elite Car Seat	Vendor will stop shipping BJ's.
Fisher-Price	Nursery Monitor	They have agreed to stop selling this item to the clubs.
Safety 1st	Swivel Bath Seat	They have agreed to stop selling the clubs this item.
Playskool Baby (a Hasbro div.)	Nighttime Feeder	We have reached a corporate agreement on the sale of this item to the club stores.
Kransco	Swim Seater	Will not be selling like items to them next year. Will change graphics/packaging to differentiate item in future.
Morey Boogie	Sting Ray Board	Admitted they screwed up—will not happen again. Will continue to sell them but in a "completely" different packaging and graphics on the boards.
Nintendo	Asst.	"Not getting it from Nintendo" per Randy. They will "look into."
Sega	Asst.	Will continue to sell as long as Nintendo is in Warehouse Clubs.

Source: *In the Matter of Toys "R" Us*, FTC Docket No. 9273, Initial Decision, James P. Timony, Administrative Law Judge, September 25, 1997, 21–22.

... In September 1991, Fisher-Price's regional manager sent [Fisher-Price sales-man John] Chase a copy of a TRU shopping report showing products of Hasbro, Fisher-Price and Playskool found in Price Club. He told Chase that a TRU execu-tive had sent the report to Byron Davis, Fisher-Price's vice-president for sales. The words "Byron, you promised this wouldn't happen" were written on the report. After this event, Fisher-Price limited its club sales to special and combination packs.[30]

TRU admitted that it acted as a conduit between firms regarding com-plaints of noncompliance:

TRU's President testified: "I would get phone calls all the time from Mattel say-ing Hasbro has this in the clubs or Fisher Price has that in the clubs. . . . So that occurred all the time." Goddu explained that, on the many occasions he received these calls, he would "always thank them and tell them we would follow up." . . . TRU would speak to the offending firm and even assure the complainant that the offending firm would be brought into line. Violations of TRU's club policy were thus detected and punished, serving to enforce the horizontal agreement. The toy companies participated in this exchange of complaints, which was frequent and continued over lengthy periods, effectively making their competitors' compliance a part of their agreements with TRU.[31]

In sum, TRU had two sources of information to aid in monitoring com-pliance with the collusive scheme. One source was TRU shopping the clubs, and the second was reports from toy manufacturers.

To pull together the preceding discussion, we will use the FTC's succinct synopsis of the case:

The record demonstrates that TRU organized and enforced a horizontal agree-ment among its various suppliers. Despite TRU's considerable market power, key toy manufacturers were unwilling to refuse to sell to or discriminate against the clubs unless they were assured that their competitors would do the same. To over-come that resistance, TRU gave initial assurances that rival toy manufacturers would commit to comparable sales programs; TRU representatives then acted as the central player in the middle of what might be called a hub-and-spoke con-spiracy, shuttling commitments back and forth between toy manufacturers and helping to hammer out points of shared understanding; toy manufacturers' com-mitments were carefully conditioned on comparable behavior by rivals; and, after the discriminatory program was in place, TRU and the toy manufacturers worked out a program to detect, bring back into line, and sometimes discipline, manufac-turers that sold to the clubs.[32]

The evidence is compelling that TRU's collusive strategy of exclusion was effective in reducing toy manufacturers' sales to the clubs. Mattel and

Hasbro's combined sales to the clubs dropped from $32.5 million in 1991 to $10.7 million in 1993.[33] The clubs' share of US toy sales, which had risen from 1.5% to 1.9% during the pre-boycott years of 1991–1992, had fallen to 1.4% by 1995.[34] TRU's internal documents revealed that, while the clubs were a competitive threat as of late 1992, they were not considered as such by 1993: "In December of 1992, TRU included clubs located near TRU stores when it calculated its [competition] index. TRU explained this decision by noting that 'warehouse clubs have been a strong competitive force this season.' Clubs were withdrawn from later competition indices in 1993—after TRU's club policy was put into effect—because clubs were then thought to have 'no significant . . . impact on TRU stores.'"[35]

The clubs' reduced supply translated into higher prices for consumers. Products sold by TRU but not by discounters had margins as high as almost 40%.[36] By expanding the set of products exclusive to it, TRU would have expanded the set of products for which it could set a high margin. For 1993, the FTC "found that the elimination of competitive pressure from the clubs cost consumers as much as an extra $55 million per year on top-selling products purchased at TRU alone."[37] As another measure of effect, TRU and three toy manufacturers settled private litigation for $56 million (Scherer 2004).

The Administrative law judge (ALJ) ruled that TRU and 14 toy manufacturers had engaged in a per se violation of Section 5 of the FTC Act. In response to the increased competition from warehouse clubs, the ALJ noted that "TRU could have announced a unilateral policy by TRU and a refusal to deal with suppliers that did not comply. The issue is whether TRU went further, entering agreements with each manufacturer."[38] The ALJ concluded that "TRU orchestrated a horizontal conspiracy among its suppliers [and] the major manufacturers knew that TRU was contacting the other manufacturers with the same proposal and that concerted action was invited."[39] TRU's appeal of the ALJ's decision was denied by the FTC. TRU then appealed that decision to the Seventh Circuit Court, which affirmed the FTC's decision and, in doing so, viewed the case as more compelling than *Interstate*: "The Commission's theory, stripped to its essentials, is that this case is a modern equivalent of the old *Interstate Circuit* decision. . . . The TRU case if anything presents a more compelling case for inferring horizontal agreement than did *Interstate Circuit*, because not only was the manufacturers' decision to stop dealing with the warehouse clubs an abrupt shift from the past, and not only is it suspicious for a manufacturer to deprive itself of a profitable sales outlet, but the record here included the direct evidence of communications that was missing in *Interstate Circuit*."[40]

In *Interstate*, the key piece of evidence was the letter sent by the hub (Interstate Circuit) to the spokes (movie distributors), which indicated that all spokes were receiving it. A spoke's inference that other spokes were intending to comply would have only been based on knowing that the other spokes had received the letter. With *Toys "R" Us*, there was instead bilateral verbal communications between the hub (TRU) and the spokes (toy manufacturers) that not only encouraged a spoke to participate but made clear that other spokes were similarly being encouraged and that some had already agreed to participate: "As in *Interstate Circuit*, there was an invitation clearly addressed to all of the participants in the proposed conspiracy. Like the listing of all the film distributors as addressees in the letter sent by Interstate Circuit, TRU, in Goddu's phrase, 'made a point of telling' its suppliers that its club 'policy' was to be extended to each and every one of them. Each therefore knew that the others were asked to make a similar decision."[41]

There was more in *Toys "R" Us*, for the spokes made clear in their communications with the hub that their participation depended on the participation of the other spokes. We then have express communication by a spoke to the hub that it needed joint action among manufacturers. That could only be inferred in *Interstate*.

5.2.3 Fiberglass Insulation (US)
The product in this case is fiberglass insulation for houses in the US.[42] At the time, almost all fiberglass insulation was produced by five manufacturers: Certainteed (CT), Guardian, Johns Manville (JM), Knauf, and Owens Corning (OC). They sold their nearly homogeneous products to distributors, retailers, and building contractors.

Masco was the largest buyer in the market, installing almost half the fiberglass insulation in new US homes. As a result, it had been able to receive lower wholesale prices compared to most other contractors. However, by late 1998, weakening demand for fiberglass insulation resulting from a decline in new housing construction had caused manufacturers to lower their prices for other contractors, which served to partly or fully erode Masco's wholesale price advantage over its competitors.

For the purpose of reclaiming its price advantage, Masco was alleged to have instigated an arrangement with the five manufacturers whereby they would provide Masco with a discount on the prices charged to other contractors and, in exchange, Masco would support an industry-wide wholesale price increase. Thus, this agreement involved both collusive price setting in the upstream market and exclusion in the downstream market. A private litigation case was brought by 377 independent contractors (who were competitors of Masco) against the fiberglass manufacturers and Masco.[43] They alleged that the agreement ran from 1999 to 2003.

Consistent with this scheme, an April 2001 internal email by a vice president of Knauf described a plan to increase the price of fiberglass insulation and emphasized the critical role of Masco: "Because the Masco companies represent better than half of the installed market, their support of the increase is essential to it sticking. We need this increase desperately. We must see that all of this increase gets passed to everyone."[44] A similar sentiment was expressed by the vice president of sales and marketing for CT: "What we really need is to convince them [Masco] that they can lead the industry in getting pricing up in the market if we commit to a reasonable gap. I don't know how we do this well without crossing the line on certain antitrust/price fixing rules. It's not about setting a price in a market, it's about making sure we can generate an appropriate return for the investment we make. If all they want is the lowest price they can manipulate from the mfgs. then there won't be investments made."[45]

Based on a February 2002 meeting with Donny DeMarie of Masco, Gary Romes of Guardian expressed that Masco would be supportive as long as they were given a price advantage: "He [DeMarie] is concerned that [with] 1.6 million [housing] starts; there is so much extra capacity on [fiberglass insulation] batts. Lower [wholesale] prices don't necessarily help them; Masco just wants to maintain a spread with everyone else; as prices go lower that becomes more difficult. They want to maintain a spread at a higher price level—we agreed."[46] According to Romes, low housing demand had intensified competition among contractors, and Masco was most interested in having a lower wholesale price relative to its rivals, even if it meant paying a higher wholesale price.

The evidence presented thus far is consistent with a series of bilateral vertical agreements between Masco and insulation manufacturers that were intended to raise prices for all contractors and provide a discount for Masco. For this to become hub-and-spoke collusion, Masco would need to have coordinated the manufacturers in their acceptance of this arrangement. We next turn to providing supportive evidence of such coordination.

Given the intense competition in the market for insulation—which is a natural consequence of excess capacity for a homogeneous good—a manufacturer would be unlikely to find much demand for its product if it raised its price substantially above that of other manufacturers. Thus, an across-the-board price increase to contractors (with a smaller price increase to Masco in order to give it an advantage) would only prove profitable to a manufacturer if it could expect the other manufacturers to consummate similar price increases. The court did comment on some parallel movement of prices: "There is no question that the insulation manufacturers involved in this case exhibited 'conscious parallelism' in their pricing decisions relative to Masco and other independent contractors. . . . The documentary evidence suggests that the manufacturers 'ha[d] allowed this spread to be a minimum of 12–15% over the years.'"[47]

However, there is no evidence of direct communication between the manufacturers to coordinate their prices and discounts. Instead, the evidence shows that Masco engaged in bilateral communications with each manufacturer. These communications included sharing pricing intentions between manufacturers, which would have facilitated the coordination of their prices. For example, a July 2001 calendar entry by an executive at CT stated: "Per Donny [DeMarie, executive at Masco]—OC [Owens Corning] going to announce an increase."[48] A September 2001 email from DeMarie to a CT executive conveyed the expectations of JM with regard to CT: "If Manville THINKS you did not go up they will not go up."[49] An undated memo from JM stated: "You can count on our support to get the prices up. You can tell my competitors that we are holding firm."[50]

Consistent with Masco having facilitated a collusive arrangement among insulation manufacturers, there is evidence of monitoring compliance. In some instances, Masco found that a manufacturer was not compliant and then shared this information with other manufacturers. For example, a JM memorandum from June 2002 stated: "OC has been found in violation of the spread. Masco has found instances where OC had independents priced at levels that reduced the spread."[51] Similarly, a CT executive "had been informed that Masco 'caught OC@ IDI with equal pricing, also 31W.'"[52]

The manufacturers were also involved in monitoring the agreement and would report deviations by rival manufacturers to Masco. For example, when a CT executive learned of JM's quote to an independent contractor, he sent an email requesting that another CT employee "tell Donny [DeMarie of Masco] that JM has dropped a medium sized retail account to within a smidge [sic] of the Masco price. We may need his help to send JM the correct message."[53] And the manufacturers knew this reporting was going on: "CT was likewise aware that if it lowered its relative price to an independent contractor, one of the other manufacturers 'would be on the phone to Masco pronto saying CT is not maintaining the increase.'"[54]

When it received reports or otherwise became aware of deviations, Masco would demand wholesale price adjustments. Interestingly, such demands were not always directed only at the deviating manufacturer. If one manufacturer was selling to Masco's competitors at a wholesale price below the agreed spread, Masco would demand wholesale price adjustments by *all* the manufacturers. In one episode, a CT executive complained: "OC gets caught and we pay with lower revenues. Cost us $422,500 a month?"[55]

There is not much publicly available evidence to assess the effect of this hub-and-spoke cartel on insulation prices. Although contested by Masco, the plaintiffs' economic expert found that "the alleged conspiracy had a clear and discernible impact" over 1999–2003.[56] The four manufacturers settled with the plaintiffs for $32 million in 2008. This left Masco to go to court, where it was denied summary judgment on the charge of collusion in 2009. Masco subsequently settled with the plaintiffs for $75 million in 2012.[57]

5.2.4   e-books (US)

In the book publishing market, the traditional pricing strategy was to initially release a book in hardcover at a high price and then later release a paperback version at a lower price. Referred to as "windowing," it allowed a publisher to generate higher profits through intertemporal price discrimination. Compared to charging a constant price over time, higher margins were earned on those consumers who most valued the product—and thus bought it early at the high price—while still selling to the broader market (who valued it less) later through its lower-priced paperback edition.

Also known as digital or electronic books, e-books presented a new format for publishers. They were introduced by Amazon in 2007 with its Kindle reader, and Amazon chose a pricing strategy that was a disruptive departure from the windowing strategy. For new releases and *New York Times* bestsellers, Amazon charged a retail price of $9.99, which was significantly below the typical $30 price of a hardcover book.[58] The $9.99 price was at or slightly below the wholesale price Amazon paid the publishers. Amazon's pricing strategy was focused more on promoting adoption of the

Kindle platform than making money on e-book sales. Amazon dominated the e-book market, with a market share of almost 90%.

The publishing industry for "trade" books (i.e., general-interest fiction and nonfiction books) was dominated by the "Big Six"—Hachette, Harper-Collins, Macmillan, Penguin, Random House, and Simon & Schuster. Their market share of *New York Times* bestsellers exceeded 90%, and they sold almost 50% of e-books. For several reasons, the Big Six "saw Amazon's $9.99 pricing strategy as a threat to their established way of doing business."[59] First, e-books at a retail price of $9.99 were taking sales away from their more profitable hardcover sales. Second, the low e-book price might create increasing consumer resistance to the hardcover price, which would force publishers to reduce the wholesale price for hardcover books. Third, while Amazon was currently selling e-books at or below the wholesale price it was paying publishers, it might eventually use its dominant position in the e-book market to demand a lower wholesale price to enable Amazon to have positive margins at a retail price of $9.99: "As Hachette's [chairman and CEO David] Young put it, the idea of the 'wretched $9.99 price point becoming a de facto standard' for e-books 'sickened' him."[60]

Starting as early as September 2008, the CEOs of the Big Six publishers were meeting privately every quarter to discuss industry matters, including Amazon's e-book retailing practices. Since publishers competed over authors and agents rather than prices, they "felt no hesitation in freely discussing Amazon's prices with each other and their joint strategies for raising those prices."[61] Some of the policies debated included raising the wholesale price for e-books and creating their own e-book platform as an alternative to Amazon's.

Though the publishers did not settle on any policy, their meetings yielded a common understanding that Amazon's pricing model had to be changed and that could only happen if the publishers adopted a unified front. As noted by Simon & Schuster's president and CEO Carolyn Reidy, "We've always known that unless other publishers follow us, there's no chance of success in getting Amazon to change its pricing practices [and] without a critical mass behind us Amazon won't 'negotiate,' so we need to be more confident of how our fellow publishers will react if we make a move."[62] This point resonated with a Penguin executive in a report made to the Penguin Group's board of directors, who stated, "It will not be possible for any individual publisher to mount an effective response [to Amazon] because of both the resources necessary and the risk of retribution, so the industry needs to develop a common strategy."[63]

At the same time that the publishers were in the midst of searching for an alternative to the current arrangement with Amazon, Apple was preparing to launch the iPad on January 27, 2010. Apple's goal was to have a well-stocked iBookstore from which iPad users could purchase and download e-books by the time of the launch. Hence, Apple needed to work out an arrangement with the Big Six publishers, and it knew that they wanted to raise the e-book price above $9.99. As a result, Apple and the publishers were natural allies; Apple wanted to effectively compete with Amazon in the e-book market, and the publishers wanted to have an alternative e-book platform to reduce the market power of Amazon.[64]

As director of Apple's digital content stores, Eddy Cue was in charge of negotiations with the Big Six. The pricing arrangement with Amazon (which was referred to as the "wholesale model") had the publisher charge a fixed wholesale price for each e-book sold by Amazon, with Amazon setting the retail price (which was $9.99). Cue proposed a wholesale model but with higher price points. Hachette (and later HarperCollins) suggested instead an "agency model" in which the publishers set the retail prices and the publisher and Apple shared the revenues. While initially resistant, Cue soon embraced it, though with Apple retaining some control over retail prices: "Apple settled on an agency model with a 30% commission, the same commission it was using in its App Store. Agency would give the Publishers the control over e-book pricing that they desired, and ensured that Apple would make a profit from every e-book sale in its iBookstore without having to compete on price. Apple realized, however, that in handing over pricing decisions to the Publishers, it needed to restrain their desire to raise e-book prices sky high. It decided to require retail prices to be restrained by pricing tiers with caps."[65] Apple proposed retail price caps of $14.99, $12.99, and $9.99, depending on the book's hardcover price.

However, this strategy would not solve the publishers' problem if Amazon continued to sell e-books at $9.99, for then the publishers would be forced to set the iBookstore retail price close to $9.99 in order to remain competitive with Amazon. In that situation, publishers would be making 70% of $9.99, while it was receiving the wholesale price of $9.99 (or larger) from Amazon. Recognizing that the agency model needed to be augmented with a plan to control price competition between Apple and Amazon, Apple devised a two-pronged strategy. First, the publishers would force Amazon to adopt the agency model. Second, Apple would add a most favored nation (MFN) clause to their contracts with publishers.

By moving Amazon to the agency model, the publishers would regain control over the retail price and thus could set a higher price. The MFN clause mandated that "if, for any particular New Release in hardcover format, the . . . Customer Price [in the iBookstore] at any time is or becomes higher than a customer price offered by any other reseller . . . , then [the] Publisher shall designate a new, lower Customer Price [in the iBookstore] to meet such lower [customer price]."[66] Thus, if a publisher offered a lower price for its e-book at Amazon (perhaps because of pressure from Amazon), it would be contractually bound to lower its price at the iBookstore to that same level. An MFN clause would weaken the incentive for Amazon to bargain for a lower retail price—since it would not result in a price advantage over Apple—and strengthen the incentive of a publisher to resist a lower retail price, as it would be forced to also lower the retail price at the iBookstore.

Apple's scheme would not necessarily make e-book sales more profitable for publishers. For example, consider a hardcover book priced at $25. Apple would cap the retail price at $12.99 and, if that was the price at which a publisher sold the e-book, it would earn 70% of $12.99, or $8.75, which is less than the wholesale price Amazon was paying. For some publishers, it was predicted that e-book gross revenue would decline by 17%.[67] Nevertheless, Apple's pricing scheme appealed to the publishers for several reasons. First, higher e-book prices would raise hardcover sales, which had a higher margin. Second, regaining control over retail prices could prove more profitable in the long run if Apple raised the price caps, which would be quite likely once the e-book market became better established. Third, it would allow Apple to effectively enter the market, and that would weaken the position of Amazon when bargaining with the publishers.

To summarize, and as argued by the DOJ in its complaint,[68] adoption of the Apple agency agreements would raise e-book prices by taking away retail pricing authority from the retailers, having e-book prices set according to the Apple price caps, and result in higher retail prices for other retailers (specifically, Amazon) through their adoption of the agency model and an MFN clause that would ensure that the price caps would not be less than those set by Apple. In addition to this anticompetitive effect, the plan was exclusionary in that it sought to use the combined market power of the publishers to force Amazon to switch from wholesale pricing to the agency model. It is also worth pointing out that Amazon was dominant in the e-book retail market, in which case the coordinated actions of the publishers could be viewed as a countervailing force to Amazon. Indeed, the mutual interests of the publishers and Apple resided in reducing Amazon's market dominance.

Having devised this plan, Apple now had to get publishers to accept it. Apple quickly learned that it would not succeed if each negotiation with a publisher was conducted in isolation from the negotiations with other publishers. Publishers were willing to go along with Apple's plan—which involved higher retail prices and pressuring Amazon to accept the agency model—only if all or almost all publishers were on board:

> Each Publisher Defendant required assurances that it would not be the only publisher to sign an agreement with Apple that would compel it either to take pricing authority from Amazon or to pull its e-books from Amazon. The Publisher Defendants continued to fear that Amazon would act to protect its ability to price e-books at $9.99 or less if any one of them acted alone. Individual Publisher Defendants also feared punishment in the marketplace if only its e-books suddenly became more expensive at retail while other publishers continued to allow retailers to compete on price. As Mr. Cue noted, "all of them were very concerned about being the only ones to sign a deal with us." Penguin explicitly communicated to Apple that it would sign an e-book distribution agreement with Apple only if at least three of the other "major" publishers did as well.[69]

Beginning in December 2009, Cue's strategy was to negotiate with a publisher while keeping it apprised of what the other publishers were intending to do. At a personal level, Cue would be the hub communicating with the spokes, who were the CEOs of the Big Six. He began by meeting with each of the Big Six in New York City over December 15–16, 2009. In the following week, he met again with executives from three publishers and

> explained that he had met with all of the Big Six the preceding week, and had come to the conclusion that the way forward would involve four components. First, the e-book "industry" needed to move to the agency model, which would allow the Publishers to set the prices and introduce what Cue euphemistically termed "some level of reasonable pricing." Second, Apple would need a 30% margin on e-books sold through Apple. Third, he proposed setting prices for New Release e-books at $12.99, that is, $3 over Amazon's $9.99 price. Finally,

to remove all retail price competition, the Publishers would have to adopt the agency model for all of their e-tailers.[70]

It is critical that Apple was telling each of those publishers that *all* publishers had to get Amazon to change its pricing policy. Over January 4–5, 2010, Cue wrote essentially identical emails to each of the publishers and, for the three that he did not meet in late December, he began by saying, "After talking to all the other publishers and seeing the overall book environment, here is what I think is the best approach for e-books."[71] On January 11, each publisher received from Apple its proposed e-book agency distribution agreement, and each was assured that all publishers were getting the same terms.

The goal was to get all publishers under contract prior to the iPad launch on January 27. As of January 16, Apple did not have a single contract signed, but then the publishers started coming on board with the plan. Simon & Schuster was the first to sign, which led Cue to send "substantively identical e-mails to Macmillan and Penguin stating that Apple had completed its first agency agreement and was 'very close' on two more."[72] On January 22, Cue informed Apple CEO Steve Jobs "that he had commitments from Hachette, S&S, Macmillan, and Penguin that they would sign. At this point, Penguin required assurance that three other Publishers were also signing Agreements. As Cue admits, in these final days the Publishers needed reassurance that they would not be alone in signing an agency agreement with Apple because they feared Amazon's reaction, reassurance that Cue readily provided."[73] Come January 26, five of the Big Six had signed, with Random House deciding it would stick with the wholesale model. As the district court noted, "In less than two months, Apple had signed agency contracts with five of the six Publishers, and those Publisher Defendants had agreed with each other and Apple to solve the 'Amazon issue' and eliminate retail price competition for e-books. . . . This would not have happened without Apple's ingenuity and persistence. Apple's task had not been easy, but it had succeeded. As Reidy acknowledged in an email to Cue on January 21, working with the Publishers had been like 'herding . . . cats.'"[74]

There were also direct communications among the publishers during this period, as "during their negotiations with Amazon, the Publisher Defendants shared their progress with one another."[75] Of particular note is how the publishers joined forces when Amazon retaliated against Macmillan. When Macmillan CEO John Sargent met with Amazon, he told Amazon that they could either adopt the agency model or not receive the Kindle versions of its new releases for seven months (which was the length of time that these books were classified as "new releases" under the contract with Apple). Amazon responded by removing the buy buttons at its websites for Macmillan print and Kindle versions; the books were still listed at Amazon, but a customer could not buy them. Macmillan expected the support of the other publishers, for Sargent wrote, "The deal that 5 of us did with Apple meant someone was gonna have to do it [first]. . . . The optics make it look like I stood alone, but in the end I had no doubt that the others would eventually follow."[76] And indeed they did:

> Hachette's Nourry [wrote] to Sargent: "I can ensure you that you are not going to find your company alone in the battle" with Amazon. The next day, Penguin's Makinson similarly wrote, "just to say that I'm full of admiration for your articulation of Macmillan's position on this. Bravo." Internally, Hachette's Nourry told Young that he wanted to "enter in the battle as soon as possible," and in an allusion to Macmillan's small size, that he was "thrilled to know how A[mazon] will react against 3 or 4 of the big guys." Over the weekend, it became obvious to Amazon that its strategy had failed. The feedback was mixed, but included intense criticism of Amazon by customers and publishers.[77]

On January 31, Amazon announced that it would adopt the agency model with Macmillan, and by March 2010 it had also done so with Hachette, HarperCollins, and Simon & Schuster. Though the key retailer to convert was Amazon, the five publishers also switched other retailers—such as Barnes & Noble (which had its own Nook e-book reader) and Google's e-bookstore—to the agency model.

In sum, Apple proved to be an effective hub in coordinating the adoption of the agency model between five of the Big Six publishers and e-book retailers Apple and Amazon. The district court summarized the coordinating role played by Apple as follows:

> A chief stumbling block to raising e-book prices was the Publishers' fear that Amazon would retaliate against any Publisher who pressured it to raise prices. Each of them could also expect to lose substantial sales if they unilaterally raised the prices of their own e-books and none of their competitors followed suit. This is where Apple's participation in the conspiracy proved essential. It assured each Publisher Defendant that it would only move forward if a critical mass of the major publishing houses agreed to its agency terms. It promised each Publisher Defendant that it was getting identical terms in its Agreement in every material way. It kept each Publisher Defendant apprised of how many others had agreed

to execute Apple's Agreements. As Cue acknowledged at trial, "I just wanted to assure them that they weren't going to be alone, so that I would take the fear away of the Amazon retribution that they were all afraid of."[78]

The evidence shows that the adoption of the agency model by Apple and Amazon caused e-book prices to rise.[79] To begin, e-book prices were generally set at Apple's price caps: "In the five months that followed [the opening of the iBookstore], the Publisher Defendants collectively priced 85.7% of their New Release titles sold through Amazon and 92.1% of their New Release titles sold through Apple within 1% of the price caps. This was also true for 99.4% of the NYT Bestseller titles on Apple's iBookstore, and 96.8% of NYT Bestsellers sold through Amazon."[80]

Figure 5.1 was offered by one of Apple's economic experts at trial. After the iBookstore opened in April 2010, Amazon's e-book prices went up for all publishers (except Random House, which did not adopt the agency model). A statistical analysis by an expert witness for the DOJ found that the average

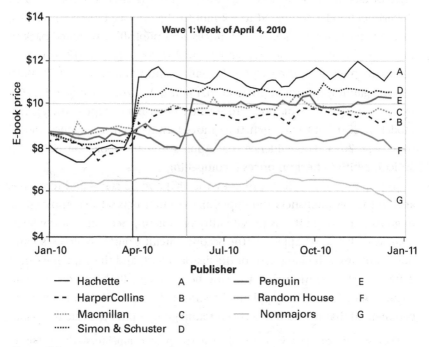

Figure 5.1
Weighted average e-book price by publisher at Amazon. *Source: United States v. Apple Inc.*, Opinion and Order, Southern District Court of New York, Judge Denise Cote, July 10, 2013, 95.

Table 5.2
Impact of collusion on e-book prices

Publisher	All e-Books	New releases	New York Times bestsellers	Backlist
Hachette	33.0%	14.1%	37.9%	37.5%
HarperCollins	13.6%	12.5%	44.0%	15.2%
Macmillan	11.6%	14.0%	—	11.2%
Penguin	18.3%	19.5%	43.6%	17.6%
Simon & Schuster	18.0%	15.1%	28.7%	19.8%
Defendant publishers	18.6%	14.2%	42.7%	19.6%
Random House	0.01%	1.9%	0.2%	0.3%
Nonmajors	–0.2%	–0.9%	1.1%	0.1%

Source: *United States v. Apple Inc.*, Opinion and Order, Southern District Court of New York, Judge Denise Cote, July 10, 2013, 96.

price of e-books rose by 16.8% in the six months after Amazon adopted the agency model compared to six months before (see table 5.2). Finally, an academic study tracked e-book prices after publishers switched back to the wholesale model from September 2012 to September 2013 as part of their settlement with the DOJ (De los Santos and Wildenbeest 2017). With retailers gaining control of prices at that point, Amazon's e-book prices fell by 18%. In sum, e-book prices rose when publishers adopted the agency model in 2010 and fell when they moved away from the agency model over 2012–2013. The evidence that Apple's hub-and-spoke cartel had an anticompetitive effect on prices is compelling.

In response to a civil suit filed by the DOJ and 33 states and territories against the five publishers and Apple, all five publishers settled. Apple chose to go to trial, where it was found guilty of violating Section 1 of the Sherman Act.[81] It lost on appeal to the Second Circuit Court,[82] which resoundingly supported the judgment of the district court, and the Supreme Court denied Apple's petition that the case be reviewed. Both the district and circuit courts found that Apple had committed a per se violation and even commented that it would have been found guilty under the rule of reason:

Because this conspiracy consisted of a group of competitors—the Publisher Defendants—assembled by Apple to increase prices, it constituted a "horizontal price-fixing conspiracy" and was a per se violation of the Sherman Act. It concluded, moreover, that even if the agreement to raise prices and eliminate retail price competition were analyzed under the rule of reason, it would still constitute an unreasonable restraint of trade in violation of § 1. In the district court's view, Plaintiffs' experts persuasively demonstrated that the agreement facilitated an "across-the-board price increase in e-books sold by the Publisher Defendants" and a corresponding drop in sales. Apple, on the other hand, failed to show that "the execution of the Agreements," as opposed to the launch of the iPad and "evolution of digital publishing more generally" (which were independent of the Agreements), "had any pro-competitive effects."[83]

Vertical agreements are a feature of hub-and-spoke cartels, so it should be emphasized that those agreements are typically legal. Exemplified in the current case, the Apple agency agreement was lawful. What was unlawful was Apple coordinating publishers so that they would collectively adopt the agreement with Apple and Amazon. Nevertheless, a remedy for the horizontal agreement could mean prohibiting the associated vertical agreement, which is what happened in the e-books case.

5.3 General Lessons

The four hub-and-spoke cartels examined are common in structure and objective. The structure is that of a downstream firm acting as the hub and upstream firms acting as spokes. The objective was to exclude competitors to the downstream hub. Here we identify some general patterns of conduct but also ways in which the cartels differed.

5.3.1 Description of the Collusive Outcome

These four cartels cover all the forms of exclusion discussed in section 5.1. In the US market for toys (hereafter Toys-US), there was naked exclusion, with manufacturers preventing warehouse clubs from carrying any toy carried by the retailer-hub Toys "R" Us (TRU). In contrast, in the e-books and cinema markets (hereafter e-books-US and Movies-US, respectively), the suppliers imposed higher retail prices on the targeted retailers. In Movies-US, this partial exclusion was complemented by the upstream distributors requiring the downstream subsequent-run theaters to limit the number of films viewed for a single ticket, thus lowering the quality of these theaters' products. In the fiberglass insulation market (hereafter Fiberglass-US), the exclusionary conduct had the suppliers coordinate on an across-the-board wholesale price increase but with a smaller price increase for the downstream hub. The purpose was to reestablish the hub's traditional wholesale price advantage over its rivals, which had recently eroded.

In all the cases except Fiberglass-US, the exclusionary conduct targeted aggressive discount retailers, with the purpose of raising their retail prices. In Toys-US, the discounters were warehouse clubs, whose business model involved selling at low prices in a less attractive setting than that of TRU. Likewise, in Movies-US, the target was subsequent-run theaters that showed films at a later date and for a lower admission price. In e-books-US, Amazon was aggressively discounting e-books for the purpose of promoting the adoption of its Kindle platform. In contrast, the firms that were excluded in Fiberglass-US were contractors that charged a higher price than the hub because they were at a cost disadvantage.

Let us next turn to commenting on the type of exclusion. In Toys-US, the hub TRU had a leading market position and was the dominant source of revenue for the upstream toy manufacturers. This arguably made naked exclusion possible because revenues from the warehouse clubs were less significant. Nevertheless, the growing revenues from the clubs still made the manufacturers reluctant to comply with their exclusion. In Movies-US, the hub movie theater chain Interstate was also one of the market leaders. However, here naked exclusion would seem to have been difficult, since the targeted movie theaters supplied a differentiated product—second-run movies at a lower price—which was a significant source of additional revenue for movie distributors. Likewise, in e-books-US, Amazon delivered a large and growing revenue stream, which would have made naked exclusion unattractive to the upstream publishers. Furthermore, exclusion of Amazon would have strengthened the position of the hub Apple when bargaining with the publisher-spokes, and that would run contrary to the primary rationale for the spokes' participation, which was to weaken the leverage of e-book retailers.

Finally, consider the source of the initiation of the collusive plan to exclude. In Movies-US and Toys-US, it was the downstream hub, as the main beneficiary, that initiated the exclusion. In contrast, the spokes in Fiberglass-US had to convince Masco to take part in an increase in input prices. However, having done so, Masco played a key role in subsequently forming and implementing the agreement. In e-books-US, the major publishers were in discussions about how to raise Amazon's retail prices, prior to Apple's involvement. Furthermore, the proposal to adopt a model in which the publishers set their retail prices was suggested by the publishers. Though initially resistant to this scheme, Apple soon embraced it and devised the strategy to control price competition between itself and Amazon.

Section 5.1 highlighted that a supplier will not want to exclude on its own and will be more likely to participate in the exclusionary conduct when other suppliers are also doing so. It is therefore not surprising that the spokes in these cartels typically comprised all the major suppliers in the market. The one exception was in e-books-US, where, despite being involved in the initial communications with the hub, one of the Big Six publishers eventually decided not to participate.

5.3.2 Communication to Achieve Mutual Understanding

The fact that a supplier will not want to exclude a retailer on its own suggests a key role for the hub in coordinating the suppliers. While the hub always played a role in promoting that coordination, the cartels varied in the amount of communication involved; more specifically, the extent to which the hub shared the intentions of one spoke (with regard to their participation in the collusive plan to exclude) with that of the other spokes.

In Movies-US, the hub sent a letter to each spoke and named all the spokes as addressees. This letter outlined the intended exclusionary conduct. Subsequently, there were bilateral meetings between the hub and each spoke. Nevertheless, each spoke had to rely on knowing that all spokes had received the same letter in order to infer that other spokes were intending to comply with the exclusionary behavior.

In Toys-US, communications were again bilateral between the hub and the spokes. However, compared to Movies-US, communication was much more explicit in indicating that other spokes were similarly being encouraged to participate, and, furthermore, the hub conveyed when another spoke had agreed to participate. During these communications, a spoke made clear to the hub that its participation depended on the other spokes participating. Similarly, the hub in e-books-US kept each spoke apprised of what the other spokes were intending to do and provided reassurance that they would not be alone. There were also direct communications among the spokes, in which they shared their progress in reaching an agreement with the hub. The extensive back-and-forth bilateral communications between the hub and spokes in Toys-US and e-books-US is in contrast to the more limited communications in Movies-US. In the latter case, the primary message was that all spokes were invited to participate in a collusive scheme—which was achieved via the common letter sent to them—with only limited communications used to provide added confidence that all were accepting that invitation.

Finally, in Fiberglass-US, coordination was restricted to bilateral communications between the hub and each spoke. These communications served to share pricing intentions between manufacturers through which they could coordinate on a price increase that gave the hub a discount relative to other downstream firms.

5.3.3 Did Upstream Spokes Benefit?

In section 5.1, it was demonstrated that, even if the suppliers acted in a coordinated fashion, the lost sales to the excluded retailer implied that the suppliers would not benefit from exclusionary conduct, other things being equal. Therefore, in order to get the suppliers to participate, the retailer would have to incentivize them by sharing the collusive rents or using the threat of not buying their products if they did not comply.

In Fiberglass-US, the spokes were in favor of the collusive scheme, as they would benefit from the across-the-board wholesale price increase even if a discount had to be given to the hub to gain its participation. In some of the other cases, the upstream spokes may well not have benefited from the exclusionary conduct. In Movies-US, the spokes initially objected to the plan, which suggests that they thought it would lower their profits. This aversion to the exclusionary plan was even clearer in Toys-US, where manufacturers appealed to be able to continue to sell to clubs because they found them to be a growing source of sales (which, of course, is exactly why TRU was determined to exclude them). The fact that in these cases the suppliers still went along with the collusive scheme suggests that the spokes were induced to comply by the hub's threat to refuse to purchase from them.

The situation is a bit different in e-books-US. Though the evidence suggests that the revenues of the spokes declined under the exclusionary conduct, the spokes still supported it. This was because it allowed them to regain some control over retail prices, it would improve their bargaining power over the longer term, and higher e-book prices would raise highly profitable hardcover book sales. Their desire for the exclusionary plan is also revealed by the fact that the publishers had communicated with each other about the need to raise Amazon's retail price even before Apple became involved.

5.3.4 Monitoring Spokes for Compliance

The difficulty in monitoring varied across the cases. In Toys-US, since naked exclusion was adopted and the products were branded, it should have been relatively easy to tell whether a supplier had deviated. All TRU would have had to do was visit the clubs to see what toys they had in stock. In addition, toy manufacturers were inclined to monitor and report any noncompliance to TRU.

In contrast, in Fiberglass-US, monitoring of wholesale prices was required, which would have been more difficult. Still, there is evidence that Masco, in its role as the hub, informed manufacturers of noncompliance by a rival manufacturer. Furthermore, when suppliers discovered a rival supplier lowering wholesale prices, presumably from its own negotiations with buyers, they would report this information to Masco.

5.3.5 Punishment

Generally, there was a clear mechanism through which the hub could punish noncompliant spokes. In Toys-US and Movies-US, the hub threatened to stop buying from a noncompliant supplier. As discussed earlier, the suppliers' participation in the collusive scheme—even when they voiced opposition to it—suggests that they found this threat credible. In e-books-US, the most favored nation clause meant that if a publisher offered a lower price to a retailer other than the hub, it would be contractually bound to lower its price to the hub to that same level. This clause then disincentivized the publishers from offering lower prices to Amazon. Finally, in Fiberglass-US, the hub would demand wholesale price adjustments following a deviation. Interestingly, rather than just being directed at the deviating manufacturer, there were instances where the hub demanded lower wholesale prices from all manufacturers.

5.4 Appendix: Automobile Retailing—General Motors (US)

Here, we discuss a cartel among vertically related firms that had the same exclusionary objective as the other cartels in this chapter. However, it differs in that there were widespread multilateral communications among the spokes pertinent to the instigation, coordination, and monitoring of the arrangement. Thus, it had communications consistent with a standard cartel but had an upstream supplier assist in cartel operations. This case provides further evidence of the critical role that an upstream hub can play through its ability to monitor compliance and to punish when there is evidence of noncompliance.

This cartel arose at the start of the 1960s and involved General Motors Corporation (GM), which manufactures the Chevrolet brand of automobiles, and three associations of Chevrolet dealers that covered all the Chevrolet dealers in the Los Angeles area.[84] In this market, dealers would ordinarily operate as a franchise of the manufacturer, purchasing cars exclusively from the manufacturer and retailing them to the public. However, toward the end of the 1950s, separate discount firms began offering "referral services" to sell new cars at low prices. Their sources of supply were the franchised dealers, and in the case of Chevrolet vehicles, the dealers did not have authorization from GM to sell their cars through these outlets.

Upon visiting a discounter, a potential buyer could examine price lists for automobiles produced by several manufacturers. If the buyer wished to purchase a vehicle, the discounter would typically either refer the buyer to a dealer to buy the car at a prearranged discounted price (with the discounter getting a cut of the profit) or negotiate the price with the buyer and then the discounter would pay the dealer a prearranged price. In this way, discounters enabled the dealers to price discriminate between price-sensitive buyers (who visited the discounter) and buyers who were less price sensitive (who did not). By 1960, discounters' sales had grown substantially and the Chevrolet dealers that did not use discounters began to suffer financially.

The purpose of the subsequent collusive agreement between GM and its Chevrolet dealers was to exclude those discounters from the market. While the exclusion of downstream competitors is similar to that of the hub-and-spoke cartels in this chapter, the structure differs in that coordination among the dealers that supplied the discounters was facilitated by an upstream firm rather than a downstream firm. Thus, the main beneficiaries of the collusion would have been the dealers that did not use the discounters; other dealers that did use them would also have benefited from reduced price competition but would have lost out on the revenue from the discounters. One way GM could have benefited from facilitating collusion between the dealers, in the absence of higher wholesale prices, would have been by enhancing the dealers' investments in nonprice promotional activities that raise demand.

The instigation of collusion was similar to that of some previously discussed cases. While the upstream hub (GM) played a pivotal role, it was the downstream spokes (dealers) that prompted GM to act. For instance, before GM became involved, Owen Keown, a director of the Losor Chevrolet Dealers Association, had already approached some of the other Chevrolet dealers (who were doing substantial business with the discounters) to discuss discontinuing their use of the discounters. However, they failed to reach an agreement because the dealers were not adequately reassured that other dealers would also comply. In particular, Keown was told that the dealers would continue the practice "'until . . . told not to by' Chevrolet and only in that event would the dealer know 'that they wouldn't let some other dealer carry on with it.'"[85] Presumably, they were concerned that unilaterally ceasing the practice would put them at a competitive disadvantage compared to their rivals that did not stop the practice. Consequently, at Losor's annual meeting in November 1960, the dealers collectively decided they would flood GM with requests for help. The scale of this coordinated act prompted GM to bilaterally discuss the matter with each of the dealers, with the main offenders being "treated to unprecedented individual confrontations."[86] These meetings were usually enough to stop the practice, although one dealer delayed its response until a week after its meeting, "to make sure that the other dealers, or most of them, had stopped their business dealings with discount houses."[87] By mid-January 1961, each dealer had promised GM not to deal with the discounters.

The method by which the cartel monitored compliance was the aspect where the cartel most resembled a standard cartel. There were numerous multilateral meetings between the three dealer associations that were organized through a joint investigating committee set up to detect deviations by dealers. The committee decided that each association should contribute $5,000 to fund a professional investigator who would "try to purchase new Chevrolets from the proscribed outlets, to tape-record the transactions, if any, and to gather all the necessary documentary evidence—which the associations would then lay 'at the doorstep of Chevrolet.'"[88] Such collaboration among the spokes would not be possible in a standard hub-and-spoke cartel, where there is rarely direct communication between them. However, similar to many of our cases, GM also conducted its own monitoring with Chevrolet Division's Los Angeles zone manager, Robert O'Connor, and a subordinate, Jere Faust, actively seeking the help of individual dealers to detect noncompliance.

The hub was actively involved in the punishment of deviators and in ensuring that nondeviators were compensated. In the event that noncompliance

was discovered, the committee passed the evidence to O'Connor, and he
or members of his staff would invite the offending dealer to a meeting at
which they would be confronted "with the car purchased by the 'shopper,'
the documents of sale, and in most cases a tape recording of the transaction."[89] In every instance, the dealer was required to repurchase the car,
sometimes at a substantial loss, with the check being made payable to an
attorney who acted jointly for the three dealer associations.

Within three months, the cartel had succeeded in eliminating the discounters' sales, and the collusive scheme lasted approximately three years.
The district court concluded that there was no violation of Section 1 of
the Sherman Act, but the decision was reversed and remanded by the US
Supreme Court.

This is a case in which the Chevrolet dealers initiated a plan to exclude
discounters and directly communicated among themselves to put it into
place. However, rather than go it alone as with a standard cartel, they solicited the assistance of the upstream supplier, GM. That they did so is evidence
of the enhanced efficacy that comes from having a vertically related hub.
GM assisted in getting dealers to agree to an exclusionary plan. Once this was
done, GM served as a clearinghouse for information on noncompliance and,
most critically, implemented a punishment that was unavailable to dealers.
As noted, a deviating dealer would have to buy back the auto it sold to a discounter. That GM could induce a dealer to comply with such a punishment
is surely because of its ability to limit or refuse to supply dealers. Even when
colluding firms communicate directly, their goal of limiting competition can
be served by inviting an upstream supplier to assist them.

5.5 Technical Appendix

In this appendix, we present a theoretical model to show when vertically
related firms will want to collude in order to nakedly exclude a retailer,
how this exclusion raises the retail price, and how the retailer can share the
resultant collusive rents with the suppliers by raising the wholesale price.
We establish that product substitutability is an important factor.

The structure of the appendix is as follows. First, we present the assumptions of the model and then derive the integrated monopolist benchmark.
Following this analysis, we solve for the equilibrium retail and wholesale

prices when the firms are vertically separated and their conduct is noncollusive. Then we consider an exclusionary strategy where one retailer and the suppliers collude to nakedly exclude the other retailer. We analyze the case where the firms operate as a vertically integrated firm that maximizes the profits of the supply chain. A hub-and-spoke cartel that seeks to maximize its profits would set the same retail price and earn the same joint profits as this vertically integrated firm. Finally, we derive conditions under which this exclusionary strategy is more profitable than competition and show how the retailer can share the collusive rents with the suppliers by raising the wholesale price above the competitive level.

5.5.1 Model

Suppose there are two suppliers, denoted 1 and 2, that sell their products through two retailers, denoted A and B. The retailers offer products that are imperfect substitutes and compete on price. Let q_{ik} denote the quantity demanded of supplier k's product from retailer i. Following Shubik and Levitan (1980), the utility function of a representative consumer is

$$U(\cdot) = v \sum_{i,k} q_{ik} - \frac{2}{(1+\mu)} \left[\sum_{i,k} q_{ik}^2 + \frac{\mu}{4} \left(\sum_{i,k} q_{ik} \right)^2 \right],$$

where $v > 0$ and $\mu \in [0, \infty)$ controls the degree of product substitutability. The products are independent when $\mu = 0$ and are increasingly substitutable as μ is raised; they are perfect substitutes as $\mu \to \infty$. From this specification, one can derive the inverse demand function for retailer i for product k:

$$p_{ik} = v - \frac{1}{1+\mu} \left(4q_{ik} + \mu \sum_{i,k} q_{ik} \right), \tag{5.1}$$

where p_{ik} is retailer i's price for product k. The price vector of all products is denoted $\mathbf{p} \equiv (p_{A1}, p_{A2}, p_{B1}, p_{B2})$.

Suppose supplier k makes a take-it-or-leave-it offer to sell its product to retailer i at a constant wholesale price of w_{ik} for each unit bought by retailer i. For simplicity, we assume that marginal cost is constant and normalize it to zero for the retailers (other than the cost for purchasing the input) and the suppliers. Hence, retailer i's marginal cost for product k is w_{ik} and the supplier's marginal cost is zero. There are no fixed costs.

The timing of the game is as follows.

Stage 1 Suppliers simultaneously make take-it-or-leave-it wholesale price offers to the retailers, and then retailers simultaneously decide whether to accept or reject these offers.

Stage 2 Retailers observe the stage 1 outcome and then simultaneously select retail prices.

The game is solved using backward induction.

Before moving on, let us address a limitation of our approach to modeling product substitutability. In the utility function above, the products are assumed to be symmetrically differentiated. This implies that product 1 from retailer A is just as substitutable as product 2 from retailer A and products 1 and 2 from retailer B. In reality, products are unlikely to be symmetrically differentiated in a setting with multiple retailers and manufacturers, because substitutability will arise from two distinct sources. The first source is intrabrand substitutability, where product 1 at retailer A is likely to be a closer substitute for product 1 at retailer B than for product 2 at retailer B, because product 1 is produced by the same manufacturer. The second source is interbrand substitutability, where product 1 at retailer A is likely to be a closer substitute for product 2 at retailer A than for product 2 at retailer B, because the products are sold by the same retailer. Our model abstracts from these issues because both intrabrand and interbrand substitutability are captured by the parameter μ. This implies that both rise as μ increases, which means that we can only analyze the case where both sources of substitutability are either strong or weak. We cannot comment on the cases where intrabrand substitutability is strong and interbrand substitutability is weak and vice versa. A more comprehensive analysis would require having separate parameters for the two types of substitutability. Our more modest objective is to offer a simple tractable exploratory analysis of the issues related to exclusionary hub-and-spoke cartels to inform our discussion of the cases. Consequently, a full analysis of intrabrand and interbrand substitutability lies beyond the scope of this book and is left for future research.

5.5.2 Integrated Monopolist Benchmark

We begin by supposing the actions of all firms are controlled by an integrated monopolist that seeks to maximize the profits of the supply chain. To do so, it would supply the input to its retailers at marginal cost, which implies $w_{ik}=0$ for all i and k, and maximize the sum of retailers' profits.

When $q_{ik} > 0$ for all i and k, the demand function of retailer i for product k is derived by inverting (5.1),

$$q_{ik}(p_{i1}, p_{i2}, p_{j1}, p_{j2}) = \frac{1}{4}(v - p_{ik} + \mu(\hat{p} - p_{ik})),$$ (5.2)

where $\hat{p} = \frac{1}{4}(p_{A1} + p_{A2} + p_{B1} + p_{B2})$ is the average retail price. We drop subscripts when there is no ambiguity. When $p_{ik} = p$ for all i and k, we write $q(p, p, p, p) = q(p) = \frac{1}{4}(v - p)$ and denote the industry profit at some common retail price p as $\Pi(p) = p4q(p)$.

Thus, when both retailers' demands are positive for both products, it follows that

$$\Pi(\mathbf{p}) = \sum_{i,k} p_{ik} \frac{1}{4}(v - p_{ik} + \mu(\hat{p} - p_{ik})).$$ (5.3)

Maximizing $\Pi(\mathbf{p})$ with respect to $\mathbf{p}$ gives us four first-order conditions:

$$\frac{1}{4}(v - 2(1 + \mu)p_{ik} + 2\mu\hat{p}) = 0, \ i \in \{A, B\}, k \in \{1, 2\}.$$ (5.4)

Solving (5.4), one obtains the monopoly price and quantity for each retailer:

$$p^m = \frac{v}{2} \text{ and } q(p^m) = \frac{v}{8}.$$

The integrated monopoly profits are $\Pi(p^m) = p^m 4q(p^m) = \frac{v^2}{4}$.

5.5.3 Competitive Equilibrium without Exclusion

Let us next solve for the equilibrium when the firms are vertically separated and their conduct is competitive. In this case, the profit functions of retailer i and supplier k are, respectively,

$$\pi_{Ri}(\mathbf{p}, w_{i1}, w_{i2}) = (p_{i1} - w_{i1})q_{i1}(\mathbf{p}) + (p_{i2} - w_{i2})q_{i2}(\mathbf{p})$$ (5.5)

and

$$\pi_{Sk}(w_{ik}, w_{jk}, \mathbf{p}) = w_{ik}q_{ik}(p_{i1}, p_{i2}, p_{j1}, p_{j2}) + w_{jk}q_{jk}(p_{i1}, p_{i2}, p_{j1}, p_{j2}).$$ (5.6)

When $w_{ik} = w$ and $p_{ik} = p$ for all i and k, we write $\pi_R(\mathbf{p}, w_{i1}, w_{i2}) = \pi_R(p, w) = (p - w)2q(p)$ and $\pi_S(w_{i1}, w_{i2}, \mathbf{p}) = \pi_S(w, p) = w2q(p)$.

Proposition 5.1 *The unique symmetric subgame perfect equilibrium has a wholesale price of* $w^N(\mu) = \dfrac{v}{2 + \dfrac{\mu}{4}\left(1 + \dfrac{1}{2 + \mu}\right)} \in \left(0, \dfrac{v}{2}\right]$

and a retail price of

$$p^N(w^N(\mu); \mu) = w^N(\mu) + \frac{2(v - w^N(\mu))}{4 + \mu} \in \left(0, \frac{3v}{4}\right]. \tag{5.7}$$

The equilibrium wholesale and retail prices are both strictly decreasing in the degree of product substitutability, μ.

To explain the role of product substitutability, first note that each manufacturer's demand is derived from consumers' demand for the retailers' differentiated products. Thus, the extent to which the consumers consider the retailers' products substitutable determines the extent to which the retailers consider the manufacturers' products differentiated. When consumers consider products perfectly substitutable at the retail level (i.e., $\mu \to \infty$), the manufacturers' products are also considered perfect substitutes by the retailers. Consequently, through standard reasoning, neither the retailers nor the suppliers place a markup on the product, $\lim_{\mu \to \infty} w^N(\mu) = 0$ and $\lim_{\mu \to \infty} p^N(w^N(\mu); \mu) = 0$ (and recall that each supplier's marginal cost is zero). As the products become less substitutable at the retail level (both within and across brands), retailers perceive greater differences between the manufacturers' products. This ensures that the retail and wholesale prices rise above costs, with the higher wholesale cost for retailers being partially passed through to consumers. When products are independent (i.e., $\mu = 0$), the retailers are local monopolies downstream and manufacturers are local monopolies upstream. Thus, the manufacturers charge the monopoly wholesale price, $w^N(0) = \frac{v}{2}$, with the retailers adding their own monopoly markup, $p^N(w^N(0); 0) = \frac{3v}{4}$.

Corollary 5.1 *There exists a critical level of product substitutability $\mu^* \in (0, \infty)$, where $p^N(\mu^*) = p^m$, such that the Nash equilibrium retail price is less than the monopoly price, $p^N(\mu^*) < p^m$, if and only if $\mu > \mu^*$.*

An implication of this corollary is that, under competition, the profits of the supply chain are maximized when $\mu = \mu^*$. Thus, the firms would increase their joint profits, $\Pi(p^m) > \Pi(p^N(\mu))$, by charging a higher retail price only when $\mu > \mu^*$, so products are sufficiently substitutable. When instead $\mu < \mu^*$, the firms would increase their joint profits by lowering their price.

5.5.4 Naked Exclusion

Next, we will calculate the joint profits that retailer A and both suppliers could earn if they formed a hub-and-spoke cartel that enabled the two suppliers to coordinate in nakedly excluding retailer B. The cartel's objective is to maximize the joint profits of the supply chain for retailer A's products. Thus, we can calculate the cartel's joint profits by analyzing the case where the cartel members operate as a vertically integrated firm that excludes retailer B.

Setting the quantities for retailer B equal to zero (because it is excluded) and presuming that the quantities for retailer A for both suppliers' products are positive, we can invert (5.1) to derive the demand function of retailer A for product k:

$$q_{Ak}(p_{Ak}, p_{Al}) = \frac{(1+\mu)}{2(2+\mu)}\left(v - p_{Ak} + \frac{\mu}{4}(p_{Ak} - p_{Al})\right).$$

A vertically integrated firm would supply the inputs to retailer A at cost (which is zero) $w_k = w_l = 0$ and maximize the retailer's profits, given by

$$\sum_k \left[p_{Ak}\frac{(1+\mu)}{2(2+\mu)}\left(v - p_{AK} + \frac{\mu}{4}(p_{AK} - p_{Al})\right)\right]. \tag{5.8}$$

Maximizing (5.8) with respect to p_{A1} and p_{A2} gives

$$\frac{(1+\mu)}{4(2+\mu)}[2v - (4+\mu)p_{Ak} - \mu p_{Al}] = 0, k \neq l, k \in \{1, 2\}. \tag{5.9}$$

Solving (5.9) delivers

$$p^m = \frac{v}{2} \quad \text{and} \quad q_A(p^m; \mu) = \frac{(1+\mu)}{2(2+\mu)}(v - p^m) \in \left(\frac{v}{8}, \frac{v}{4}\right].$$

Hence, the profits of the supply chain are $\Pi^E(\mu) = p^m 2q_A(p^m; \mu) = \frac{v^2(1+\mu)}{4(2+\mu)}$ $\in \left[\frac{v^2}{8}, \frac{v^2}{4}\right)$ and $\Pi^E(\mu) < \Pi(p^m)$ for all $\mu < \infty$.

Despite the vertically integrated firm always charging the monopoly retail price p^m, the profits from naked exclusion are less than the profits of a vertically integrated monopolist (with four products). That is because some consumers will not purchase when their preferred product is not available, though the number of lost consumers is less when interbrand and intrabrand substitutability are stronger. For instance, when the products are independent ($\mu = 0$), no consumers will purchase an alternative product when their preferred product is unavailable. In contrast, when the products are perfect substitutes ($\mu \to \infty$), then, at a given price, all consumers that purchase a product when it is available are still willing to purchase when that product is not available. For this reason, the profits from naked exclusion are higher when the products are more substitutable.

5.5.5 Incentives for Naked Exclusion

We are now in a position to examine firms' incentives to form a hub-and-spoke cartel that excludes retailer B. In order to maximize the cartel's joint profit, retailer A will set the same retail prices as the vertically integrated firm in subsection 5.5.4. We first solve for the conditions under which forming such a hub-and-spoke cartel is more profitable than competition and show that higher profits are associated with higher retail prices. Next, we demonstrate that retailer A can share the collusive rents with the suppliers by raising wholesale prices above competitive levels. As in section 3.5, we focus on the participation constraints and do not model the stability constraints, which would be satisfied when firms are sufficiently patient.

The hub-and-spoke cartel would earn the same joint profits as the vertically integrated firm in subsection 5.5.4, $\Pi^E(\mu)$. Using the analysis in subsection 5.5.3, we now calculate the total profits of the retailer and two suppliers when they compete,

$$\pi_R(p^N(w^N(\mu); \mu), w^N(\mu)) = (p^N(w^N(\mu); \mu) - w^N(\mu))2q(p^N(w^N(\mu); \mu))$$

and

$$\pi_S(w^N(\mu), p^N(w^N(\mu); \mu)) = w^N(\mu)2q(p^N(w^N(\mu); \mu)).$$

Their joint profits are

$$\Pi^N(\mu) = \pi_R(p^N(w^N(\mu); \mu), w^N(\mu)) + 2\pi_S(w^N(\mu), p^N(w^N(\mu); \mu)),$$

which can be simplified to

$$\Pi^N(\mu) = (p^N(w^N(\mu); \mu) + w^N(\mu))2q(p^N(w^N(\mu); \mu)).$$

We can now use the preceding equation to write $\Pi^E(\mu) - \Pi^N(\mu)$ as

$$\left[\frac{\Pi(p^m) - \Pi(p^N(w^N(\mu); \mu))}{2} \right] - w^N(\mu)2q(p^N(w^N(\mu); \mu)) \tag{5.10}$$
$$+ p^m 2[q_A(p^m; \mu) - q(p^m)]$$

Compared to competition, the three terms in (5.10) capture three effects of the exclusionary strategy on the cartel's profits. The first effect results from higher profits on retailer A's products because of higher prices at the retail level, and the second and third effects result from the exclusion of retailer B's products. More specifically, the first term in square brackets represents the increase in the cartel's profit from raising retail prices from $p^N(w^N(\mu); \mu)$ to p^m and thereby providing the cartel with the vertically integrated monopolist's profits for both retailer A's products. The second term captures the decrease in the cartel's profit because each supplier is no longer selling $q(p^N(w^N(\mu); \mu))$ units to retailer B at a price $w^N(\mu)$. The third term represents the increase in the cartel's profit resulting from retailer A now supplying an extra $2[q_A(p^m; \mu) - q(p^m)] > 0$ units of its products at a price of p^m to some of the consumers that otherwise would have purchased one of retailer B's products at p^m.

Proposition 5.2 states the conditions under which the suppliers and a retailer have a collective incentive to nakedly exclude the other retailer.

Proposition 5.2 *The two suppliers and a retailer have a joint incentive for naked exclusion if and only if $\mu > \mu^*$; that is, $\Pi^E(\mu) > \Pi^N(\mu)$ if and only if $\mu > \mu^*$.*

Together with corollary 5.1, proposition 5.2 implies that the exclusionary strategy will be profitable for the cartel if and only if it raises the retail price. This occurs when substitutability is sufficiently great; that is, $\mu > \mu^*$. Intuitively, when products are nearly perfect substitutes, the retailers and manufacturers do not impose markups on the products under competition, $\lim_{\mu \to \infty} w^N(\mu) = 0$ and $\lim_{\mu \to \infty} p^N(w^N(\mu); \mu) = 0$. Consequently, the suppliers lose next to no profit by reducing how much they sell to retailer B, implying that the second term in (5.10) is zero. However, the cartel still profits by charging a higher price to retailer A's consumers and by selling additional units to some of the consumers that prefer retailer B's products. In fact, the first and third terms in (5.10) sum to $\Pi(p^m) = p^m 4 q^m(p^m)$, implying that the cartel is able to obtain the vertically integrated monopoly profits. As substitutability increases, there is less incentive for naked exclusion, because the third term in (5.10) gets smaller since the cartel sells to fewer of retailer B's consumers. This effect can dominate the counteracting effects from the first and second terms. At the level of product substitutability where the retail prices are the same under competition and collusion, μ^*, both the retailers and manufacturers impose a markup on the product under competition but the retail price is at the monopoly level, $p^N(w^N(\mu^*); \mu^*) = p^m$. This implies that the first term in (5.10) is zero. The two other effects remain but exactly offset each other, so $\Pi^E(\mu^*) = \Pi^N(\mu^*)$.

Having established that the exclusionary strategy can be profitable, we now show that the retailer can share the resultant collusive rents with the suppliers by raising the wholesale price.

Proposition 5.3 *If $\mu > \mu^*$, then there exists a unique $\underline{w} > w^N(\mu)$ and a unique $\bar{w} \in (\underline{w}, p^m)$ such that if and only if the wholesale price is raised from $w^N(\mu)$ to some $w \in (\underline{w}, \bar{w})$ will the suppliers' and the retailer's participation constraints be satisfied.*

There is a range of wholesale prices between $w^N(\mu)$ and p^m for which the suppliers' and the retailer's participation constraints are satisfied. The wholesale price has to increase above $w^N(\mu)$ to compensate the suppliers; otherwise, the exclusionary strategy would not be profitable for the suppliers, because it reduces demand for each of the supplier's products. This is so for two reasons. First, given that two of the four differentiated products are no longer available, the quantity of a supplier's product that is demanded is less than before. Second, exclusion eliminates competition at the retail level, which raises the retail prices to the monopoly level, further reducing the demand for the suppliers' products. However, while the wholesale price must increase to ensure that the suppliers' participation constraints are satisfied, it cannot increase beyond an upper threshold that lies below the monopoly price p^m. That is because when the wholesale price is close to p^m, the retailer's profits will be close to zero, and consequently the retailer's participation constraint will not be satisfied. Similar to that found in section 3.5, this range is as wide as possible when products are nearly perfect substitutes, with $\lim_{\mu \to \infty} \underline{w} = w^N(\mu)$ and $\lim_{\mu \to \infty} \bar{w} = p^m$. That is because neither a supplier nor a retailer has a markup under competition. Therefore, a supplier's profit will increase even if the new wholesale price is positive yet very close to zero, and the retailers' profits will increase when the new wholesale price is below but very close to p^m. The range gets smaller as substitutability increases.

To summarize, we have shown that forming a hub-and-spoke cartel to nakedly exclude a downstream firm is profitable when it raises retail prices to the monopoly level. This occurs when intrabrand and interbrand substitutability are sufficiently great. Furthermore, we showed that the retailer can share the collusive rents with the upstream suppliers by raising the wholesale price above competitive levels and that this can result in each of the cartel members earning higher profits.

5.5.6　Proofs
Proof of proposition 5.1　First, we solve for the equilibrium retail prices and quantities in stage 2 for given wholesale prices. Maximizing (5.5) with respect to the price of product $k \neq l$ gives

$$\frac{1}{4}\left[(v - p_{ik} + \mu(\hat{p} - p_{ik})) - (p_{ik} - w_{ik})\left(1 + \frac{3\mu}{4}\right) + (p_{il} - w_{il})\frac{\mu}{4}\right] = 0. \tag{5.11}$$

Solving (5.11) simultaneously for $i=\{A, B\}$ and $k=\{1, 2\}$ gives

$$p_{ik}^N(\mathbf{w}; \mu) = w_{ik} + \frac{2(v - w_{ik})}{4 + \mu}$$

$$+ \frac{\mu^2(w_{il} - w_{ik}) + 2\mu(2 + \mu)(w_{jk} + w_{jl} - 2w_{ik})}{4(4 + \mu)(4 + 3\mu)}, \qquad (5.12)$$

so the equilibrium average retail price is

$$\hat{p}^N(\mathbf{w}; \mu) \equiv \frac{1}{4} \sum_{i,k} p_{ik}^N(\mathbf{w}; \mu) = \hat{w} + \frac{2(v - \hat{w})}{4 + \mu}, \qquad (5.13)$$

where $\hat{w} \equiv \dfrac{1}{4}(w_{i1} + w_{i2} + w_{j1} + w_{j2})$ denotes the average wholesale price.

Next, we solve for the equilibrium wholesale prices in stage 1. Substituting (5.12) and (5.13) into $\pi_{Sk}(\cdot) = w_{ik}q_{ik}(\cdot) + w_{jk}q_{ik}(\cdot)$ and maximizing with respect to w_{ik} gives

$$\frac{\partial \pi_{Sk}}{\partial w_{ik}} = q_{ik}(\cdot) + \frac{w_{ik}}{4}\left[-\frac{\partial p_{ik}^N}{\partial w_{ik}} + \mu\left(\frac{\partial \hat{p}^N}{\partial w_{ik}} - \frac{\partial p_{ik}^N}{\partial w_{ik}}\right)\right]$$

$$+ \frac{w_{jk}}{4}\left[-\frac{\partial p_{jk}^N}{\partial w_{ik}} + \mu\left(\frac{\partial \hat{p}^N}{\partial w_{ik}} - \frac{\partial p_{jk}^N}{\partial w_{ik}}\right)\right] = 0, \qquad (5.14)$$

where

$$q_{ik}(\cdot) = \frac{1}{4}(v - p_{ik}^N(\cdot) + \mu(\hat{p}^N(\cdot) - p_{ik}^N(\cdot))),$$

$$\frac{\partial p_{ik}^N}{\partial w_{ik}} = \frac{32 + 32\mu + 7\mu^2}{4(4 + \mu)(4 + 3\mu)} > 0,$$

$$\frac{\partial p_{jk}^N}{\partial w_{ik}} = \frac{\mu(2 + \mu)}{2(4 + \mu)(4 + 3\mu)} > 0, \text{ and } \frac{\partial \hat{p}^N}{\partial w_{ik}} = \frac{2 + \mu}{4(4 + \mu)} > 0 \text{ for all } \mu \geq 0.$$

Solving (5.14) for $i = \{A, B\}$ and $k = \{1, 2\}$ then shows that $w^N(\mu)$ is as claimed. Substituting $w^N(\mu)$ into (5.12) shows that $p^N(w^N(\mu); \mu)$ is as claimed.

Finally, totally differentiating $p^N(w^N(\mu); \mu)$ with respect to μ yields

$$\frac{dp^N}{d\mu} = \frac{\partial p^N}{\partial \mu} + \frac{\partial p^N}{\partial w}\frac{\partial w^N}{\partial \mu} = -\frac{2(v - w^N)}{(4 + \mu)^2} + \left(\frac{2 + \mu}{4 + \mu}\right)\frac{\partial w^N}{\partial \mu} < 0$$

from

$$\frac{\partial w^N}{\partial \mu} = -\frac{w^N(\mu)}{2 + \frac{\mu}{4}\left(1 + \frac{1}{2 + \mu}\right)}\left(\frac{1}{4} + \frac{1}{2(2 + \mu)^2}\right) < 0,$$

where $w^N(0) = \dfrac{v}{2}$ and $p^N(w^N(0); 0) = \dfrac{3v}{4}$, and $\lim\limits_{\mu \to \infty} w^N(\mu) = 0$ and $\lim\limits_{\mu \to \infty} p^N(w^N(\mu); \mu) = 0$. ∎

Proof of proposition 5.2 We first establish that there exists a unique level of μ, initially denoted $\underline{\mu}$, that sets $\Pi^E(\underline{\mu}) = \Pi^N(\underline{\mu})$, where $\Pi^E(\mu) > \Pi^N(\mu)$ for all $\mu > \underline{\mu}$. It follows from $\Pi^E(0) = \dfrac{v^2}{8}$, $\Pi^N(0) = \dfrac{5v^2}{32} > \dfrac{v^2}{8}$, $\lim\limits_{\mu \to \infty} \Pi^E(\mu) = \dfrac{v^2}{4} > 0$, and $\lim\limits_{\mu \to \infty} \Pi^N(\mu) = 0$ that if $\dfrac{\partial \Pi^E(\mu)}{\partial \mu} > \dfrac{\partial \Pi^N(\mu)}{\partial \mu}$, then $\underline{\mu}$ exists and is unique.

Differentiating $\Pi^E(\mu)$ and $\Pi^N(\mu)$ with respect to μ yields

$$\frac{\partial \Pi^E(\mu)}{\partial \mu} = \frac{v^2}{4(2+\mu)^2} > 0$$

and

$$\frac{\partial \Pi^N(\mu)}{\partial \mu} = \frac{v^2}{4(2+\mu)^2}\left[1 - \frac{X(\mu)}{(4+\mu)^2(16+11\mu+\mu^2)^3}\right],$$

where

$$X(\mu) \equiv 81920 + 194560\mu + 202240\mu^2 + 143040\mu^3 + 90560\mu^4$$
$$+ 47876\mu^5 + 17203\mu^6 + 3715\mu^7 + 433\mu^8 + 21\mu^9 > 0.$$

Given that the expression in square brackets is less than 1, it follows that $\dfrac{\partial \Pi^E(\mu)}{\partial \mu} > \dfrac{\partial \Pi^N(\mu)}{\partial \mu}$. Note that the former is equivalent to the derivative of the third term in (5.10) and the latter is equivalent to the derivative of the sum of the first two terms.

Next, we prove $\underline{\mu} = \mu^*$. It suffices to show that $\Pi^E(\mu^*) = \Pi^N(\mu^*)$ when $p^m = p^N(w^N(\mu^*); \mu^*)$. Rearranging (5.7) yields $w^N(\mu^*) = \dfrac{p^m(4+\mu^*) - 2v}{2+\mu^*}$, and substituting into $\Pi^N(\mu^*) = (p^m + w^N(\mu^*))\, 2q(p^m)$ gives

$$\Pi^N(\mu^*) = \frac{v}{4}\left(p^m + \frac{p^m(4+\mu^*)-2v}{2+\mu^*}\right) = \frac{v}{4}\left(\frac{p^m(6+2\mu^*)-2v}{2+\mu^*}\right).$$

Noting that

$$\Pi^E(\mu^*) - \Pi^N(\mu^*) = p^m\frac{v(1+\mu^*)}{2(2+\mu^*)} - \frac{v}{4}\left(\frac{p^m(6+2\mu^*)-2v}{2+\mu^*}\right) = \frac{v(v-2p^m)}{2(2+\mu^*)},$$

it follows from $p^m = \dfrac{v}{2}$ that $\Pi^E(\mu^*) - \Pi^N(\mu^*) = 0$, which then implies $\mu^* = \underline{\mu}$. ∎

Proof of proposition 5.3 Supplier k's participation constraint is satisfied if $wq_A(p^m; \mu) > \pi_S(w^N(\cdot), p^N(\cdot))$. Substituting for $\pi_S(w^N(\cdot), p^N(\cdot))$ yields

$$wq_A(p^m; \mu) > w^N(\mu)2q(p^N(w^N(\mu); \mu)).$$

Rearranging shows that $w > w^N(\mu)\dfrac{2q(p^N(w^N(\mu); \mu))}{q_A(p^m; \mu)} \equiv \underline{w}$, where $\underline{w} > w^N(\mu)$ if $2q(p^N(w^N(\mu); \mu)) > q_A(p^m; \mu)$, which is true for all $\mu > \mu^*$.

The retailer's participation constraint is satisfied if $(p^m - w)2q_A(p^m; \mu) > \pi_R(p^N(\cdot), w^N(\cdot))$. Substituting for $\pi_R(p^N(\cdot), w^N(\cdot))$ yields

$$(p^m - w)2q_A(p^m; \mu) > (p^N(w^N(\mu); \mu) - w^N(\mu))2q(p^N(w^N(\mu); \mu)).$$

Rearranging shows that

$$w < p^m - (p^N(w^N(\mu); \mu) - w^N(\mu))\frac{q(p^N(w^N(\mu); \mu))}{q_A(p^m; \mu)} \equiv \bar{w},$$

where $\bar{w} < p^m$ and $\bar{w} > \underline{w}$ if and only if $\mu > \mu^*$, where $\Pi^E(\mu) > \Pi^N(\mu)$. ∎

6   General Assessment of Hub-and-Spoke Cartels

The 16 hub-and-spoke cartels examined in chapters 3–5 tell 16 different stories of collusion. While the specific elements of those stories may differ, there is a common set of events and driving forces that helps in understanding why a cartel formed, how the cartel operated, and how effective collusion was. In this chapter, we identify those common forces to derive some general lessons and recognize critical sources of heterogeneity in these cartels.

To begin, table 6.1 provides a summary of the main features of these cartels that will be a useful reference throughout this chapter.

Table 6.1 reminds us where in the vertical chain the hub and spokes can reside and whether the intent of the cartel was to raise prices or exclude a competitor. To elaborate on the location of the cartel's effect (far-right column), chapters 3 and 4 focused on cartels that coordinated spokes' prices, so competition was constrained at the same stage of the supply chain as the spokes. In contrast, chapter 5 considered the coordination of upstream firms to exclude a downstream firm, so despite collusion occurring upstream, the effect of this collusion was to dampen competition downstream. In all the cartels, the harm from collusion was always experienced by the buyers of the downstream firms. This is even true for the cartels in chapter 4. Though collusion affected upstream prices, those higher upstream prices were passed through to downstream buyers by a "cost-plus" contract between the downstream intermediary-hub and the buyer.

The discussion that follows will revolve around three of the questions central to the study of cartels: (1) How do cartels form?; (2) How do cartels operate?; and (3) How effective are cartels? Much of our discussion will focus on the role of the hub. As we have seen in the previous chapters, the hub acted as the nexus of the communication network in all but one of the

Table 6.1
Summary of cartel types

Chapter	Location of the hub	Location of the spokes	Intent of collusion	Location of the effect of collusion on competition
3	upstream	downstream	raising prices	downstream
4	downstream	upstream	raising prices	upstream
5	downstream	upstream	exclusion	downstream

cases (Pipes-US), and it played a critical role in enforcing the agreed collusive arrangement, both in terms of monitoring compliance and punishing when there was evidence of noncompliance.

6.1 Cartel Formation

Let us begin by identifying the firm responsible for instigating collusion. In the vast majority of cases across all three cartel types, collusion was initiated by the hub. There is clear evidence of this in Kits-UK, Paints-Poland, Drugs-US, Bread-Canada, Automobiles-US, Insurance-US, Movies-US, and Toys-US. In Toys-UK, Desiccant-UK, and e-books-US, the spokes might have voiced complaints for which collusion could be an appropriate response, but it was the hub that was energetic and entrepreneurial in developing a collusive plan. Only in Dairy-UK (for which farmers were primarily responsible) and Fiberglass-US (for which it was the upstream spokes) can we not conclude that the hub was the primary force behind the cartel's formation. In the other cases (Drugstores-Belgium, Chicken-Chile, and Pipes-US), a lack of documentary evidence prevents us from determining which firm instigated the collusion.

Given a proposed collusive arrangement, it was common for a hub to exert extraordinary effort in convincing the spokes to agree to that arrangement. A common challenge was that a spoke would not comply unless it believed enough other spokes were intending to comply. It is particularly well documented in Toys-UK, Toys-US, and e-books-US that a spoke needed the assurance that the other spokes were going to abide by the plan. Coordinated adoption often required a series of extensive bilateral communications between the hub and each spoke, where the hub would go back and forth between spokes to obtain their consent to the collusive plan and then share that information with the other spokes. An essential part of these communications was the hub convincing each spoke that their rivals would go through with their reported intentions. While a regular cartel would have all firms meet together to agree, the hub had to achieve that same level of mutual understanding through back-and-forth bilateral communications between spokes that often did not trust each other.

The task of instigating collusion was complicated further in a few cases where it is arguable that some spokes did not want to comply even if other spokes did. Such a situation arose when a downstream firm was looking to increase its market share, as documented in Kits-UK and Drugs-US, or when an upstream manufacturer-spoke did not want to participate in the exclusion of a downstream retailer because of the expected loss of sales of their product, as occurred in Toys-US and Movies-US. When a spoke was not interested in collusion, cooperation was commonly obtained by having an upstream hub threaten to deny supply or a downstream hub threaten to refuse to buy. Because of this threat of exclusion, the spokes reluctantly participated in the cartel.

Let us end our discussion of cartel formation by considering why one type of cartel formed rather than another. This is most relevant for the cartels that had the objective of dampening downstream competition, because they differed in how they went about achieving this objective. The reason for this variation likely lies in the specific market structure and industry characteristics prior to cartel formation. The exclusionary cartels were often formed to counter the threat of smaller retailers trying to increase their market share at the expense of the downstream hub. The hub was usually the dominant downstream supplier in its market. It was well placed to coordinate the upstream firms to exclude their rivals, because it offered a wide product range and the threat of refusal to buy was sufficient to coerce suppliers into cooperating. In contrast, the cartels with downstream price collusion formed to facilitate collusion between two or more firms that were usually well established in the market and thus more interested in achieving high margins than in expanding their market presence. Prior to collusion, there was often intense price competition downstream and/or interbrand competition, so profits throughout the chain were probably low. This provided the hub with the opportunity to facilitate downstream collusion for mutual gain. In some cartels, the hub initiated downstream collusion with the intention of also raising wholesale prices. In other cartels, the hub initiated downstream collusion to raise the retail profits of its products with the expectation that this would reduce the chances of its product being delisted in favor of other more profitable alternatives. Though the hub was rarely the sole dominant player in the upstream sector, this obstacle could be overcome by encouraging the spokes to raise the prices of rival products or forming multiple hub-and-spoke cartels with their rival suppliers.

6.2 Cartel Operations

Let us next turn our attention to cartel operations, which encompass coordinating on a collusive outcome, monitoring compliance with that outcome, and punishing deviations from that outcome. Communications intended to coordinate on an outcome (e.g., what price to set or which firms to exclude) are closely related to communications to achieve mutual understanding among firms to collude. The latter was discussed earlier, and there is little to add concerning the former. Therefore, we will focus on monitoring protocols and punishment devices.

Both the hub and the spokes were often active in monitoring compliance, and this is well documented in Toys-UK, Paints-Poland, Drugstores-Belgium, and Toys-US. In many cartels, the hub had a pivotal role in acting as a mediator of disputes when a claimed episode of noncompliance was brought forward by a spoke. In the event that a spoke discovered a rival deviating, the spoke would convey its findings to the hub, upon which the hub would contact the deviant spoke and seek to get it back into compliance. The hub also served to assure spokes that others were complying, which may have been crucial to avoiding a temporary price war or the collapse of the collusive agreement. Such communications are evident in Toys-UK, Desiccant-UK, Bread-Canada, and Toys-US. The hub was in a prime position to monitor the agreement in Pipes-US and Insurance-US because the upstream spokes had to submit their bids to the downstream hub to gain business.

With regard to the punishment of deviants, the hub was able to add to the cartel's armory in two crucial respects. One common punishment across the three cartel structures was that the hub would exclude a noncompliant spoke. This is clearly documented in Kits-UK, Paints-Poland, and Chicken-Chile, where the upstream hub would refuse to supply a deviant downstream spoke. Similarly, in Insurance-US, Toys-US, and Movies-US, there is evidence that the downstream hubs were willing to refuse to buy from upstream deviants. A second type of punishment was available to an upstream hub: it could threaten to increase the wholesale prices it charged to a noncompliant spoke, as was evident in Desiccant-UK and Paints-Poland. This would limit the gain from any deviation and incentivize the firms to comply. In Desiccant-UK, the hub also proposed a scheme in which it would lower wholesale prices for nondeviants in order to compensate them.

When the factors of monitoring and punishment are compared across the cartels in which collusion was on prices, it is reasonable to conclude that collusion would be easier to sustain when the hub was an intermediary (and spokes were upstream suppliers) compared to an upstream supplier (and spokes were downstream firms). This conclusion is based on three features. First, monitoring was perfect in the cartels with an intermediary-hub, because the upstream spokes had to submit their bids to the hub, so any deviation would be immediately and unambiguously detected. In contrast, while the spokes of the cartels with downstream price collusion were mainly at the retail level, so that prices were publicly available, monitoring compliance was not a costless activity, because the firms had to invest resources in checking each other's prices. Second, punishment could be more rapid in the cartels with an intermediary-hub, because the hub could exclude a deviant spoke from the list of suppliers it provided to its client. Hence, an upstream spoke could not expect to benefit from a deviation even in the short term in the same way that a retailer-spoke could with an upstream hub. Third, it is easier for both the spokes and hub to profit from higher downstream prices when the hub is an intermediary, because collusion could result in higher prices without any loss in sales. This results from the downstream hub being contracted by the client before the suppliers' prices were revealed to that client, so the hub would not lose business to rivals.[1]

While our focus in this book is on cartels for which the hub was the primary player when it came to communications, it is still striking how little direct communication there was among horizontally related firms, whether it was to instigate collusion, convey future pricing intentions, or report noncompliance. Even in the cartels where communications were not exclusively through the hub, the spokes rarely communicated with each other and such communications only served to supplement the bilateral communications between the hub and spokes. In Kits-UK, Desiccant-UK, and Automobiles-US, the hub organized a meeting among the spokes when the cartel arrangement was being instigated. In e-books-US, there were direct communications among the upstream publisher-spokes preceding the entry of Apple (the hub) into the market. Pipes-US was unique among our cases in that it was the only one where the hub delegated an information exchange role to one of the upstream spokes, so there was frequent communication between the spokes. Even so, all documented meetings except one were bilateral between the ringleader spoke and another spoke. The exception was when the spokes needed to decide how to divide an unusually large order. Finally, in Dairy-UK and Bread-Canada, where there were multiple upstream hubs, there is evidence of direct communication between the hubs at the outset of a cartel episode.

It is natural to ask why there was not more communication between the spokes in these cartels. While the multiple crucial roles played by the hub suggest that collusion would not have occurred without the hub's intervention, some direct communication would have helped ensure that the messages were truthful and not distorted (unintentionally or otherwise). This is especially true when the firms were initially setting up the arrangement, and the few examples of multilateral communication described here did seem to happen at an early stage. Once the cartel was up and running, communication was likely to be less necessary, and there is evidence in Toys-UK and Desiccant-UK that the firms found running the collusive scheme easier over time once it became clear that the scheme was working.

The lack of direct communication between the spokes could reflect the recognition that it was more dangerous from a legal perspective. While communications between an upstream firm and a downstream firm are to be expected in a competitive market, communications between competitors are not. This may mean that hub-and-spoke cartels communicate more frequently than standard cartels, and this frequency may replace the need for one message to be received by all firms. The firms may have also understood that there is a greater burden of proof on competition authorities to prove guilt when communications are bilateral between a supplier and its retailers. It is even possible that the firms did not realize that communicating indirectly via a supplier or buyer was illegal. However, that seems implausible in light of documented evidence in many of the cases. For example, in Toys-UK, a senior manager of the hub Hasbro warned his subordinates to "never ever put anything in writing, it's highly illegal."[2] In Desiccant-UK, a spoke's initial response to a coordinated price rise proposed by the hub was to say "I have run it past my solicitors, who advise me not to accept this policy."[3] Furthermore, in both Kits-UK and Dairy-UK, the Office of Fair Trading was made aware of similar conduct in the market just before the formation of these cartels, and it had advised the firms that it would likely be a breach of the law. Likewise, in Fiberglass-US, a manager expressed the following about the scheme he was instigating: "I don't know how we do this well without crossing the line on certain antitrust/price fixing rules."[4] In many of the cases, it seems unlikely that cartel members were unaware of the possible illegality of their actions.

6.3   Cartel Efficacy

The two key measures of cartel efficacy are the overcharge (how much higher the price is) and duration (the length of time during which prices are higher and, more generally, collusion is affecting market outcomes). The case material generally does not have overcharge estimates (with e-books-US being an exception), so our attention will focus on duration. As a point of comparison, most past studies of (discovered) cartels report a mean duration between 5 and 8 years. For instance, Levenstein and Suslow (2006) surveyed several studies and found a mean cartel duration between 4.5 and 7.5 years. Taking account of selection bias in having been discovered, Harrington and Wei (2017) found a mean duration for all cartels (both discovered and undiscovered) in the range of 5.3 to 6.8 years.

The duration of the cartels in our sample is reported in table 6.2. What is striking is their brevity. Overall, these cartels had a median duration of 3 years and a mean duration slightly above 3.5 years. This is roughly half the length of more standard cartels.

Available information shows that these cartels were active at the time of detection (though to varying degrees of effectiveness), which means that cartel death was caused by detection and prosecution rather than internal collapse. Thus, the relatively short duration of hub-and-spoke cartels can be traced to the rapidity with which the cartel was detected. In light of the significant role of discovery in a cartel's demise, let us explore how detection occurred. For eight of the 16 cartel cases in our sample, there is no information pertaining to the cartel's discovery. That includes all four of the exclusionary cartel cases where the hub was downstream. Our discussion will therefore focus on the remaining eight cases.

Table 6.2
Cartel detection and duration

Market	Country	Chapter subsection	Time until detection	Duration (of effect)
Toys	UK	3.2.1	2.5 years	2.5 years
Desiccant	UK	3.2.2	3 years	3 years[a]
Paints and varnishes	Poland	3.2.3	?	3 years
Drugstore, perfumery, and hygiene products	Belgium	3.2.4	4 years	4.5 years
Replica football kits	UK	3.2.5	6 months	1 year
Pharmaceutical products	US	3.2.6	3 months	3 months
Dairy	UK	3.2.7	1 year	1.5 years
Bread	Canada	3.2.8	13.5 years	16 years
Chicken	Chile	3.2.9	?	3.5 years
Automobile retailing	US	3.2.10	1 year	1 year
Commercial insurance	US	4.2.1	7 years	7 years
Specialty pipes	US	4.2.2	?	3.5 years
Movie exhibition	US	5.2.1	6 months	1 year
Toys	US	5.2.2	2 years	3 years
Fiberglass insulation	US	5.2.3	?	5 years
e-books	US	5.2.4	2 years	3 years

Note: The time of detection is the earliest time for which there is evidence that a competition authority suspected collusion, as reflected in receiving a complaint, requesting information from a cartel member, opening an investigation, or having a leniency application. In many cases, the documentation is incomplete and we have provided our best guess as to time until detection and duration length.
[a] While it was suspected that the cartel in Desiccant-UK may have existed in some form for an additional 11 years, it was only prosecuted for the final 3 years.

Leniency applications were responsible for the detection (and subsequent collapse) of three of the cartels—Drugstores-Belgium, Dairy-UK, and Bread-Canada—all of which were cartels with downstream price collusion (and multiple upstream hubs). In these cases, it was an upstream hub that applied for leniency. We may expect that the hub would be in a prime position to apply for and receive leniency because, as the nexus of a communication network, it would have had the necessary evidence to assist the competition authority in prosecuting the other cartel members. In contrast, a spoke's evidence would be indirect. At most, it would possess documented messages from the hub expressing its intent to share rivals' future pricing intentions but without evidence that the hub actually did so. This would put a spoke at a disadvantage compared with the hub, because it might fear its limited information would be insufficient to receive leniency. Furthermore, the fact that there were multiple hubs in each of the three cases may have motivated a race to apply for leniency. The incentive to be the first leniency applicant is likely to be lower for a hub when it is the only one.

It was an investigation by the competition authority on another matter that unearthed the Toys-UK and Desiccant-UK cartels, both of which involved downstream price collusion. The information was discovered at the hub in Toys-UK and at a spoke in Desiccant-UK. In both cases, the firms responded by filing a leniency application. While such events may be unlikely, the chances of it happening to a hub may be greater than for a spoke, because the hub will possess more potential evidence about the cartel. In the case of Desiccant-UK, there were some multilateral communications among the firms, and this may have meant that the spoke had more information than if there were just bilateral communications between the hub and each spoke.

Another two cartels—Kits-UK and Drugs-US—were discovered following a spoke's complaint to the competition authority. Both cartels involved downstream price collusion. In Kits-UK, spoke Sports Soccer complained to the Office of Fair Trading, and in Drugs-US, spoke Dart Drug complained to the Antitrust Division of the US Department of Justice. Prior to the cartel's formation, both Sports Soccer and Dart Drug were low-priced retailers seeking to expand their market shares and thus proved to be recalcitrant spokes. Such retailers may have preferred competition to collusion but were induced to cooperate by the threat of not receiving supply from the upstream hub. Their desire to expand market share, rather than margins, may have led them to report collusion. It is not surprising that these two cartels had the shortest lives in our sample, with the cartels being detected in less than six months. This may also explain how the exclusionary cartels were detected, as perhaps the spokes—which may have preferred competition to collusion—reported it or engaged in little effort to hide it.

The remaining cartel, Insurance-US, was discovered during a public investigation into an industry-wide business practice. This was the second-longest cartel episode in our sample, lasting more than twice as long as average. Its longevity may reflect that collusion is more effective when the hub is an intermediary, as explained earlier.

Let us finish by speculating on other reasons that may explain why detection is easier for hub-and-spoke cartels. The first is that detection may occur because of "leaky" information flows. In standard cartels, the members strive to keep their communications secret because they know that revealing any such communications creates a high likelihood of prosecution and conviction. That is not the case with a hub-and-spoke cartel, for an upstream firm and a downstream firm regularly communicate under competition. Furthermore, it is perfectly reasonable, and sometimes necessary, for a retailer to convey its pricing intentions to an upstream supplier. Perhaps the normalcy of those communications led members of a hub-and-spoke cartel not to be as diligent in keeping them confidential, which could then result in other parties learning of the collusion. The widespread flow of such information is consistent with the presence of simultaneous hub-and-spoke cartels, as occurred in Paints-Poland, Drugstores-Belgium, and Dairy-UK.

Another reason why detection may be more likely for a hub-and-spoke cartel is that it may involve a larger number of employees. As documented in Toys-UK, collusion engaged senior management to organize and set up the collusive scheme and account managers of both the hub and the spokes to operationalize it by passing messages not only between the hub and spokes but also between other account managers internally within the hub. Having a large group of employees concerned with possible sanctions increases the chances of a leniency application. Furthermore, trusting one's co-conspirators is likely to be more difficult when there are more of them so each conspirator may be more eager to be the first to report the cartel to the competition authority, which further raises the probability of an early leniency application. In contrast, in standard cartels, where it may be possible to control the strategy and operation of the cartel at the level of senior management, there may be fewer people with knowledge of the cartel and thus a lower chance of a leniency application and, more generally, detection.

7 Competition Law and Hub-and-Spoke Collusion

The preceding chapters have explored why hub-and-spoke cartels form and how they operate. This information is of practical value only if it can be used to deter the formation of hub-and-spoke cartels and, when they do form, assist in detection and prosecution. To that end, this chapter reviews how hub-and-spoke collusion is treated by competition law, examines the legal challenges posed by this brand of collusion, and offers new legal strategies. In doing so, our coverage of jurisprudence is not meant to be comprehensive. For more extensive treatments, the interested reader is referred to Odudu (2011) for the UK, Prewitt and Fails (2015) for the EU, and Orbach (2016) for the US.

Hub-and-spoke collusion involves an information exchange in which a firm (hub) collects and disseminates information on price or supply intentions among its upstream suppliers or downstream customers (spokes) for the purpose of restraining competition. Restraining competition can mean raising downstream (as well as upstream) prices, which was covered in chapters 3 and 4, or excluding some downstream firms, which was covered in chapter 5.

7.1 Defining Liability

An immediate enforcement challenge is that many vertical information exchanges are lawful, for it is necessary that an upstream supplier and a downstream customer communicate in order to transact. For example, in bargaining over the upstream price, a downstream retailer might express its pricing intentions to an upstream supplier. Thus, the communication of pricing intentions, which is so central to unlawful collusion intended to raise prices, can have a legitimate rationale when it is between firms with a vertical relationship. When the goal of hub-and-spoke collusion is exclusion, there is analogously the challenge of determining whether unequal treatment of a firm's suppliers or customers is part of a coordinated strategy to exclude. In evaluating such conduct, US law gives considerable discretion to upstream and downstream firms in laying out the terms of their arrangement, and that includes a downstream firm agreeing not to buy from an upstream supplier or an upstream firm agreeing not to sell to a downstream firm. In considering whether Toys "R" Us was in violation of Section 5 of the FTC Act, the FTC made clear that it would "not intrude on the right of a trader unilaterally to announce terms on which it will deal with suppliers, even if those terms disadvantage a rival. That is a company's long-recognized right under *United States v. Colgate & Co.*, 250 U.S. 300 (1919), reaffirmed by the Supreme Court in 1984 in *Monsanto Co. v. Spray-Rite Servs. Co.*, 465 U.S. 752 (1984)."[1]

The point is that some of the communications and conduct that are integral to unlawful hub-and-spoke collusion—sharing pricing intentions and excluding firms—can be consistent with lawful competition. In order to clarify when vertical information exchanges and agreements cross over into illegal territory, the FTC went on to say that "what a firm cannot do is to coordinate with rival firms on the terms of that arrangement."[2] It is the presence of a *rim*—a horizontal agreement among the spokes—that moves vertical agreements into illegal territory.[3] Hub-and-spoke arrangements can be interpreted as tacit agreements: "The critical elements of tacit agreement [are]: the communication of pricing intent; interdependent pricing; and a basis for an inference of a causal relationship. . . . It makes sense to treat at least some hub-and-spoke conspiracies as a species of tacit agreement because express vertical agreements may serve a function similar to a direct communication of intention among rivals; the agreements coordinate the interdependent responses of the rivals by providing strategic information that each recipient knows its rivals are also receiving" (Page 2017, 619, 624). Multiple vertical agreements between a hub and spokes that do not connect and coordinate the spokes (and thus are "rimless") are not actionable.

A few examples from some cases previously discussed will elucidate what it means for there to be a rim. In Toys-UK, Hasbro was seeking to convince retailers Argos and Littlewoods to price at the recommended level, an obstacle being each retailer's concern that the other retailer would not do so:

Littlewoods . . . expressed doubts about Hasbro's ability to prevent undercutting by Argos. . . . "It was at this point that Mike McCulloch intimated . . . that he had been having discussions with the major opposition (Argos) and they were of the same opinion, i.e. that they could not agree to the new pricing structure for fear of being undercut. It did need the agreement of both parties in order for the plan to work, but that if [Littlewoods] would agree to go along with it then Mike McCulloch, using this knowledge, was confident that he could persuade them to do the same."[4]

By sharing one retailer's concern with the other and expressing that the retailer would be willing to price at the higher level if the other retailer was assured of doing so, Hasbro established an agreement between the two retailer-spokes that each would price at the recommended level if the other did so. That mutual understanding formed the rim that turned those vertical relationships into a horizontal agreement.

In Kits-UK, there was a well-documented series of bilateral communications between manufacturer Umbro, which was acting as the hub, and retailer-spokes JJB and Sports Soccer. JJB conveyed to Umbro that "JJB would sell at High Street prices unless others discounted."[5] Umbro then took that information and conveyed it to Sports Soccer, which agreed to raise its price "conditionally on the others also raising or maintaining their prices to or at the same level."[6] Finally, Umbro went back to JJB and conveyed that "Sports Soccer had agreed to raise their prices and to sell at High Street prices."[7] These bilateral communications effectively substituted for direct communications between JJB and Sports Soccer and thereby formed an agreement between those retailers.

In the case of Automobiles-US, the rim was formed when Mid-Atlantic Toyota (hub) announced a plan at a meeting with Toyota dealers (spokes) that they adopt the Total Concept Protective Program and raise the sticker price of their automobiles by $533. The hub then "facilitated the dealers' adherence to the scheme by circulating sign-up sheets. The use of these sheets allowed each dealer to observe which other dealers were joining the program."[8] This public announcement with publicly observed actions formed the basis for dealers' conduct being coordinated, not independent.

A related tactic served to form the rim in Movies-US, where theater chain Interstate, acting as the hub, wrote a letter to each of eight distributors in which it described a proposed course of action to exclude theater chains that priced too low. Most critically, it made clear in the letter that the same letter had been sent to all eight distributors. Thus, there was an overt act of communication that delivered the mutual understanding of a plan among the distributor-spokes that would result in the coordinated adoption of this plan.

An example of a case for which the evidence fell short of establishing a rim was one pursued by PepsiCo against Coca-Cola.[9] Coca-Cola had been supplying its syrup to independent food service distributors under contracts with an exclusivity clause. When PepsiCo decided that it would also like to supply its product to those same distributors, Coca-Cola exercised that clause. In response, PepsiCo claimed that Coca-Cola acted as a hub in coordinating an agreement among those distributors to exclude PepsiCo. While Coca-Cola did convey to the distributors that it would uniformly enforce exclusivity, there was no evidence of communication that facilitated an agreement between the distributors. For example, there was no evidence that a distributor expressed to Coca-Cola the necessity that other distributors also exclude PepsiCo. By way of comparison, in the Toys-US case, a toy manufacturer-spoke agreed to exclude club warehouses only if retailer-hub Toys "R" Us assured them that the other toy manufacturers were also participating in this exclusionary plan. Such communications were absent between Coca-Cola and the distributors, and therefore there was no basis to conclude that the common conduct of the distributors was the result of coordinated action.

When a horizontal agreement among the spokes is established, the law has treated hub-and-spoke cartels in the same way as standard cartels, which do not engage an upstream supplier or downstream buyer: "There is some question whether the conspiracy provisions of Sections 1 and 2 of the Sherman Act apply to a hub-and-spoke conspiracy. We believe that they do. Two federal courts addressing this question have recognized—at least implicitly—that such a conspiracy is cognizable under the Sherman Act if the plaintiff introduces sufficient evidence to demonstrate that one exists."[10] This view was underscored in e-books-US: "Horizontal agreements with the purpose and effect of raising prices are *per se* unreasonable because they pose a 'threat to the central nervous system of the economy,' *United States v. Socony-Vacuum Oil Co.*, 310 U.S. 150, 224 n.59 (1940); that threat is just as significant when a vertical market participant organizes the conspiracy."[11]

Courts then consider hub-and-spoke cartels as pernicious and unlawful as those cartels that exclusively involve firms that ought to be competing.

Furthermore, the hub is as liable (and often at least as culpable) as the spokes whose market conduct was distorted. The defining issue is whether a party participated in a restraint of trade: "The Sherman Act outlaws *agreements* that unreasonably restrain trade and therefore requires evaluating the nature of the restraint, rather than the identity of each party who joins in to impose it, in determining whether the *per se* rule is properly invoked. . . . The Supreme Court and our Sister Circuits have held all participants in 'hub-and-spoke' conspiracies liable when the objective of the conspiracy was a *per se* unreasonable restraint of trade."[12]

Though vertical agreements—such as resale price maintenance and tying—are evaluated using the rule of reason in the US, hub-and-spoke cartels are per se illegal when there is evidence of communication sufficient to establish a horizontal agreement among the spokes.[13] Per se illegality clearly applies to the spokes, for they are the ones with the horizontal agreement. In implicating the hub, "plaintiffs must demonstrate both that a horizontal conspiracy existed, and that the vertical player was a knowing participant in that agreement and facilitated the scheme."[14]

While per se illegality pertains to the horizontal agreement, it is not applied to the individual vertical agreements. Nevertheless, the court may choose to prohibit certain vertical agreements as part of a remedy, as it did in e-books-US. While the Apple agency agreement was lawful, the US Court of Appeals for the Second Circuit prohibited its adoption, because publishers had illegally coordinated its nearly industry-wide adoption.

7.2 Proving Liability

The next issue is how one proves that firms are engaged in unlawful hub-and-spoke collusion. One must establish that firms in a market have a horizontal agreement, even though they did not directly communicate, and that it was facilitated by an upstream or downstream firm. *Interstate* (1939) set a key precedent when it stated: "It was enough that, knowing that concerted action was contemplated and invited, the distributors gave their adherence to the scheme and participated in it. Each distributor was advised that the others were asked to participate; each knew that cooperation was essential to successful operation of the plan. They knew that the plan, if carried out, would result in a restraint of commerce, . . . and knowing it, all participated in the plan."[15]

It is argued that the current interpretation of *Interstate* (1939) is that vertical relations comprise illegal hub-and-spoke collusion when "(1) two or more competitors enter into vertical agreements with a single upstream or downstream firm; (2) the vertical agreements could benefit each competitor only if its rivals enter into similar agreements; and (3) the firm that facilitates all the vertical agreements persuades each competitor that its competitors will take a similar action" (Orbach 2016, 6).

Toward providing a test for proving that there is an unlawful hub-and-spoke cartel, the US Court of Appeals for the Sixth Circuit put forth three requirements: "(1) that there is an overall-unlawful plan or 'common design' in existence; (2) that knowledge that others must be involved is inferable to each member because of his knowledge of the unlawful nature of the subject of the conspiracy but knowledge on the part of each member of the exact scope of the operation or the number of people involved is not required; and (3) there must be a showing of each alleged member's participation."[16]

Though fundamentally sound, this perspective leaves unanswered how to operationalize it. To establish a violation of the law regarding a restraint of trade, it is crucial to show that the conduct of competitors was not independent. Drawing on the Office of Fair Trading and the European Court of Justice, one needs to show that conduct "breached the 'obligation of independence' as set out in *Suiker*, when the Court of Justice recognised that for competition to occur it is necessary for competing undertakings to act independently, so that: 'the concept inherent in the provisions of the Treaty relating to competition [requires] that each economic operator must determine independently the policy which it intends to adopt on the common market'" (Odudu 2011, 207).Similarly, in the US, courts have been guided by the requirement that "there must be evidence that tends to exclude the possibility that the [firms] were acting independently."[17] While many avenues have been pursued by plaintiffs to argue that firms' conduct could not have been reached independently, successful recipes for convincing a court of that claim have almost always had a common ingredient: evidence of an overt act of communication. According to Hovenkamp (2016, 243), "few courts have found a conspiracy without some evidence of communication tending to show an agreement." Page (2007, 447) adds that "in the search for evidence that tends to exclude independent action, courts have focused primarily on evidence tending to suggest communication has occurred. Although some cases do not involve testimony or documents detailing communication, the courts nevertheless require proof that they conclude justifies an inference that communications took place. In essence, there is no longer an open-ended plus factors analysis; the only evidence that actually distinguishes interdependent and concerted action is evidence that tends to show that the defendants have communicated in the requisite ways."

When firms communicate in a manner pertinent to future conduct (either expressing intentions or conveying information relevant to intentions), they create the legitimate concern that they have influenced each other's conduct and therefore that their behavior was not reached independently. With a standard cartel, these acts of communication take place between the firms whose conduct will be affected in a manner that restrains competition. However, such communication is lacking in a hub-and-spoke cartel when the spokes directly communicate only with the hub. The challenge is to determine when firms (spokes) indirectly communicating through a third party (hub) is sufficiently comparable to direct communications between those firms to conclude that firms' conduct is coordinated.

The UK's Competition Appeal Tribunal developed an approach referred to as the "A to B to C" test. Hub-and-spoke collusion is said to exist if

> (i) retailer A discloses to supplier B its future pricing intentions in circumstances where A may be taken to intend that B will make use of that information to influence market conditions by passing that information to other retailers (of whom C is or may be one), (ii) B does, in fact, pass that information to C in circumstances where C may be taken to know the circumstances in which the information was disclosed by A to B, and (iii) C does, in fact, use the information in determining its own future pricing intentions, then A, B, and C are all to be regarded as parties to a concerted practice having as its object the restriction or distortion of competition.[18]

Alternatively stated, the conditions are that (1) spoke A discloses intentions on future conduct (such as prices) to hub B for which A intends that B will pass them on to spoke C; (2) B passes information to C, where C knows it was passed on with A's understanding; and (3) C uses the information in determining its own conduct (such as pricing). In its contribution to an OECD report on information exchanges, the UK summarized this test by stating that "the provision of, receipt of or passing on of information between competitors through an intermediary in circumstances where it can be taken for one to have intended to influence the market conduct of the other is anticompetitive."[19]

The "A to B to C" test gets us closer to operational criteria for determining when a series of vertical relations embodies a horizontal agreement. Though challenging, the third condition is typical in cases that seek to determine the effect of information sharing on firms' prices. It can entail assessing whether C acted in a manner consistent with the information that it received from B and whether the timing between the receipt of that information and a change in C's conduct is consistent with that information having a causal effect. Turning to the second condition, it can be straightforward to document that information that A passed to B was then passed to C. Further establishing that C is cognizant of the "circumstances" whereby A gave this information to C can be formidable, but again that could be documented in communications between B and C. The most challenging condition to satisfy is the first one. While one can document that A conveyed certain information to B, it is quite another matter to determine whether it was A's intent for B to pass that information to C for the purpose of influencing C's behavior.

The relevance of the "A to B to C" test for the US is not immediately clear because the law in the UK is more expansive than that in the US. Like the EU, the UK prohibits "concerted practices," which is a category of practices that falls short of an agreement. A concerted practice could be an information exchange that, by reducing uncertainty between firms, results in supracompetitive prices but does not go so far as to form an agreement. This means plaintiffs could prove that there is a violation of Chapter I of the UK Competition Act 1998 (or Article 101 of the Treaty on the Functioning of the European Union) without showing that there is an agreement, which must be done to establish a violation of Section 1 of the Sherman Act.[20]

Following US jurisprudence, let us develop an operational test rooted in agreement. Such a test should answer the following question: when do communications between vertically related firms form a per se illegal horizontal agreement? Consider a vertical information exchange between firm A (spoke) and firm B (hub) and between firm C (spoke) and firm B, where firms A and C are competitors and firm B is either an upstream supplier to or downstream buyer from firms A and C. A horizontal agreement has two elements: firm A invites firm C to collude, and firm C accepts that invitation. In the context of a hub-and-spoke cartel, we propose that firm A invites firm C to collude when

(1) the information conveyed by firm A to firm B would have facilitated a horizontal agreement had it been conveyed directly to firm C; and

(2) when conveying the information to firm B, firm A would have reasonably foreseen that firm B would convey the information to firm C.

It is the second condition that captures the intent of firm A. In determining when these two conditions are satisfied, there is considerable jurisprudence regarding condition (1).[21] Regarding condition (2), we will describe four approaches for substantiating that a spoke would have reasonably foreseen that the hub would share the information with another spoke.[22]

First, spoke A requested that the information be shared by the hub with spoke C or the hub expressed to spoke A that it intends to share A's information with spoke C. While it is possible that a spoke may not believe the hub, the burden should be on the spoke to convince the court why the hub should not have been believed.

Second, the hub provided information from spoke C to spoke A that is of a type similar to the information that spoke A had previously provided to the hub for spoke C. In concluding that condition (2) is satisfied, one is drawing the inference that spoke A understands that the information exchange is reciprocal. This is a point emphasized in the Toys-UK case, where "those reciprocal contacts reduced uncertainty on Argos' part as to what other retailers' pricing intentions were, and reduced uncertainty on Hasbro's part on what Argos' prices would be. That, in turn, facilitated Hasbro's conversations with other retailers, especially Littlewoods, with a view to ensuring that they too priced at [recommended retail prices]."[23]

If hub B conveyed the pricing intention of spoke C to spoke A, then, when spoke A conveys its pricing intentions to hub B, it is reasonable for spoke A to expect that hub B will convey spoke A's pricing intentions to spoke C. This makes sense because if it is optimal for the hub to share such information from spoke C to spoke A, it is likely to be optimal for the hub to share similar information from spoke A to spoke C.[24] However, one does want to be careful, for spoke A might have provided its pricing intentions to B without any intention that it be shared by B to C, and it was solely on B's own initiative that B collected C's pricing intentions and conveyed them to A. In that instance, B might be culpable even if A is not. The following requirement should suffice to deal with that situation: if A shares its pricing intentions with B *after* having received C's pricing intentions from B, then

A would have reasonably foreseen that the pricing intentions it shared with B would be passed on to C.

Third, it is in the hub's best interest to share a spoke's information with other spokes, and it is reasonable for a spoke to be aware that it is in the hub's best interest to share it. A spoke's own conduct can serve to satisfy this requirement. Suppose the hub is better off if all spokes choose some common course of action (e.g., raising prices), and suppose a spoke conveys to the hub that it is willing to adopt that action *if all other spokes do so* (e.g., it is willing to raise prices if all other spokes raise their prices). It would then be in the best interest of the hub to share the spoke's intention with the other spokes and, furthermore, the spoke would be cognizant of it because its message to B is implicitly a request for it to do exactly that.[25]

Fourth, it is in the spoke's best interest to convey this information to the hub only if the information is shared with other spokes or, more to the point, it will influence the conduct of other spokes. An example is when A complains to B about C's low prices. While it could be that A is simply venting, the default assumption should be that A is sharing this information with B in order for B to act on it. Firm A could be doing so as part of a plan to negotiate a lower wholesale price with B, which would then allow A to set a lower price to compete with C. Such a rationale is procompetitive. However, a more obvious explanation is that A is complaining in order to cause B to stop C from charging low prices. If it can be argued that, in light of the evidence, the only plausible explanation for A to voice such a complaint is to have B affect the conduct of C, then that supports the hypothesis that A's complaint is an invitation to collude. Or suppose a retailer (spoke) expresses to an upstream supplier (hub) its intention to raise prices. If this information was not to be shared with other spokes (and thus was not to be used to enact a coordinated rise in retail prices), then it might not be in the best interest of the retailer to share this information, for it could be the basis for the upstream firm to raise its wholesale price to the retailer (knowing that the retailer could maintain its current margin given it is raising its retail price). If instead the pricing intention was shared with other retailers, then it could lead them all to raise their prices. Thus, by this argument, a spoke would share its intention to raise prices only if it expected the hub to share this information with other spokes. Of course, whether the information that is shared by a spoke to the hub is in its best interest only if it was intended to affect the conduct of another spoke will depend on the specifics of the case.

If any of the four conditions are satisfied, that should be sufficient to conclude that firm A invited firm C to collude. In the US, that would be a violation of Section 2 of the Sherman Act (as an attempt to monopolize) or Section 5 of the FTC Act (as an unfair practice). For there to be an agreement in violation of Section 1 of the Sherman Act, US law also requires acceptance of A's invitation by C. That evidence could take the form of communication or market conduct. Obviously, if A conveys to B that it will raise prices if C does, B conveys that information to C, and C expresses to B that it will raise prices as long as A is assured of doing so, then C has accepted A's invitation and there is an agreement. Alternatively, evidence of such an acceptance could be market conduct by C that is consistent with its acceptance. For example, if A tells B that A and C should enact a common price increase (or A complains to B that C was pricing too low), B conveys that information to C, and C subsequently raises its price, C is signaling its acceptance with a price increase that would only be in its best interest if it expected A to do likewise. Finally, we can conclude that A and C have an agreement when the previously mentioned conditions to substantiate an invitation to collude by A to C also apply for C to A; that is, if firm C also conveyed information to firm B that, had it been conveyed directly to firm A, would have facilitated a horizontal agreement, and firm C would have reasonably foreseen that firm B would convey the information to firm A. If that condition holds with regard to C's communications with B (as well as A's communications with B), then we can conclude that firms A and C have the requisite "meeting of minds."

Our discussion has focused on when the invitation to collude is initiated by a spoke. The canonical sequence of communications is

$$A \to B \to C \to B \to A.$$

In other words, spoke A conveys a message to hub B regarding a plan to coordinate the conduct of spokes A and C, and hub B passes that message along to spoke C, which responds affirmatively to hub B, which then conveys C's message to A. This process is exemplified by Kits-UK:

$A \to B$: Retailer JJB (A) complained to manufacturer Umbro (B) that retailer Sports Soccer (C) was discounting off the recommended retail price (RRP). This complaint is an implicit proposal for all retailers to charge the RRP.

$B \to C$: Umbro communicated to Sports Soccer that it should stop offering discounts off the RRP. Umbro also conveyed that it was having similar discussions with other retailers.

C→B: Sports Soccer responded to Umbro by stating that it would comply as long as other retailers did so.

B→A: Umbro conveyed to JJB that Sports Soccer would charge the RRP and that JJB was expected to do so.

While this sequence of communications is present in several cases, our review in chapter 6 revealed that the vast majority of hub-and-spoke cartels were initiated by the hub, not a spoke. The initial invitation to collude typically came from an upstream supplier when collusion involved coordinating on higher downstream prices or a downstream buyer when collusion involved coordinating upstream suppliers on the exclusion of a rival to that downstream buyer. This sequence is depicted in the following diagram.

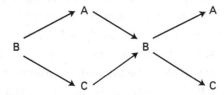

Hub B communicates a plan to spokes A and C, as well as conveying that the plan is being shared with the other spoke. A and C each convey their acceptance of the plan to B. That acceptance may be conditional on whether the other spoke complies with the plan. Next, B conveys C's acceptance (or conditional acceptance) to A and A's acceptance to C. A and C then adopt the agreed actions.

This sequence, or some variant of it, was well documented in several cases. As an example, consider Toys-UK, in which upstream manufacturer Hasbro developed a plan to have downstream retailers Argos and Littlewoods set a common price. Hasbro's sales agent for Argos conveyed the plan to Argos (B→A), while its agent in charge of Littlewoods conveyed it to Littlewoods (B→C). In doing so, it was made clear to each retailer that the other retailer was being informed of the plan. The retailer-spokes expressed their willingness to charge the proposed price but also their concern that the other retailer would not comply (A→B, C→B). Hasbro then assured each of them that both retailers were on board (B→A, B→C). An identical pattern can be found in Toys-US. Similarly, in Desiccant-UK, upstream supplier UOP sought to have a coordinated increase in the prices of its retailers so that they would accept a rise in the wholesale price. This led UOP to propose to all retailers that they raise their prices by 4%. Through a series of bilateral communications with the retailers, this uniform price hike was conveyed along with the assurances that all the retailers had expressed that they would comply.

While the examples just provided had express communication at every stage of the process, this is not necessary in order to conclude that there is an agreement. For example, after hub B conveys its plan to spokes A and C, A and C may adopt the proposed actions without further communications. In doing so, they have implicitly accepted the invitation put before them. That occurred in the Movies-US case, where the critical message from downstream theater chain Interstate (B) was the letter sent simultaneously to the upstream distributors (A and C) along with the knowledge that all had been sent that letter. Subsequent conduct by the distributors consistent with that plan established that they accepted it.

However, it is not enough that there are communications that could have been sufficient for the spokes to coordinate their conduct. It must also be true that a shared understanding of coordinated action was necessary for the spokes to pursue their course of action. If it was in the independent interest of a retailer-spoke to raise its price or a manufacturer-spoke to stop supplying a retailer, then there is no unlawful agreement: "In [the hub-and-spoke] variant of tacit agreement, . . . the rivals interdependently accept a common proposal by a trading partner, thereby reducing competition to their joint benefit. The decisive issue in cases like this is whether the rivals act interdependently because of the vertical agreements; it is insufficient that they act in the same way if they had independent reasons for doing so" (Page 2017, 623).

Given the lack of direct communication between the spokes and that a series of vertical agreements are unlawful only if they form a horizontal agreement, it is essential in establishing hub-and-spoke collusion that a spoke's conduct was contingent on the other spokes acting in the same manner. However, proving that competitors' conduct is coordinated can be more difficult when a cartel is hub-and-spoke.[26] That is because the hub may have means at its disposal to incentivize a spoke to comply even without the participation of other spokes. For example, a manufacturer that desires that retailers raise their prices might be able to get them to do so by threatening to deny supply. That threatened punishment could make it optimal for a retailer to raise its price independent of what other retailers do. Thus, even if there are communications between the manufacturer and each retailer and the content of those communications includes how other retailers will also be raising their prices, one could argue that each retailer's conduct was independent of what other retailers did because the threatened punishment by the manufacturer was sufficient in and of itself. In that case, the hub's communications with each spoke about other spokes' intended conduct were incidental and irrelevant to the observed conduct. For this reason, it is more difficult to establish the existence of a rim: "Because a hub with market power is more likely to have the ability to impose a sufficient sanction to obtain unilateral universal compliance, it is less likely that unambiguous evidence of an agreement among the spokes will exist" (Klein 2020, 164).

However, the matter becomes more nuanced when one considers the credibility of a hub's threatened punishment. As we discussed in several cases, including Drugs-US and Toys-US, the credibility of the threat to deny supply to a retailer may be contingent on other retailers complying. Consider an upstream supplier that threatens to deny supply to a retailer that does not raise its price. While an upstream supplier may be willing to fulfill that threat with regard to one retailer, as then some of that lost demand will be picked up by other retailers, would it really be willing to deny supply to many retailers? Wouldn't that prove highly unprofitable for the manufacturer? Thus, the credibility of the threat to deny supply is undermined unless most of the other retailers are complying. We are then back to the existence of a rim, because coordinated conduct was essential for each spoke to act according to plan. A retailer-spoke complies if it believes other retailer-spokes will comply, because only then does it believe the manufacturer-hub's threat to deny supply should it not comply.

In seeking to determine whether there is a rim, Klein (2020) argues that evidence against there being a horizontal agreement is that adoption of the vertical agreements was done quickly. If the spoke's acceptance of a vertical agreement is in its best interest regardless of what the other spokes do, then one could expect a spoke to sign on as soon as it is presented with the agreement. In contrast, if a spoke's acceptance is contingent on other spokes doing so as well, it could take a sustained period of negotiations and communications as the hub seeks to convince each spoke that the other spokes are planning to comply. The need for coordinated action would then manifest itself as a delay followed by a spate of adoptions by the spokes within a short time.

Consistent with the need for coordinated action, a protracted series of discussions between a hub and spokes is well documented in many of our cases. Klein (2020) finds such evidence in support of the existence of a rim in the Toys-US case but that it is lacking in the General Motors case (section 5.4). Even though there were direct communications among the auto dealer–spokes, it is argued that it was in the independent interest of each dealer to stop selling to unauthorized dealers, because of General Motors' threat to take away its dealership. Consistent with the claim that coordinated conduct was not needed is that the dealerships quickly complied. However, going back to the issue of credibility, would a dealer have believed that General Motors would implement its threat if it meant closing down a large number of dealerships? It may then follow that a dealer would only believe the threat if it expected other dealers to comply. It is then essential that General Motors communicate to each dealer that the other dealers are on board, in which case we are working our way back to there being a rim. This is a subtle matter that can only be properly accessed with a close inspection of the evidence.

Another case in which these evidentiary issues arose involved Guitar Center, which was one of the largest retailers of musical instruments.[27] Guitar Center was accused of coordinating musical instrument manufacturers in the adoption of a minimum advertised price (MAP) policy. Under this policy, retailers could charge below the minimum price set by a manufacturer but could not advertise such a price. Plaintiffs claimed there was a hub-and-spoke cartel with Guitar Center as the hub and manufacturers as spokes, where the objective was to restrain price competition from Guitar Center's competitors.

In affirming the motion to dismiss, the US Court of Appeals for the Ninth Circuit noted that the plaintiffs' own claim provided "ample independent business reasons why each of the manufacturers adopted and enforced MAP policies even absent an agreement among the defendant manufacturers."[28] It was noted that Guitar Center offered to buy large volumes from a manufacturer if it adopted a MAP policy, which could be seen as sufficient inducement to comply regardless of what other manufacturers did. Manufacturers adopted the MAP policy over a span of several years and "such slow adoption of similar policies does not raise the specter of collusion."[29]

In concluding our discussion of legal strategies, we raise a potentially serious obstacle to prosecuting hub-and-spoke collusion in the US. To prosecute any cartel case, it is critical to obtain evidence from the defendants that documents the communications used to form an unlawful agreement. Prior to reaching the discovery stage, when those documents could be procured, plaintiffs face the challenge of having their claim dismissed at the pleading stage. With its decision in *Bell Atlantic Corp. v. Twombly* (2007), the US Supreme Court erected a plausibility standard in order for a claim not to be dismissed.[30] In pleading an antitrust claim, "an allegation of parallel conduct and a bare assertion of conspiracy will not suffice."[31] The plaintiff must present "enough facts to state a claim to relief that is plausible on its face."[32] In other words, sufficient evidence (and not simply unsubstantiated claims and speculation) must be provided at the pleading phase in order to move to the discovery phase. Many claims of violation of Section 1 of the Sherman Act have been dismissed for lacking such evidence.[33]

In a standard cartel case, evidence that could suffice to surmount the plausibility standard would be market conduct suggesting coordinated action (e.g., parallel price movements) along with details as to when firms might have communicated that are consistent with the claimed coordinated actions. Those details would have to be more than pure speculation but are not required to be the documentation that would generally only come out of discovery. The reason that this standard could prove more challenging in hub-and-spoke cartel cases is that the unlawful communications between a hub and a spoke are likely to take place within what are otherwise legitimate relations. It is natural for an upstream manufacturer to communicate regularly with a downstream retailer, in which case it could be difficult to identify which of those encounters contained unlawful messages. In comparison, communication between competitors is inherently suspect. Putting it in the simplest and coarsest terms, the default for when two competitors communicate in private is that it is anticompetitive, while the default for when an upstream supplier and downstream customer communicate in private is that it is procompetitive. This makes it more difficult to identify what could be the times and places of unlawful communication, and such information may be needed for the case to survive dismissal at the pleading stage.

Notes

Preface

1. Analogously, Harrington (2006) offered a set of facts for around 20 standard cartels, which led to several new collusive theories, including those in Harrington and Skrzypacz (2007, 2011), Awaya and Krishna (2016), and Sugaya and Wolitsky (2018).

Chapter 1

1. The administrative law judge of the Federal Trade Commission concluded that there were 14 toy manufacturers (spokes) involved. On appeal, the commission reduced the number to seven, which included the three companies appearing in figure 1.2.

2. European Commission decision of December 10, 2003, relating to a proceeding under Article 81 of the EC Treaty and Article 53 of the EEA Agreement (Case COMP/E-2/37.857—organic peroxides).

3. *Official Journal of the European Union*, L 152/24, 7.6.2001, Case COMP/36.545/F3—amino acids, decision of June 7, 2000.

4. While "prosecute" is commonly used for criminal cases in the US, it is regularly used in the UK for both civil and criminal cases. Our usage of the term is the more encompassing definition in that prosecute refers to any legal action by a lawyer on behalf of a client in either a criminal or civil case.

5. This is not coincidental because it was the legal case that provided the factual evidence that allowed the cartel to be studied.

6. Fersthman and Pakes (2000) show this is possible when firms collude on prices and compete on product quality. Collusion raises prices but also raises quality to such an extent that consumer welfare can rise.

7. One possible exception to the general rule that price collusion reduces welfare is a hub-and-spoke cartel where the hub is a manufacturer and the spokes are

retailers who sell that manufacturer's product. As explained in section 3.1, competition may systematically result in retailers providing too little service from a welfare perspective and therefore welfare could increase if both prices and service were to rise. In that case, hub-and-spoke collusion that constrains intrabrand price competition could raise welfare and even make consumers better off. This is the rationale for resale price maintenance—whereby a manufacturer sets a minimum price that retailers can charge—not being per se illegal in the US. Since 2007, it has been evaluated according to the rule of reason. See the discussion in subsection 3.1.5.

8. It is possible that some cartels did not form when nonprice competition would have intensified enough to dissipate much of the incremental profit from higher collusive prices. Thus, we may only be observing hub-and-spoke cartels where price collusion would not lead to much intensification of nonprice competition.

9. Because of inadequate documentation, we do not include the case of a cartel in Estonia that involved an upstream supplier of vodka and downstream retailers (cited in OECD 2019).

10. See the appendices in sections 3.4 and 5.4 for cases where, in contrast, communications between competitors were consistent with those of a standard cartel. However, an upstream supplier assisted in the cartel operations, so the case provides further evidence of the critical role that an upstream hub can play.

11. It has also been argued by Klein (2012) that the famous Standard Oil case, *Standard Oil Co. v. United States*, 221 U.S. 1 (1911), can be reinterpreted as a hub-and-spoke case. The case brought against Standard Oil was under Section 2 of the Sherman Act for acting unilaterally to monopolize the petroleum industry. However, Klein argues that this was achieved by colluding with the railroads in a hub-and-spoke conspiracy that allowed Standard Oil to receive preferential rebates from the railroads, which then charged higher rates to rival refiner shipments. Under this interpretation, this case would then be consistent with the class of hub-and-spoke cartel we examine in chapter 5.

12. Our sample encompasses cartels discovered and thus excludes cartels that were not discovered and those that were discovered but where the evidence was inconclusive regarding collusion. As a result, ineffective cartels could be undersampled (as they quickly collapsed and avoided discovery) or oversampled (as their ineffectiveness extended to revealing evidence), while effective cartels could be undersampled (as they were skilled at avoiding detection) or oversampled (as they remained active long enough to be discovered).

13. There is also a recent OECD (2019) background paper on hub-and-spoke arrangements that draws on Harrington (2018).

Chapter 2

1. These conditions can be found in Harrington (2015).

2. Motta (2004) reviews the many factors that influence whether a self-enforcing collusive arrangement exists.

3. *Am. Tobacco Co. v. United States*, 328 U.S. 781, 810 (1946).

4. *Monsanto Co. v. Spray-Rite Serv. Corp.*, 465 U.S. 752, 765 (1984).

5. Judgment of the Court of July 15, 1970, *ACF Chemiefarma NV v. Commission of the European Communities*, Case 41–69.

6. Judgment of the Court of First Instance of October 26, 2000, *Bayer AG v. Commission of the European Communities*.

7. For an episode in the German cement market, see Harrington et al. (2015).

8. For example, see Centorrino et al. (2015), Sparks, Burleigh, and Barclay (2016), and Manzini, Sadrieh, and Vriend (2009), the latter of which offers a novel approach to measuring the signaling value of nonverbal gestures.

9. Examples in which a neutral third party was hired to assist a cartel include a taxi driver for a bidding ring at stamp auctions (Asker 2010) and a consulting company, AC Treuhand, for the organic peroxides cartel (Marshall and Marx 2012). In those cartels, firms communicated directly and the third party's role was to assist in implementing and monitoring the collusive outcome and organizing meetings among cartel members.

10. In the context of the preceding example, A's private information is where A will be, A's message refers to a location, B draws inferences from A's message about where A will be, and B then decides where to go.

11. Though that is not always the case. A counterexample is a gasoline cartel in Quebec for which the preferred collusive price probably differed between vertically integrated chains, chains with convenience stores, and independent chains (Clark and Houde 2013).

12. A notable example is the Organization of Petroleum Exporting Countries (OPEC), where some countries are notorious for agreeing with a particular sales quota and then willfully supplying in excess of it. It seems clear that their expression of support for the allocation was not truthful.

13. This result is proven in Ambrus, Azevedo, and Kamada (2013) and holds as long as parties do not randomize their actions.

14. For a broader discussion of how vertical restraints can aid collusion, see Levenstein and Suslow (2014).

15. A regular cartel could also elicit the assistance of an upstream supplier to enforce a collusive agreement. For example, in *JTC Petroleum Co. v. Piasa Motor Fuels, Inc.*, 190 F.3d 775 (7th Cir. 1999), six road contractors formed a cartel to rig bids at local government tenders. (Since the cartel involved direct communication between the contractors, the case is not included in our sample.) One of the contractors, JTC, did not abide by the collusive arrangement, so the cartel enlisted three emulsified asphalt producers to refuse to supply this essential input to JTC. Nevertheless, most standard cartels do not involve upstream or downstream firms and thus lack their assistance in making collusion more effective.

16. An exception is when competing firms engage in interfirm sales as part of their normal business practice. Such sales allowed firms to consummate transfers in the citric acid, lysine, and vitamin cartels; see Harrington (2006) and Harrington and Skrzypacz (2011).

17. This point will be explored at length in chapter 7.

18. Though there are ample counterexamples, such as the vitamin cartel. For a study of the various corporate levels involved in global cartels, see Ashton and Pressey (2012).

Chapter 3

1. When there is perfect competition among retailers, so they are forced to price at cost, an upstream monopolist will optimally set the wholesale price w equal to the retail price that a vertically integrated monopolist would set, denoted p^m, less the unit cost of a retailer for inputs other than that provided by this upstream firm, denoted c; that is, $w = p^m - c$. A retailer's unit cost inclusive of the wholesale price w is then $w + c = (p^m - c) + c = p^m$. With perfect competition forcing retailers to price at cost, the retail price is p^m, which is the same as would be set by a vertically integrated firm and thus is the retail price that maximizes total profits for the vertical chain. Note that the upstream firm captures the entire profit since the downstream firms are pricing at cost.

2. This scheme is referred to as linear pricing, in that the total expenditure by a downstream buyer is linear in the number of units purchased.

3. For a more comprehensive discussion of the use of vertical agreements to correct inefficiencies, see Mathewson and Winter (1984). A useful general reference is Rey and Vergé (2008).

4. In the US, for example, maximum resale price maintenance was per se (or by object) illegal from 1968, due to *Albrecht v. Herald Co.*, 390 U.S. 145 (1968), to 1997, when, in *State Oil Company v. Khan*, 522 U.S. 3 (1997), it was ruled to be neither per se illegal nor legal and was to be judged by the rule of reason.

5. In the jargon of bargaining theory, these properties pertain to the profit (or utility) possibilities set.

6. We refer the reader to section 3.5 for an explanation of this latter effect, because there are four forces at play, which makes providing a simple intuitive explanation difficult.

7. One advantage of raising wholesale prices is that it can help facilitate the sustainability of retail collusion. For example, by agreeing on a unit wholesale price as high as the retail price, the retailers can eliminate their incentives to deviate. However, this would require a fixed fee payment from the supplier to the retailers. See Piccolo and Miklós-Thal (2012) for a theoretical model with these features.

8. It has long been recognized in the literature (see, for example, Yamey 1954) that this provides the rival retailers with an incentive to pressure the supplier to adopt (minimum) resale price maintenance (RPM) in order to prevent such undercutting.

9. One possible solution for a cartel comprising only retailers is for more market share to be allocated to those retailers focused on growing their market shares. However, this solution has a limit in that the more market share given away by a retailer to placate these more aggressive retailers, the less inclined that retailer is to participate in the cartel. In addition, it can be challenging for a cartel to control market shares in retail markets where there are many consumers who independently decide who to buy from.

10. It is possible that a retailer could provide customer-specific discounts, which could make monitoring more challenging.

11. Monitoring could also occur in terms of sales. If one retailer is undercutting the collusive price and selling more, other retailers will observe lower sales and the upstream supplier will observe a rise in the deviating retailer's market share. In principle, that information can be used to monitor compliance. With intermediate goods cartels for which prices are not publicly observed, the use of sales monitoring is common (see, for example, Harrington 2006; Harrington and Skrzypacz 2011). We have chosen not to emphasize it here because price monitoring is far superior in retail markets and there is no evidence that hub-and-spoke cartels have monitored sales.

12. For a theoretical analysis of collusion supported by the threat of denial of supply, see Van Cayselle and Miegielsen (2014).

13. It can be feasible for retailers to impose a harsher punishment than competitive pricing by, for example, pricing at lower levels for some length of time. However, such punishments are not commonly observed in practice. Though a proper theoretical analysis has not been done, we conjecture that it would be easier (in the sense of satisfying incentive compatibility constraints) for an upstream firm to impose a low payoff by denying supply than for rival retailers to do so by pricing low.

14. There is also maximum RPM, whereby the manufacturer specifies a maximum retail price that can be charged. However, that is not relevant to the current discussion.

15. European Commission, "Guidelines on Vertical Restraints," SEC (2010) 411, at 48.

16. For details, see Giovannetti and Stallibrass (2009).

17. *Leegin Creative Leather Products, Inc. v. PSKS, Inc.*, 551 U.S. 877 (2007).

18. *Id.* at 889, 894.

19. In section 3.1, it was explained that competition can result in retailers providing too little service from the perspective of the vertical chain's profits and, after including consumer surplus, social welfare. This implies that it is possible that higher prices (such as obtained through RPM) along with more service could benefit both firms and consumers.

20. Ensuing facts are from CA/98/8/2003 Agreements between Hasbro UK Ltd, Argos Ltd & Littlewoods Ltd fixing the price of Hasbro toys and games, [2004] 4 UKCLR 717.

21. See *Argos Ltd & Anor v. Office of Fair Trading* [2006] EWCA Civ 1318 [114].

22. *Sup.* note 20 at 98.

23. *Id.* at 48.

24. *Id.* at 55.

25. *Id.* at 47.

26. *Id.* at 96.

27. *Id.* at 49.

28. *Id.* at 53.

29. *Id.* at 97.

30. *Id.* at 97.

31. *Id.* at 103.

32. *Id.* at 140.

33. *Id.* at 65.

34. *Id.* at 65.

35. *Id.* at 65.

36. *Id.* at 84.

37. *Id.* at 89.

38. *Id.* at 75.

39. *Id.* at 75.

40. *Id.* at 75.

41. *Id.* at 85.

42. *Id.* at 86.

43. *Id.* at 90.

44. *Id.* at 91.

45. *Id.* at 58.

46. *Id.* at 289.

47. *Id.* at 385.

48. *Id.* at 42.

49. *Id.* at 383.

50. *Id.* at 382.

51. *Id.* at 383.

52. *Id.* at 67.

53. *Id.* at 73.

54. The OFT fined Hasbro £4.95 million for these infringements (see Agreements between Hasbro UK Ltd and distributors fixing the price of Hasbro toys and games, OFT Decision, Case CP/0239–01, November 28, 2002). The reason underlying such infringements was that some of the larger retailers felt they could get a better deal on Hasbro toys from the independent distributors rather than from Hasbro directly. Consequently, Hasbro instructed the distributors to sell only at a given wholesale price.

55. *Sup.* note 20 at 703.

56. All facts are from CA98/08/2004 Agreement between UOP Limited, UKae Limited, Thermoseal Supplies Ltd, Double Quick Supplyline Ltd and Double Glazing Supplies Ltd to fix and/or maintain prices for desiccant, OFT, November 8, 2004.

57. *Id.* at 89.

58. *Id.* at 177.

59. *Id.* at 183.

60. *Id.* at 188, 189.

61. *Id.* at 191.

62. *Id.* at 221.

63. *Id.* at 211.

64. *Id.* at 213, 214.

65. *Id.* at 226.

66. *Id.* at 227.

67. *Id.* at 228.

68. *Id.* at 230.

69. *Id.* at 66.

70. *Id.* at 150.

71. *Id.* at 141.

72. *Id.* at 129.

73. *Id.* at 132.

74. *Id.* at 90.

75. *Id.* at 104.

76. *Id.* at 105.

77. *Id.* at 105.

78. *Id.* at 106.

79. *Id.* at 108.

80. *Id.* at 113.

81. *Id.* at 117.

82. *Id.* at 65, 66.

83. "As discussed in November last year please find attached a fax giving advice of a 4 per cent price increase for UOP desiccant. This is to allow [distributor] to implement a price increase in the market and does not represent a price increase from UOP to [distributor]. The intention is to allow [distributor] to increase margins on UOP products, and hopefully gain an added incentive to sell more product as a result." *Id.* at 191.

84. *Id.* at 315.

85. *Id.* at 379.

86. *Id.* at 21.

87. The ensuing facts are from Bolecki (2011).

88. *Id.* at 32.

89. *Id.* at 33.

90. *Id.* at 32.

91. *Id.* at 36.

92. *Id.* at 39.

93. Facts are based on a Google translation of Autorite Belge de la Concurrence, Décision no. ABC-2015- I/O-19-AUD du 22 juin 2015, Affaire CONC-I/O-06/0038—Hausses coordonnées des prix de vente de produits de parfumerie, d'hygiène et de droguerie (which translates as Belgian Authority of Competition, Decision No. ABC-2015-I / O-19-AUD of June 22, 2015, Case CONC-I / O-06/0038—Coordinated increases in the selling prices of perfumery, hygiene and drugstore products). Other references are "Belgian Competition Authority settles its first cartel case," www .elexica.com/en/legal-topics/antitrust-and-merger-control/29-belgian-competition -authority-settles-its-first-cartel-case (accessed May 22, 2018); and Mattioli (2016).

94. Google translation of Belgian Authority of Competition, Decision No. ABC-2015-I / O-19-AUD of June 22, 2015, Case CONC-I / O-06/0038—Coordinated increases in the selling prices of perfumery, hygiene and drugstore products, at 20.

95. As with the Paints and Varnishes case in Poland, it is possible that one of the suppliers implemented a hub-and-spoke cartel and, upon learning about its success, other suppliers imitated it by creating their own.

96. The description in Mattioli (2016, 262) confirms the translation of Autorite Belge de la Concurrence, Décision no. ABC-2015-I/O-19-AUD du 22 juin 2015, Affaire CONC-I/O-06/0038—Hausses coordonnées des prix de vente de produits de parfumerie, d'hygiène et de droguerie.

97. CA/98/06/2003 Price-fixing of Replica Football Kit, OFT, August 1, 2003, at 70.

98. *Id.* at 157.

99. The case also covered several purely vertical agreements between Umbro and some of its retailers. In particular, the OFT concluded that Umbro had agreements in place with Sports Soccer for a longer period for a range of major Umbro replica kits. Over this period, Sports Soccer received assurances from Umbro regarding the pricing intentions of other retailers. The OFT believed that it was probable that the other major retailers were also involved and that the agreement reached through the hub-and-spoke arrangement described earlier extended throughout this period. However, the OFT did not prosecute the other retailers for their involvement here.

100. *Sup.* note 97 at 120.

101. *Id.* at 166.

102. Royal Courts of Justice, *Argos Ltd and Littlewoods Ltd v. OFT* and *JJB Sports Plc v. OFT*, Case No. 2005/1071, 1074, and 1623, at 94.

103. *Id.* at 97.

104. *Id.* at 98.

105. *Sup.* note 97 at 187.

106. *Id.* at 197.

107. *Id.* at 187.

108. *Id.* at 165.

109. *Id.* at 165.

110. *Id.* at 484.

111. *Id.* at 172.

112. *Id.* at 171.

113. *Id.* at 158.

114. *Id.* at 241.

115. *Id.* at 240.

116. The OFT did not specifically object to this selective distribution policy. However, they were clear that it facilitated and reinforced the collusive behavior.

117. *Sup.* note 97 at 358.

118. *Id.*, annexes 3 and 4.

119. Sports Soccer provided crucial assistance with this matter. However, their original complaint did not relate to Umbro replica kits, and they continued to take part in the agreements with Umbro. The OFT was also critical of Sports Soccer for informing other parties of the ongoing investigation and for not cooperating quickly and effectively with them. For these reasons, while Sports Soccer's fine was reduced to reflect its cooperating role, it was not granted full immunity.

120. *Sup.* note 97 at 125.

121. *Sup.* note 102 at 102.

122. Ensuing facts are from *United States v. Parke, Davis & Company*, 164 F. Supp. 827 (D.D.C. 1958) and *United States v. Parke, Davis & Co.*, 362 U.S. 29 (1960).

123. *United States v. Parke, Davis & Co.*, 362 U.S. 29 (1960), syllabus.

124. *Id.* at 362 U.S. 33.

125. *Id.* at 362 U.S. 35.

126. *United States v. Parke, Davis & Company*, 164 F. Supp. 827 (D.D.C. 1958), at 55.

127. *Sup.* note 123 at 362 U.S. 37, 38.

128. *Id.* at 362 U.S. 46.

129. Facts are from Decision of the Office of Fair Trading, CA98/03/2011, Dairy retail price initiatives, July 26, 2011 (Case CE/3094–03).

130. In October 2003, Arla merged with Express.

131. The OFT suspected that Tesco was also involved but that there was not enough evidence to prosecute. *Sup.* note 129 at 2.100.

132. *Id.* at 5.43.

133. *Id.* at 5.158.

134. *Id.* at 5.532.

135. *Id.* at 5.836.

136. *Id.* at 5.14.

137. *Id.* at 5.14.

138. *Id.* at 5.22.

139. *Id.* at 5.23.

140. *Id.* at 5.5.

141. *Id.* at 5.767.

142. *Id.* at 5.200.

143. *Id.* at 5.114.

144. *Id.* at 5.78. Such price increases for milk almost certainly relate to the OFT's abandoned investigation into the 2002 Liquid Milk Initiative allegation.

145. *Id.* at 5.80.

146. *Id.* at 5.119.

147. *Id.* at 5.122.

148. *Id.* at 5.122.

149. *Id.* at 5.171.

150. *Id.* at 5.127.

151. *Id.* at 5.171.

152. *Id.* at 5.332.

153. *Id.* at 5.335.

154. *Id.* at 5.194.

155. *Id.* at 5.213.

156. *Id.* at 5.213.

157. *Id.* at 5.231.

158. *Id.* at 5.687.

159. *Id.* at 5.754.

160. *Id.* at 5.510.

161. *Id.* at 5.510.

162. *Id.* at 5.45.

163. *Id.* at 5.661.

164. *Id.* at 5.756.

165. *Id.* at 5.413.

166. *Id.* at 5.530.

167. *Id.* at 5.838.

168. *Id.* at 5.847.

169. *Id.* at 5.846.

170. *Id.* at 5.849.

171. *Id.* at 5.850–5.853.

172. *Id.* at 5.518.

173. *Id.* at 5.56.

174. *Id.* at 5.57.

175. *Id.* at 5.59.

176. *Id.* at 5.150.

177. *Id.* at 5.86.

178. *Id.* at 5.131.

179. *Id.* at 4.28.

180. *Id.* at 5.24.

181. The facts are mainly from Redacted Information to Obtain (ITO) Warrants, Ontario, Superior Court of Justice (East Region), November 1, 2017. We also draw on

Clark, Horstmann, and Houde (2020), who have conducted an empirical analysis of the effects of the alleged cartel on Canadian bread prices, and where we have done so, we include the appropriate reference.

182. Redacted Information to Obtain (ITO) Warrants, Ontario, Superior Court of Justice (East Region), November 1, 2017, at 1.12.

183. *Id.* at 1.12.1.

184. *Id.* at 1.12.2.

185. www.canadabread.com/media-statement-%E2%80%93-update-canada-bread-response-release-ito-related-industry-wide-competition-bureau# (accessed October 26, 2020).

186. www.ctvnews.ca/canada/bakers-grocers-involved-in-16-year-price-fixing-conspiracy-competition-bureau-1.3783528 (accessed October 26, 2020).

187. *Sup.* note 182 at 4.24.

188. *Id.* at 4.26.

189. *Id.* at 4.26.

190. *Id.* at 4.27.

191. *Id.* at 4.27.

192. *Id.* at 4.94.

193. *Id.* at 4.95.

194. *Id.* at 4.96.

195. *Id.* at 4.97.

196. *Id.* at 4.98.

197. *Id.* at 4.99.

198. *Id.* at 1.12.1.

199. *Id.* at 4.142.

200. *Id.* at 4.80.

201. *Id.* at 4.81.

202. *Id.* at 4.82.

203. *Id.* at 4.83.

204. *Id.* at 4.79.

205. *Id.* at 4.107.

206. *Id.* at 4.62.

207. *Id.* 4.62.

208. *Id.* at 4.85.

209. *Id.* at 4.86.

210. *Id.* at 4.87.

211. *Id.* at 4.69.

212. *Id.* at 4.81.

213. *Id.* at 4.88.

214. *Id.* at 4.90.

215. *Id.* at 4.91.

216. *Id.* at 4.34.

217. Though not discussed in Clark, Horstmann, and Houde (2020), the price index for US bread also appears to have fallen after the cartel's collapse.

218. We would like to thank Juan-Pablo Montero for suggesting this case.

219. Google translation of Fiscalía Nacional Económica, "FNE Accuses Cencosud, SMU and Walmart of Collusion in the Market for Fresh Chicken Meat," press release, January 6, 2016, www.fne.gob.cl/fne-acusa-a-cencosud-smu-y-walmart-por-colusion-en-el-mercado-de-la-carne-de-pollo-fresca/ (accessed November 13, 2018).

220. Translation by Diana Harrington of Fiscalía Nacional Económica to Tribunal de Defensa de La Libre Competencia (Court of Defense of Free Competition), "Interpone Requerimiento en Contra de Cencosud S.A. y Otros" ("Files a Request against Cencosud S.A. and Others"), January 6, 2016, at 9, 21.

221. "The Chilean Competition Tribunal Upholds the FNE's Collusion Claim against Cencosud, SMU and Walmart," February 28, 2019, www.fne.gob.cl/en/tdlc-acoge-requerimiento-de-la-fne-sancionando-a-cencosud-smu-y-walmart-por-colusion-en-el-mercado-de-la-carne-de-pollo-fresca (accessed October 26, 2020).

222. *Id.*

223. These emails are from Section V of "Final Expert Opinion and Declaration of Professor Spencer Weber Waller Regarding Horizontal Price Fixing Investigation in the Retail Sale of Poultry in Supermarkets," December 23, 2015.

224. *Id.* at 39.

225. *Sup.* note 219.

226. For the second email, the year was reported as "20" though it is likely to be "2010." *Sup.* note 223.

227. *Id.* at Section V.

228. *Id.* at Section V.

229. *Id.* at Section VI.

230. *Id.* at Section VI.

231. *Sup.* note 219.

232. Google translation of "Supreme Court Confirms Fines for Collusion against Agrosuper, Ariztía and Don Pollo and Tightens Sanction against the Union That Brings Them Together," www.fne.gob.cl/corte-suprema-confirma-multas-por-colusion-contra-agrosuper-ariztia-y-don-pollo-y-endurece-sancion-contra-el-gremio-que-las-reune/ (accessed November 13, 2018).

233. Facts are based on *In re Mid-Atlantic Toyota Antitrust Litigation*, 560 F.Supp. 760 (1983), United States District Court, D. Maryland, April 4, 1983, Memorandum Opinion and Order, Joseph H. Young, District Judge.

234. *Id.* at 760.

235. *Id.* at 769.

236. *Id.* at 770.

237. *Id.* at 770.

238. *Id.* at 775.

239. *Id.* at 768, 770, 776.

240. *In re Mid-Atlantic Toyota Antitrust Litigation*, 605 F.Supp. 440 (1984), at 443.

241. *Sup.* note 233.

242. *Sup.* note 240 at 444.

243. For an analysis of how coordination on list prices can be effective and a collection of cases involving coordination on list prices, see Harrington and Ye (2019).

244. We would like to thank Tom Ross for suggesting this case. Our discussion is largely based on Asker and Hemphill (2020), with some use of Hoffman (2013).

245. See Motta (2004, 568) for more details on this functional form. Note $q_i = \frac{1}{2}\left[v - p_i - \frac{\mu}{2}(p_i - p_j)\right]$ when $q_i > 0$ and $q_j > 0$ in (3.1) and $q_i(p_i, p_j) = \left(\frac{1+\mu}{2+\mu}\right)(v - p_i)$ when $q_i > 0$ and $q_j = 0$.

246. This static bargaining solution can be interpreted in terms of a noncooperative dynamic process (as proposed by Rubinstein 1982) in which the two bargaining players make alternating offers and counteroffers to each other (see Binmore, Rubinstein, and Wolinsky 1986).

247. This is an important aspect of our model because we assume that the supplier negotiates simultaneously with both retailers. For certain parameter values, the supplier may in fact do better by negotiating with just one retailer, as it strengthens the supplier's overall bargaining position relative to retailer i. However, this result relies on retailer i believing that the supplier is not negotiating with retailer j despite the fact that the supplier will have an incentive to do so in order to mitigate the consequences of possible disagreement with retailer i.

248. See the proof of proposition 3.1 for a formal demonstration of each effect described here.

Chapter 4

1. We will elaborate on such intermediaries when the Specialty Pipe case is covered.

2. At the end of this section, an explanation is provided for why we should not expect to find hub-and-spoke cartels with a downstream intermediary of the first type.

3. For a nontechnical treatment of auction theory, see Klemperer (2004). For a technical treatment, see Krishna (2010).

4. "Roundtable on Collusion and Corruption in Public Procurement," Global Forum on Competition, OECD DAF/COMP/GF(2010)6, October 15, 2010.

5. By definition, the monopoly price maximizes the intermediary's profit. A price exceeding that would sufficiently reduce the demand for its services, so its profit would decline.

6. For example, it could result in the cartel choosing to compete at the next few tenders. Though that will reduce their profits, such an episode of competition acts as a punishment designed to incentivize firms not to deviate in the future. For a theoretical analysis of such a mechanism, see Skrzypacz and Hopenhayn (2004).

7. Chapter 5 will explore cartels with a retailer as the hub when the objective is instead to exclude rivals to the downstream hub.

8. If a buyer is able to learn what upstream suppliers are charging other buyers who are not using this intermediary, it might eventually learn that the prices it is getting out of this intermediary are excessively high. If that occurred, demand for the intermediary's services would decline. However, it could take considerable effort and time for a buyer to determine that it is paying too much, so collusion may prove effective for a reasonable length of time.

9. Unless otherwise stated, the ensuing facts are taken from Second Amended Complaint, *In re: Insurance Brokerage Antitrust Litigation* (MDL No. 1663), 04–5184, Docket Entry No. 1240 (filed June 29, 2007) (hereafter SAC), and *In re: Insurance Brokerage Antitrust Litigation* (MDL No. 1663), No. 07–4046 (3rd Cir., filed August 16, 2010) (hereafter Appeal).

10. *Id.* SAC at 72.

11. *Id.* at 83.

12. *Sup.* note 9, Appeal at 17.

13. For more details on these lawsuits, see Kolasky and McNeece (2015, 3).

14. *Sup.* note 9, SAC at 92.

15. *Id.* at 92.

16. *Sup.* note 9, Appeal at 28.

17. *Id.* at 104.

18. *In re Insurance Brokerage Antitrust Litigation*, MDL No. 1663, Civil Action No. 04–5184, U.S. District Court (DNJ), opinion by Cecchi, U.S. District Judge, filed August 1, 2013.

19. The US Supreme Court erected a plausibility standard in order for a claim not to be dismissed and thus be able to move to discovery. The plaintiff must present "enough facts to state a claim to relief that is plausible on its face." *Bell Atlantic Corp. v. Twombly*, 550 U.S. 544, 570 (2007).

20. *Sup.* note 9, SAC at 115.

21. *Id.* at 105.

22. *Id.* at 84.

23. *Id.* at 105.

24. *Id.* at 116.

25. *Id.* at 105.

26. *Id.* at 97.

27. *Id.* at 135.

28. *Id.* at 138.

29. *Id.* at 115.

30. *Id.* at 118.

31. *Id.* at 99.

32. *Id.* at 117.

33. *Id.* at 117.

34. *Id.* at 148.

35. *Id.* at 128.

36. *Id.* at 125.

37. *Id.* at 141.

38. *Sup.* note 9, Appeal at 104.

39. *Sup.* note 9, SAC at 107.

40. *Id.* at 114.

41. *Id.* at 153–154.

42. *Id.* at 154.

43. *Id.* at 155.

44. *Id.* at 155.

45. *Id.* at 155.

46. Unless otherwise stated, the facts are taken from Brief for Appellant Midco Pipe & Tube, *U.S. v. All Star Industries*, No. 91–2439 (5th Cir., filed October 11, 1991) (hereafter Midco Brief), Brief for Appellee U.S., *U.S. v. All Star Industries*, No. 91–2439 (5th Cir., filed November 27, 1991) (hereafter U.S. Brief), and Decision, *U.S. v. All Star Industries*, No. 91–2439 (5th Cir., filed May 28, 1992) (hereafter Decision).

47. *Id.*, U.S. Brief at 4.

48. "By the time a fabricator contracted with a pipe distributor, the contract between the fabricator and the architect, engineer or contractor was already in place." *Sup.* note 46, Midco Brief at 7.

49. *Sup.* note 46, Midco Brief at 12.

50. *Id.* at 4–5.

51. *Id.* at 5.

52. *Id.* at 4–5.

53. Reply Brief for Appellants Mannesmann International Alloys Inc. and Richard A. Brazzale (5th Cir., filed December 12, 1991), at 2.

54. *Sup.* note 46, Midco Brief at fn 6.

55. *Sup.* note 46, Decision at fn 15 (see also fn 16).

56. *Sup.* note 46, Midco Brief at 7. Midco claimed that it did not benefit from the conspiracy, arguing that its "prices to TPB were raised by the same percentage as the subsequent rebate to TPB." (Reply Brief for Appellant Midco Pipe & Tube, *U.S. v. All Star Industries*, No. 91–2439 (5th Cir., filed December 12, 1991), at 8.)

57. *Sup.* note 46, Midco Brief at 5.

58. Reply Brief for Appellant Midco Pipe & Tube, *U.S. v. All Star Industries*, No. 91–2439 (5th Cir., filed December 12, 1991), at 3.

59. *Id.* at 3–4.

60. *Id.* at 4.

61. *Sup.* note 46, Midco Brief at 16.

62. *Id.* at 16.

63. *Id.* at 16.

64. *Sup.* note 58 at 3.

65. *Sup.* note 46, Midco Brief at 8–9.

66. *Id.* at fn 10.

67. *Id.* at 10.

68. *Sup.* note 58 at fn 13.

69. *Id.* at 14.

70. *U.S. v. All Star Industries*, No. 91–2439, Federal Enforcement Actions, U.S. Antitrust Cases, Criminal N. Cr. H-88–29, 3488, at 1.

71. *Sup.* note 46, Midco Brief at 12.

72. *Sup.* note 58 at 15–16.

Chapter 5

1. Naked exclusion need not create a monopoly to benefit the nonexcluded retailers. When there are more than two retailers, the exclusion of some subset of them benefits the remaining nonexcluded retailers because it means more demand and more market power, which allows them to raise prices and earn higher profits.

2. It has proven intractable to derive the effect of changing product differentiation holding retailer differentiation fixed and the effect of changing retailer differentiation holding product differentiation fixed. Our formal results are derived for when both product and store differentiation change.

3. *Interstate Circuit, Inc., et al. v. United States*, 306 U.S. 208 (1939). The following discussion draws on Orbach (2019).

4. *Interstate Circuit, Inc., et al. v. United States*, 306 U.S. 208 (1939), at 215.

5. *Id.* at 217–218.

6. For evidence, see Orbach (2019) at 1478.

7. Cited in Orbach (2019) at 1493.

8. *Sup.* note 4 at 216n3.

9. *Id.* at 222.

10. *Id.* at 227.

11. Facts are from *In re Toys "R" Us*, 126 F.T.C. 415 (F.T.C., September 25, 1997) (initial decision, James P. Timony) (hereafter *Toys "R" Us* 1997); *Toys "R" Us, Inc. v. FTC*, 126 F.T.C. 415 (F.T.C., October 14, 1998) (opinion of the Federal Trade Commission, Chairman Robert Pitofsky) (hereafter *Toys "R" Us* 1998); and *Toys "R" Us, Inc. v. F.T.C.*, 1999 U.S. 7th Cir. Briefs (on Petition for Review of a Final Order of the Federal Trade Commission. Opinion of the Commission: Chairman Robert Pitofsky) (hereafter *Toys "R" Us* 1999).

12. *Id., Toys "R" Us* 1998 at 427.

13. *Sup.* note 11, *Toys "R" Us* 1997 at 436–437.

14. *Id.* at 448.

15. *Sup.* note 11, *Toys "R" Us* 1998 at 552.

16. *Id.* at 60.

17. *Sup.* note 11, *Toys "R" Us* 1997 at 436–437.

18. *Id.* at 430.

19. *Id.* at 432.

20. *Id.* at 447.

21. *Sup.* note 11, *Toys "R" Us* 1998 at 555.

22. *Sup.* note 11, *Toys "R" Us* 1997 at 432–434.

23. *Id.* at 449.

24. *Sup.* note 11, *Toys "R" Us* 1998 at 586.

25. *Id.* at 552.

26. "In May of 1992, at a toy manufacturers' conference, Hasbro's CEO Allan Hassenfeld discussed with Tyco's CEO Richard Grey what each company was doing or not doing with respect to the clubs." *Sup.* note 11, *Toys "R" Us* 1997 at 450.

27. *Sup.* note 11, *Toys "R" Us* 1998 at 575.

28. *Sup.* note 11, *Toys "R" Us* 1997 at 431.

29. *Id.* at 434.

30. *Id.* at 454.

31. *Sup.* note 11, *Toys "R" Us* 1998 at 558.

32. *Id.* at 575.

33. *Sup.* note 11, *Toys "R" Us* 1999 at 18.

34. *Sup.* note 11, *Toys "R" Us* 1998 at 600.

35. *Id.* at 13.

36. *Id.* at 530.

37. *Sup.* note 11, *Toys "R" Us* 1999 at 30. Scherer (2004) provides some of the economic analysis.

38. *Sup.* note 11, *Toys "R" Us* 1997 at 147.

39. *Id.* at 162.

40. *Toys "R" Us, Inc., v. Federal Trade Commission,* Appellee. No. 98–4107, U.S. Court of Appeals for the Seventh Circuit, 221 F.3d 928, 935, August 1, 2000.

41. *Sup.* note 11, *Toys "R" Us* 1998 at 54.

42. Unless otherwise noted, facts are from *Columbus Drywall & Insulation, Inc. v. Masco Corporation,* U.S. District Court for the Northern District of Georgia Atlanta Division. Civil Action No. 1:04-CV-3066-JEC. Filed February 9, 2009.

43. Owens Corning was excluded as a defendant because of insolvency. https://www.stollberne.com/class-actions-blog/class-actions-of-interest/masco-corp-settles-price-fixing-class-action-for-75-million/ (accessed October 26, 2020).

44. *Sup.* note 42 at 36.

45. *Id.* at 35.

46. *Id.* at 35.

47. *Id.* at 31–32.

48. *Id.* at 37.

49. *Id.* at 37.

50. *Id.* at 37.

51. *Id.* at 33.

52. *Id.* at 33. 31W is another contractor.

53. *Id.* at 34.

54. *Id.* at 34.

55. *Id.* at 34.

56. *Id.* at 8.

57. "Masco Settles Price-Fixing Lawsuit," https://www.hbsdealer.com/news/masco
-settles-price-fixing-lawsuit/ (accessed January 31, 2019).

58. Facts are from Complaint, *United States v. Apple, et al.,* No. 12 CV 2826, 2012
WL 1193205 (S.D.N.Y., April 11, 2012) (hereafter *Apple* 2012); *United States v. Apple
Inc.,* 952 F. Supp. 2d 638 (Opinion and Order, Southern District Court of New York,
Judge Denise Cote, July 10, 2013) (hereafter *Apple* 2013); and *United States v. Apple,
Inc.,* 791 F.3d 290 (2d Cir. 2015) (hereafter *Apple* 2015). For some analyses of the
case, see Gilbert (2015) and Klein (2017).

59. *Id., Apple* 2015 at 299.

60. *Id.* at 300.

61. *Id.* at 300.

62. *Sup.* note 58, *Apple* 2013 at 651.

63. *Id.* at 650.

64. "As [Apple senior vice president] Cue saw it, Apple's most valuable bargaining
chip came from the fact that the publishers were desperate 'for an alternative to
Amazon's pricing policies and excited about . . . the prospect that [Apple's] entry
[into the e-book market] would give them leverage in their negotiations with
Amazon.'" *Sup.* note 58, *Apple* 2013 at 659.

65. *Sup.* note 58, *Apple* 2013 at 659.

66. *Sup.* note 58, *Apple* 2015 at 304.

67. *Sup.* note 58, *Apple* 2013 at 667.

68. *Sup.* note 58, *Apple* 2012 at 91.

69. *Id.* at 69.

70. *Sup.* note 58, *Apple* 2013 at 660.

71. *Id.* at 661.

72. *Id.* at 674.

73. *Id.* at 674.

74. *Id.* at 678.

75. *Id.* at 681.

76. *Id.* at 680.

77. *Id.* at 680.

78. *Id.* at 692–693.

79. For recent theories exploring the rationale for and implications of the agency model in the context of a market like e-books, see Gaudin and White (2014), Foros, Kind, and Shaffer (2017), and Johnson (2017). De los Santos and Wildenbeest (2017) offer a test of these various theories.

80. *Sup.* note 58, *Apple* 2013 at 682.

81. *Id.*

82. *Sup.* note 58, *Apple* 2015.

83. *Id.* at 312.

84. The facts are from *United States v. General Motors Corporation*, 348 (U.S.) 127, April 28, 1966.

85. *Id.* at 134.

86. *Id.* at 135.

87. *Id.* at 136.

88. *Id.* at 137.

89. *Id.* at 137.

Chapter 6

1. Or at least there would not be any loss of demand *in the short run*. There could be some loss in the long run if a client learned that the input prices from this intermediary were higher than those from another intermediary (who was not part of a cartel).

2. CA/98/8/2003 Agreements between Hasbro UK Ltd, Argos Ltd & Littlewoods Ltd fixing the price of Hasbro toys and games, [2004] 4 UKCLR 717, at 73.

3. CA98/08/2004 Agreement between UOP Limited, UKae Limited, Thermoseal Supplies Ltd, Double Quick Supplyline Ltd and Double Glazing Supplies Ltd to fix and/ or maintain prices for desiccant, OFT, November 8, 2004, at 117.

4. *Columbus Drywall & Insulation, Inc. v. Masco Corporation*, U.S. District Court for the Northern District of Georgia Atlanta Division. Civil Action No. 1:04-CV-3066-JEC. Filed February 9, 2009; at 35.

Chapter 7

1. *Toys "R" Us, Inc. v. FTC*, 126 F.T.C. 415 (F.T.C., October 14, 1998) (opinion of the Federal Trade Commission, Chairman Robert Pitofsky), at 1.

2. *Id.* at 1.

3. The term *rim* is from US jurisprudence, but the property it captures is applicable to all jurisdictions.

4. CA/98/8/2003 Agreements between Hasbro UK Ltd, Argos Ltd & Littlewoods Ltd fixing the price of Hasbro toys and games, [2004] 4 UKCLR 717, at 49.

5. CA/98/06/2003 Price-fixing of Replica Football Kit, OFT, August 1, 2003, at 94.

6. *Id.* at 97.

7. *Id.* at 98.

8. *In re Mid-Atlantic Toyota Antitrust Litigation,* 560 F. Supp. 760 (1983), United States District Court, D. Maryland, April 4, 1983, Memorandum Opinion and Order, Joseph H. Young, District Judge, at 775.

9. *PepsiCo., Inc. v. The Coca-Cola Company,* 315 F.3d 101 (2nd Cir. 2002).

10. *Impro Products, Inc. v. Herrick,* 715 F.2d 1267 (8th Cir. 1983), f. 14.

11. *United States v. Apple, Inc.,* 791 F.3d 290 (2d Cir. 2015), at 75–76.

12. *Id.* at 8, 73.

13. The per se illegality of hub-and-spoke cartels was reaffirmed in *Toys "R" Us, Inc., v. Federal Trade Commission,* Appellee. No. 98–4107, U.S. Court of Appeals for the Seventh Circuit, 221 F.3d 928, 935, August 1, 2000.

14. *United States v. Apple Inc.,* 952 F. Supp. 2d 638 (Opinion and Order, Southern District Court of New York, Judge Denise Cote, July 10, 2013), at 112–113.

15. *Interstate Circuit, Inc., et al. v. United States,* 306 U.S. 208 (1939).

16. *Elder-Beerman Stores Corp. v. Federated Department Stores, Inc.,* 459 F.2d 138, 146–147 (6th Cir. 1972).

17. *Monsanto Co. v. Spray-Rite Serv. Corp.,* 465 U.S. 752, 768 (1984).

18. Royal Courts of Justice, *Argos Ltd and Littlewoods Ltd v. OFT* and *JJB Sports Plc v. OFT,* Case No. 2005/1071, 1074, and 1623, at 141.

19. OECD, "Information Exchange between Competitors under Competition Law," DAF/COMP(2010)37, 2010, 286–287.

20. The preceding passage from the UK's Competition Appeal Tribunal focuses specifically on the conveyance of "future pricing intentions" and later refers to the practices of which it speaks as "concerted." However, concerted practices are thought to be more expansive than sharing future pricing intentions in that they include sharing other commercially sensitive information that could reduce uncertainty

between firms and have a supracompetitive effect on prices. For example, it could mean exchanging actual current prices rather than future pricing intentions.

21. For example, see Areeda and Hovenkamp (2016).

22. Some of these approaches have been suggested by others, and proper attribution is accordingly provided.

23. *Sup.* note 18 at 127.

24. "When A not only gives commercially sensitive information to B, but also receives commercially sensitive information from B originating from C, i.e. there is a bidirectional flow of information, A can reasonably assume that information it provides to B will or is likely to be passed on to C" (Odudu 2011, 234).

25. "Problematic vertical information exchanges often occur when suppliers are attempting to cajole retailers into accepting the case for higher wholesale prices as a result of higher costs. A retailer may individually accept the case for higher prices but might take the view that it will only move its prices if the 'market' moves too. By sharing information on individual retailers' willingness to increase prices, the supplier can manipulate market sentiment and facilitate the wider acceptance of the case for a price increase" (Prewitt and Fails 2015, 69).

26. The ensuing discussion is based on Klein (2020).

27. *In re Musical Instruments & Equip. Antitrust Litig.*, 798 F.3d 1186 (9th Cir. 2015).

28. *Id.* at 1195.

29. *Id.*

30. In *Ashcroft v. Iqbal*, 556 U.S. 662 (2009), the pleading standard established in *Twombly* (2007) was extended to "all civil actions and proceedings in the United States district courts."

31. *Bell Atlantic Corp. v. Twombly*, 550 U.S. 544, 545 (2007).

32. *Id.* at 547.

33. For an interpretation and assessment of the impact of the plausibility standard, see Gelbach (2012) and Page (2018).

References

Ambrus, Attila, Eduardo M. Azevedo, and Yuichiro Kamada. 2013. "Hierarchical Cheap Talk." *Theoretical Economics* 8 (1): 233–261.

Areeda, Phillip E., and Herbert Hovenkamp. 2016. *Antitrust Law: An Analysis of Antitrust Principles and Their Application*, vols. 6 and 7, 4th ed. New York: Kluwer/Aspen.

Ashton, John K., and Andrew D. Pressey. 2012. "Who Manages Cartels? The Roles of Sales and Marketing Managers within International Cartels: Evidence from the European Union 1990–2009." CCP Working Paper 12-11, Centre for Competition Policy, University of East Anglia.

Asker, John. 2010. "A Study of the Internal Organization of a Bidding Cartel." *American Economic Review* 100 (3): 724–762.

Asker, John, and C. Scott Hemphill. 2020. "A Study of Exclusionary Coalitions: The Canadian Sugar Combination, 1887–1889." *Antitrust Law Journal* 83 (1): 99–126.

Awaya, Yu, and Vijay Krishna. 2016. "On Communication and Collusion." *American Economic Review* 106 (2): 285–315.

Binmore, Ken, Ariel Rubinstein, and Asher Wolinsky. 1986. "The Nash Bargaining Solution in Economic Modelling." *RAND Journal of Economics* 17 (2): 176–188.

Bolecki, Antoni. 2011. "Polish Antitrust Experience with Hub-and-Spoke Conspiracies." *Yearbook of Antitrust and Regulatory Studies* 4 (5): 25–46.

Bork, Robert H. 1993. *The Antitrust Paradox*. New York: Free Press.

Centorrino, Samuele, Elodie Djemai, Astrid Hopfensitz, Manfred Milinski, and Paul Seabright. 2015. "Honest Signaling in Trust Interactions: Smiles Rated as Genuine Induce Trust and Signal Higher Earning Opportunities." *Evolution and Human Behavior* 36 (1): 8–15.

Clark, Robert, Ig Horstmann, and Jean-François Houde. 2020. "Two-Sided Hub-and-Spoke Collusion: Evidence from the Grocery Supply Chain." Queens University, May 28, 2020.

Clark, Robert, and Jean-François Houde. 2013. "Collusion with Asymmetric Retailers: Evidence from a Gasoline Price-Fixing Case." *American Economic Journal: Microeconomics* 5 (3): 97–123.

Connor, John M. 2008. *Global Price Fixing.* 2nd ed. Berlin: Springer.

Crawford, Vincent, and Joel Sobel. 1982. "Strategic Information Transmission." *Econometrica* 50 (6): 1431–1451.

Cummins, J. David, and Neil A. Doherty. "The Economics of Insurance Intermediaries." *Journal of Risk and Insurance* 73 (3): 359–396.

De los Santos, Babur, and Matthijs R. Wildenbeest. 2017. "E-book Pricing and Vertical Restraints." *Quantitative Marketing and Economics* 15:85–122.

Dobson, Paul W., and Michael Waterson. 1997. "Countervailing Power and Consumer Prices." *Economic Journal* 107 (441): 418–430.

Dobson, Paul W., and Michael Waterson. 2007. "The Competition Effects of Industry-Wide Vertical Price Fixing in Bilateral Oligopoly." *International Journal of Industrial Organization* 25 (5): 935–962.

Fersthman, Chaim, and Ariel Pakes. 2000. "A Dynamic Oligopoly with Collusion and Price Wars." *RAND Journal of Economics* 31 (2): 207–236.

Foros, Øystein, Hans Jarle Kind, and Greg Shaffer. 2017. "Apple's Agency Model and the Role of Most-Favored-Nation Clauses." *RAND Journal of Economics* 48 (3): 673–703.

Garrod, Luke, and Matthew Olczak. 2018. "How Do Hub-and-Spoke Cartels Operate? The UK Experience." Unpublished manuscript, September 2018.

Gaudin, Germain, and Alexander White. 2014. "On the Antitrust Economics of the Electronic Books Industry." Tsinghua University, September 2014.

Gelbach, Jonah B. 2012. "Locking the Door to Discovery—Assessing the Effect of Twombly and Iqbal on Access to Discovery." *Yale Law Journal* 121:2270–2345.

Gilbert, Richard J. 2015. "E-books: A Tale of Digital Disruption." *Journal of Economic Perspectives* 29 (3): 165–184.

Giovannetti, Emanuele, and David Stallibrass. 2009. "Three Cases in Search of a Theory: Resale Price Maintenance in the UK." *European Competition Journal* 5 (3): 641–654.

Harrington, Joseph E., Jr. 2006. "How Do Cartels Operate?" *Foundations and Trends in Microeconomics* 2 (1): 1–105.

Harrington, Joseph E., Jr. 2015. "Thoughts on Why Certain Markets Are More Susceptible to Collusion and Some Policy Suggestions for Dealing with Them." OECD background paper, Global Forum on Competition, October 19, 2015.

Harrington, Joseph E., Jr. 2018. "How Do Hub-and-Spoke Cartels Operate? Lessons from Nine Case Studies." SSRN Working Paper 3238244, Social Science Research Network, August 2018.

Harrington, Joseph E., Jr., Hai Hüschelrath, Ulrich Laitenberger, and Florian Smuda. 2015. "The Discontent Cartel Member and Cartel Collapse: The Case of the German Cement Cartel." *International Journal of Industrial Organization* 42:106–119.

Harrington, Joseph E., Jr., and Andrzej Skrzypacz. 2007. "Collusion under Monitoring of Sales." *RAND Journal of Economics* 38 (2): 314–331.

Harrington, Joseph E., Jr., and Andrzej Skrzypacz. 2011. "Private Monitoring and Communication in Cartels: Explaining Recent Collusive Practices." *American Economic Review* 101 (6): 2425–2449.

Harrington, Joseph E., Jr., and Yanhao Wei. 2017. "What Can the Duration of Discovered Cartels Tell Us About the Duration of All Cartels?" *Economic Journal* 127 (604): 1977–2005.

Harrington, Joseph E., Jr., and Lixin Ye. 2019. "Collusion through Coordination of Announcements." *Journal of Industrial Economics* 67 (2): 209–241.

Hoffman, Charles Paul. 2013. "A Reappraisal of the Canadian Anti-Combines Act of 1889." *Queen's Law Journal* 39 (1): 127–174.

Hovenkamp, Herbert. 2016. *Federal Antitrust Policy: The Law of Competition and Its Practice.* 5th ed. St. Paul: West Academic Publishing.

Johnson, Justin P. 2017. "The Agency Model and MFN Clauses." *Review of Economic Studies* 84 (3): 1151–1185.

Klein, Benjamin. 2012. "The Hub-and-Spoke Conspiracy That Created the Standard Oil Monopoly." *Southern California Law Review* 85 (3): 459–498.

Klein, Benjamin. 2017. "The Apple E-Books Case: When Is a Vertical Contract a Hub in a Hub-and-Spoke Conspiracy?" *Journal of Competition Law & Economics* 13 (3): 423–474.

Klein, Benjamin. 2020. "Inferring Agreement in Hub-and-Spoke Conspiracies." *Antitrust Law Journal* 83 (1): 127–164.

Klemperer, Paul. 2004. *Auctions: Theory and Practice.* Princeton, NJ: Princeton University Press.

Kolasky, William, and Kathryn McNeece. 2015. "Contingent Commissions and the Antitrust Laws: What Can We Learn from the *In re Insurance Brokerage Antitrust Litigation?*" *Antitrust and Trade Regulation Report* 108 (2691): 1–4.

Krishna, Vijay. 2010. *Auction Theory.* 2nd ed. Burlington, MA: Academic Press/ Elsevier.

Lengwiler, Yvan, and Elmar Wolfstetter. 2006. "Corruption in Procurement Auctions." In *Handbook of Procurement*, edited by Nicola Dimitri, Gustavo Piga, and Giancarlo Spagnolo, 412–429. Cambridge: Cambridge University Press.

Levenstein, Margaret C., and Valerie Y. Suslow. 2004. "Contemporary International Cartels and Developing Countries: Economic Effects and Implications for Competition Policy." *Antitrust Law Journal* 71:801–852.

Levenstein, Margaret C., and Valerie Y. Suslow. 2006. "What Determines Cartel Success?" *Journal of Economic Literature* 44 (1): 43–95.

Levenstein, Margaret C., and Valerie Y. Suslow. 2014. "How Do Cartels Use Vertical Restraints? Reflections on Bork's *The Antitrust Paradox*." *Journal of Law and Economics* 57 (S3): 33–50.

Manzini, Paola, Abdolkarim Sadrieh, and Nicolaas J. Vriend. 2009. "On Smiles, Winks and Handshakes as Coordination Devices." *Economic Journal* 119 (537): 826–854.

Marshall, Robert C., and Leslie M. Marx. 2012. *The Economics of Collusion—Cartels and Bidding Rings*. Cambridge, MA: MIT Press.

Mason, Christopher. 2004. *The Art of the Steal: Inside the Sotheby's-Christie's Auction House Scandal*. New York: Berkley Books.

Mathewson, G. Frank, and Ralph A. Winter. 1984. "An Economic Theory of Vertical Restraints." *RAND Journal of Economics* 15 (1): 27–38.

Mattioli, Eva. 2016. "Hub and Spoke: Towards a Belgian Precedent?" *Journal of European Competition Law and Practice* 7 (4): 261–266.

Motta, Massimo. 2004. *Competition Policy: Theory and Practice*. Cambridge: Cambridge University Press.

Odudu, Okeoghene. 2011. "Indirect Information Exchange: The Constituent Elements of Hub and Spoke Collusion." *Journal of European Competition Law and Practice* 7 (2): 205–242.

OECD (Organization for Economic Cooperation and Development). 2019. "Hub-and-Spoke Arrangements—Note by the European Union." DAF/COMP/WD(2019)89.

Orbach, Barak. 2016. "Hub-and-Spoke Conspiracies." *Antitrust Source* 15 (4): 1–15.

Orbach, Barak. 2019. "Interstate Circuit and Conspiracy Theories." *University of Illinois Law Review* 2019 (5): 1447–1495.

Page, William H. 2007. "Communication and Concerted Action." *Loyola University Chicago Law Journal* 38:405–460.

Page, William H. 2017. "Tacit Agreement under Section 1 of the Sherman Act." *Antitrust Law Journal* 81 (2): 593–639.

Page, William H. 2018. "Pleading, Discovery, and Proof of Sherman Act Agreements: Harmonizing *Twombly* and *Matsushita.*" *Antitrust Law Journal* 82 (1): 123–166.

Piccolo, Salvatore, and Jeanine Miklós-Thal. 2012. "Colluding through Suppliers." *RAND Journal of Economics* 43 (3): 492–513.

Prewitt, Elizabeth, and Greta Fails. 2015. "Indirect Information Exchanges to Hub-and-Spoke Cartels: Enforcement and Litigation Trends in the United States and Europe." *Competition Law and Policy Debate* 1 (2): 63–72.

Rey, Patrick, and Thibaud Vergé. 2008. "Economics of Vertical Restraints." In *Handbook of Antitrust Economics*, edited by Paolo Buccirossi, 353–390. Cambridge, MA: MIT Press.

Rubinstein, Ariel. 1982. "Perfect Equilibrium in a Bargaining Model." *Econometrica* 50 (1): 97–110.

Sahuguet, Nicholas, and Alexis Walckiers. 2013. "The Economics of Hub-and-Spoke Collusion." Unpublished manuscript, February 2013.

Sahuguet, Nicholas, and Alexis Walckiers. 2014. "Hub-and-Spoke Conspiracies: The Vertical Expression of a Horizontal Desire?" *Journal of European Competition Law and Practice* 5 (10): 711–716.

Sahuguet, Nicholas, and Alexis Walckiers. 2017. "A Theory of Hub-and-Spoke Collusion." *International Journal of Industrial Organization* 53:353–370.

Scherer, Frederic M. 2004. "Retailer-Instigated Restraints on Suppliers' Sales: Toys "R" Us." In *The Antitrust Revolution: Economics, Competition, and Policy*, 4th ed., edited by John E. Kwoka and Lawrence J. White. Oxford: Oxford University Press.

Shamir, Noam. 2017. "Cartel Formation through Strategic Information Leakage in a Distribution Channel." *Marketing Science* 36 (1): 70–88.

Shubik, Martin, and Richard Levitan. 1980. *Market Structure and Behavior.* Cambridge, MA: Harvard University Press.

Skrzypacz, Andrzej, and Hugo Hopenhayn. 2004. "Tacit Collusion in Repeated Auctions." *Journal of Economic Theory* 114 (1): 153–169.

Sparks, Adam, Tyler Burleigh, and Pat Barclay. 2016. "We Can See Inside: Accurate Prediction of Prisoner's Dilemma Decisions in Announced Games Following a Face-to-Face Interaction." *Evolution and Human Behavior* 37 (3): 210–216.

Spengler, Joseph J. 1950. "Vertical Integration and Antitrust Policy." *Journal of Political Economy* 58 (4): 347–352.

Spulber, Daniel F. 1996. "Market Microstructure and Intermediation." *Journal of Economic Perspectives* 10 (3): 135–152.

Sugaya, Takuo, and Alexander Wolitzky. 2018. "Maintaining Privacy in Cartels." *Journal of Political Economy* 126 (6): 2569–2607.

Telser, Lester G. 1960. "Why Should Manufacturers Want Fair Trade?" *Journal of Law and Economics* 3:86–105.

Van Cayseele, Patrick, and Simon Miegelsen. 2013. "Hub and Spoke Collusion by Embargo." Discussion Paper Series DPS 13.24, KU Leuven, Center for Economic Studies, December 2013.

Van Cayseele, Patrick J. G. 2014. "Hub-and-Spoke Collusion: Some Nagging Questions Raised by Economists." *Journal of European Competition Law and Practice* 5 (3): 164–168.

Yamey, Basil S. 1954. *The Economics of Resale Price Maintenance.* London: Pitman.

Zampa, Gian Luca, and Paolo Buccirossi. 2013. "Hub and Spoke Practices: Law and Economics of the New Antitrust Frontier." *Competition Law International* 9 (1): 91–110.

Index

Page numbers followed by *f* and *t* refer to figures and tables respectively.